once a·day

nurturing great kids

DEVOTIONAL

365 practical insights for
parenting with grace

ZONDERVAN®

We want to hear from you. Please send your comments about this book to us in care of zreview@zondervan.com. Thank you.

ZONDERVAN

Once-A-Day Nurturing Great Kids Devotional
Copyright © 2014 by Dan Seaborn

This title is also available as a Zondervan ebook.
Visit www.zondervan.com/ebooks.

Requests for information should be addressed to:

Zondervan, 3900 *Sparks Drive, Grand Rapids, Michigan 49546*

Published in association with the literary agency of Credo Communications, LLC, Grand Rapids, Michigan, www. credocommunications.net.

ISBN: 978-0-310-43192-3

Printed in the United States of America

14 15 16 17 18 19 20 21 22 23 24 25 /DCI/ 15 14 13 12 11 10 9 8 7 6 5 4 3 2 1

about the author

Dan Seaborn founded Winning At Home in 1995 to develop marriages and families by producing media resources and hosting special events. Prior to establishing Winning At Home, Dan served at a large church in Michigan as Pastor of Student Ministries and then as Pastor of Family Life. Dan's mission then and now is to encourage individuals and families to build Christ-centered homes.

Dan is the Director of the Marriage and Family Network for the American Association of Christian Counselors where he provides leadership to the nearly 50,000 members worldwide. In addition, he holds a Master's degree in Christian Ministries. Dan has authored eleven books and has established himself as a radio and television personality in West Michigan and around the country.

As a featured speaker at various churches and large-scale events, Dan has earned recognition as a powerful and passionate communicator. At marriage and family conferences, including the Winning At Home signature events—The Marriage Rendezvous and The Wonders of the World of Parenting—his practical illustrations and memorable real-life examples show others how to *win* at home.

Dan talks openly about family life—often by revealing his own struggles and failures. His sincerity leaves audiences nodding in agreement, and his quick wit leaves them laughing. But ultimately, Dan hopes he achieves his one desire in life: to teach practical, Biblical insights to families and to grow and live that example himself.

Dan and his wife Jane have four children and live in West Michigan where they like to golf together, take long walks and spend time with their family.

This work would not be possible without the guidance of Timothy J. Beals, our project manager, and his valued advisor, Susan Lewis.

CHANGE IT UP

Unless you change and become like little children, you will never enter the kingdom of heaven.   MATTHEW 18:3

Throughout the Bible are lessons that point to making changes when we aren't living up to God's standards. Jesus was serious about change, and he expects you to have a teachable spirit like that of a little child. Then, when you do make changes, you are greatly rewarded.

But if nothing changes, nothing changes. For instance, as a parent you will find yourself in situations where you know a change is needed if your child is going to make progress. It's tempting to sit back and wait for that change to somehow occur instead of intentionally implementing change—so you do nothing. But what will develop if you do nothing is a pattern of bad behavior that becomes the norm.

The cure for this downward spiral with your child is moving forward with change. You must create a new environment or a new pattern for healthy patterns to be established or to re-emerge. Go do it. Don't think about it; just do it! The short-term pain of adjusting to the change will result in long-term gain. ✤

PARENTING PRINCIPLE

If nothing changes, nothing changes.

POINTS TO PONDER

- How flexible are you when it comes to making changes? Do you only talk about change without taking action?
- Do you have a teachable spirit? How do you think God wants you to develop such a spirit?
- What is a pattern of behavior with your child that could use a change?

day**2**

LIVE HONESTLY

Keep me from deceitful ways.   PSALM 119:29

One of the greatest weapons of destruction for a parent-child relationship is deceit. That word often conjures up thoughts of a child who is lying or sneaking around behind their parent's back. Although that can be true, the child's behavior may not be the source of deceit.

As parents, we need to first live by the standards we expect our children to meet. If you expect honesty from your child, that should be the standard for you. Children have built-in lie detectors. You may fool them with deceit for a while, but you will be the fool in the end.

Live a lifestyle of honesty in front of your children, and you will have set the bar high for their future behavior. ✣

PARENTING PRINCIPLE

The truth will set you free is not only an axiom. Honesty is a scriptural mandate.

POINTS TO PONDER

- Do you expect honesty from your child but allow yourself a little leeway when it comes to your own behavior?
- If you do have any areas of deceit in your life, what are they?
- How are you establishing the expectation of honesty in your family?

GOD GUIDES

Direct me in the path of your commands.   PSALM 119:35

Sometimes making the right decision as a parent is next to impossible. If you choose one path, it may have undesirable consequences. On the other hand, another decision may net equally negative results. Parenting is filled with these moments.

Another difficult aspect of making decisions for your children is the input from other parents and friends who would not have made the same decision you did. They will often tell you why because people usually aren't afraid of sharing their opinions.

This difficulty may not have happened to you yet, but it will. In those moments, your peace will come from knowing you have prayed and listened for God to direct your path. At times, it will be the only peace you feel. That's why it's important to remember that he does see your need and he will guide you as you seek him. It's his promise. ❖

PARENTING PRINCIPLE

Only with God's strength can crooked paths be straightened.

POINTS TO PONDER

- Have you ever felt all alone in making a decision for your children? Did you still have peace? Why?
- How do you respond when other people disagree with a decision you make?
- For what decision do you need to seek God's wisdom right now?

day4

SEE CLEARLY

Turn my eyes away from worthless things.   PSALM 119:37

The thought in Psalm 119:37 is often used for conventions on pornography or other objectionable material. However, to stop there is to sell this thought short. Our world is full of worthless things and temptations.

For instance, have you ever thought about the worth of comparing yourself to other families or, as parents, comparing your children to other children? Those families and those children aren't yours, and to spend countless hours focusing on them is not only worthless but fruitless.

What is worthy, however, is to look at what you have and determine to honor Christ. As you do honor him with your possessions and blessings, your children will learn to be content with who they are and what they have. It will hopefully help prompt them to turn their eyes away from worthless things. Their roots and foundations will stay with them through potential years of rebellion and will be what they come back to as adults. ✤

PARENTING PRINCIPLE

Keep your eyes turned on the things of Christ.

POINTS TO PONDER

- What worthless things get too much of your time or focus? Do you compare yourself or your children to others?
- How do you begin to eliminate the worthless and love the worthwhile?
- Are your children seeing good examples from you of focusing on what is worthy?

day5

SPEAK SOFTLY

Never take your word of truth from my mouth. 	Psalm 119:43

Your mouth speaks many words. And you would probably be shocked if you evaluated what you spoke in the last week only to see what emerged from your vocal tunnel that could be classified as fibs. Always speaking the truth is difficult, even for the most seasoned Christians.

But if you begin to think of your words as Christ's words spoken through you, your next evaluation might be more favorable. Take the time to choose your words carefully and to speak softly—or to recognize when you should simply hold your tongue.

Too often our children will hear talk that sounds more like a barroom bash than a Christ connection, even in their own homes. To help you remember their ever-present ears in the room, you need to realize that what you speak to your children will likely be spoken to your grandchildren. Sobering! ✤

PARENTING PRINCIPLE

Lord, help me speak softly and carry a big stick—in case I need to shove it down my own throat.

POINTS TO PONDER

- Who did you learn your speaking pattern from? Was the pattern helpful or damaging?
- Who is learning from you? Do you like the example you're setting? Why or why not?
- What can you do to ensure that you speak more softly more often?

 **day6** january 6

SEEK FREEDOM

I will walk about in freedom, for I have sought out your precepts. PSALM 119:45

The definition of freedom will vary from person to person. What one person calls freedom another sees as bondage. A non-believer in Christ may look at a Christian and consider their life tied up in religious representation, while a Christ-believer calls the freedom of those engaged in sinful acts the ultimate in bondage and destruction. It's a matter of perspective.

True freedom is not a man-made set of guidelines. It is a heart and art project of God. When you understand that God owns, guides and allows all that happens, your freedom exists within his limitless boundaries.

The tricky part is grasping this concept and then getting your children to embrace it. Freedom to a teen is anywhere a parent isn't. Most parents understand that this is a stage, and in their wisdom continue to direct their children to the precepts of God even through these defining days. ❖

PARENTING PRINCIPLE

Freedom isn't free—but God did all he could to pay the price through Christ.

POINTS TO PONDER

- What is your definition of freedom?
- How does your relationship with Christ affect what you teach your children about freedom?
- How do you teach this concept to your children?

BE BOLD

I will speak of your statutes before kings and will not be put to shame. PSALM 119:46

Do you ever get frustrated because your child/teen seems to be a bit ashamed of your family's faith? Have you ever seen them cower a little around their peers when someone mentions the name of Christ? If so, you have a normal child.

Our society's move away from "Christian-ness" can be intimidating for even the strongest of believers. Remember how the apostle Peter hung out with Jesus and yet peer pressure got the best of him in his moments of denial. To be appropriately bold is a high calling. Don't be ashamed of your love for Christ. In addition, let your children see your love for all people whether it's an annoying neighbor or public figures you disagree with politically. Show them how allowing Christ to live in you increases your ability to love others.

Don't use the platform of parenting as a bashing field against pundits. Instead, wisely proclaim that Christ is the answer in and on all occasions. Your contagious faith will be a shining example in a contentious world. ✤

PARENTING PRINCIPLE

Boldness isn't defined by how loud you are. It is defined by how loving you are.

POINTS TO PONDER

- What's an example of boldness you want to follow?
- Is your level of boldness for Christ appropriate for your children to emulate?
- In what ways do you show your children how you love Christ?

day8

A RECIPE FOR HOPE

My comfort in my suffering is this: Your promise preserves my life.　　　PSALM 119:50

I remember as a youngster watching my mom make homemade preserves. What that meant for me was that I would see some terrific jam or jelly on the table for dinner.

God will sometimes stir up ingredients in your life like suffering, struggling and pain to remind you to depend on him. Even though it may not seem like it at the time, what God has prepared for you will yield a much sweeter and more desirable person if you can endure the testing and hurt.

God promises he will be with you in it and through it, and he will preserve your life. The process is not always enjoyable in any realm of thinking, but parenting will occasionally test you to preserving moments. In those moments, you must be aware that the promise of his presence on the other side is your hope! ✤

PARENTING PRINCIPLE

Thank God for his promises as they make the best preserves.

POINTS TO PONDER

- What has God brought you through?
- How have you learned from that experience?
- What have been some experiences you can share with your children so they can learn in this area?

A TIME TO REMEMBER

In the night, LORD, I remember your name. PSALM 119:55

The silence of night has a way of helping us remember just about everything we had hoped to forget. The nights of stress and worry for parents can accumulate over time like blown leaves against the outside corner of a house. All of a sudden, without warning, circumstances arise and night will get even darker.

It seems almost unfathomable that in those moments we could forget to remember the name above all names. But we do. Not purposefully, not disrespectfully, not for lack of love or worship, but because the accumulation of life's stresses and worries is overwhelming.

Then it comes to us—just a whisper at first, maybe because we are praying for our child, but it comes. *Jesus*—his name is a penetrating ray of hope. We remember it. We lift our head. Our hope reappears! When morning comes, we are thankful again that he is the light of our night. ✤

PARENTING PRINCIPLE

Try to remember the One who always remembers you.

POINTS TO PONDER

- Why does the darkness of worry and stress frighten you?
- Why does his name help you?
- What could you do to remember his name more often?

HEALTHY FEAR

I am a friend to all who fear you.   Psalm 119:63

When fear is spoken of, it's usually associated with danger. But there is another type of fear—one that parents must teach to their children.

This fear comes out of respect. For example, I respect my marriage, and I fear causing a problem in my marriage if I disrespect my wife and do not treat her with love and care. Appropriate fear is a wonderful motivator for obedience.

Your children need to see that you and your spouse live with a mutual desire to love God and live by his commands. This is especially true as you befriend other families and build relationships with them, showing your children that you have a healthy respect for God's command to love others.

The concept of "healthy fear" is a concept they will not learn quickly. It will be a lifelong lesson, and your consistency in teaching healthy fear by your example will be crucial for their future relationships with Christ and other people. ❧

PARENTING PRINCIPLE

God doesn't want you to be afraid of him, but he wants you to appropriately fear his power.

POINTS TO PONDER

- How do you understand the concept of "healthy fear"?
- How do you maintain a healthy fear of the Lord while remaining a friend to God?
- How do you think your children are learning this lesson from you?

day11

NO BOUNDS

To all perfection I see a limit, but your commands are boundless.   PSALM 119:96

Have you ever wondered if you're parenting the right way? Welcome to life! There are no perfect parents. Stop putting that type of pressure on yourself, even if you sometimes wish you had handled a situation with your child differently.

To parent the best way you know how, seek advice from good role models of parenting. Be open to learning new ideas that could be helpful for your family. When you think you have all the information you need, make your decisions, move forward. Be willing to accept the fact that sometimes you will make the perfect decision and other times you won't.

The great news is that God is boundless. No matter how we may stumble, we still live well within his boundless love. That's perfect to know! ✤

PARENTING PRINCIPLE

Be thankful your burdens fall within his boundaries.

POINTS TO PONDER

- Where do you try too hard to be a "perfect parent"?
- How does this add to your stress level?
- What are some practical ways you can adjust your decision-making process to alleviate undue stress?

TRUST IN PROMISES

Your promises have been thoroughly tested, and your servant loves them. PSALM 119:140

After you have parented a few years, you begin to realize that there are some proven parenting techniques that work. For example, giving your children responsibilities early in life will help them develop certain character traits that hopefully will carry them throughout their lives.

God teaches that his promises have been tested over and over again, and throughout the generations they have proven true. The next logical step for a parent is to know these promises and teach them to their children. The most obvious promise is that Christ promises eternal life to all those who accept him and believe he is their Savior. That's a promise your children need to know. It's a choice they will need to make but one that we must lay before them.

Wise parents will study and know God's promises and instill them into the hearts and minds of their children. ✤

PARENTING PRINCIPLE

Tell the Biblical stories—store the Biblical promises!

POINTS TO PONDER

- Which of God's promises did you learn as a child that have stuck with you?
- What promises from God's Word have you been teaching your children?
- How can you study and learn more of the promises that are in God's Word?

DON'T GIVE IN

My son, if sinful men entice you, do not give in to them. PROVERBS 1:10

This verse applies to either a son or daughter and, like never before, we need to talk openly and age-appropriately about how sin is enticing. Sin is perceived crazy fun—for a season. It may taste good in the moment, but its bitter taste in the end will sour any memories of the fun and leave people incredibly empty.

For most parents, this is a lesson we can teach because of our own struggles with the enticement of sin. Now that you've matured, remember those struggles whenever you are trying to get your children to understand your rants and lectures. It's easy to forget the sins of our youth, although sometimes lingering consequences will remind us of the past and can be painful. But when you recall those times, think of them as a way of understanding what your children are experiencing.

Seek to help them understand how only the power of Christ can protect them and prevent them from giving in to sin! ✤

PARENTING PRINCIPLE

If it looks, smells, tastes and woos—be careful. It probably bites!

POINTS TO PONDER

- What have you learned about the enticement of sin that you can pass on to your children?
- Will you have patience as your child struggles through enticements? What could help you have more patience?
- What are ways you can protect your children from enticements?

BE DISCREET

Discretion will protect you, and understanding will guard you. PROVERBS 2:11

How long has it been since you heard someone say the phrase, "Use discretion." It's probably been a while. We don't talk about discretion a lot in our society because it requires discipline, which doesn't give us permission to do whatever we want.

If you try to teach discretion to your children, you might find it's a new concept for them. It will require them to think, analyze and realize there are consequences to the decisions they make and the actions they take. Children today are used to doing everything instantly and without giving much thought to others.

Show your children how discretion should be used when choosing friends, spending money, watching TV or browsing the web. The opportunity to teach discretion is all around us. As a parent, make sure you don't always make your child's decisions for them. Let them choose and, in that way, you can teach them the art of discretion. ♣

PARENTING PRINCIPLE

An ounce of discretion might protect you from a pounding.

POINTS TO PONDER

- Do you use good discretion? Be honest with yourself!
- What are some ways you can teach your child to use discretion?
- Do you try to control or dictate discretion in your child's life? If so, how can you let them grow in this area? How can you grow?

GROW IN WISDOM

Do not be wise in your own eyes.   PROVERBS 3:7

Are you a know-it-all parent? Better yet, do the people you know think that of you? One of the best techniques to protect yourself from getting this reputation with your friends and children is to keep your mouth closed more often than open. If you are listening, you are usually learning.

If you haven't reached a place of total humility yet as a parent, be forewarned that it is coming. At that moment, you will be sure to learn that you are not the wisest person in the world and possibly not even in your own family.

Remember—wisdom comes from God. Continue to seek and model this for your children. ✤

PARENTING PRINCIPLE

If you are a "know-it-all," the people around you would rather not know you at all.

POINTS TO PONDER

- What do you think of others who are know-it-alls?
- In what area do you think you have a tendency to act like you know it all?
- What would people say about you in this area?

day16

GET HEALTHY

Fear the LORD and shun evil. This will bring health to your body and nourishment to your bones.   PROVERBS 3:7–8

One of the biggest expenses for most families in our nation is health care, but most parents will spend whatever it takes to keep their children healthy.

Setting a good example for them by practicing healthy habits is a step in the right direction. But Proverbs 3:7–8 deserves a thoughtful look when it comes to considering what evil can do to our health. If you can teach your children to fear the Lord and run from the evils of Satan, there will be some health benefits for them. For example, steering your children away from sin will help eliminate some of the harmful effects they could experience from stress or addiction.

People need to see the Bible as a book from the Great Physician. He knows us and our children. He made our bodies to function under his care. Be aware of the blessings you can receive as you look more dutifully to him in these health areas of your life. ✤

PARENTING PRINCIPLE

It makes sense that the creator of our bodies would have the best lifestyle choices in mind to help us maintain healthy bodies.

POINTS TO PONDER

- What are some steps you could take to be a healthier family?
- Do you recognize God's desire for your healthy lifestyles?
- What are some of the benefits of shunning evil?

GIVE FIRST

Honor the LORD with your wealth, with the firstfruits of all your crops. PROVERBS 3:9

Giving is a sensitive subject. People can be quite defensive even dealing with it themselves much less talking about it with their children. It's ironic because every time people give and see the resulting blessing to others, they are usually filled with joy.

Establishing giving as a regular part of your family's development is a wise parenting move. It's a good kind of habit. Certainly you can give money, but your children may actually be much more motivated in this area if they see you give goods in kind or time to those who are less fortunate.

Our theme verse teaches that giving should be one of the first things you do, not an afterthought. Be creative and think of ways to bless another family or organization, and let your children be a part of it! Your family will be blessed in ways unseen. ❖

PARENTING PRINCIPLE

Keep giving and love living.

POINTS TO PONDER

- Is giving easy for you? Why or why not?
- How has someone else's giving impacted you?
- What is a practical way your family could give more often?

BE DISCIPLINED

Because the LORD disciplines those he loves, as a father the son he delights in.

PROVERBS 3:12

Discipline is training that corrects, molds or perfects the mental faculties or moral character. Most people want to grow and be molded into a better person. They just wish it could happen without all the work. Not gonna happen!

To be a parent who teaches and holds firm in the disciplining moments, you must be disciplined yourself. You have to have been through the trials of life and weathered some storms of pain to develop this character Proverbs 3:12 implies.

An undisciplined parent will be thought fraudulent if they impose discipline on their children. Many try, and the results are usually not favorable as the years go on. That's why it's important to be disciplined in your lifestyle and choices. Then your children will understand by your example the things you are trying to teach. ✤

PARENTING PRINCIPLE

Discipline is not a natural by-product of family life. It is the by-product of supernatural growth.

POINTS TO PONDER

- What is an area of discipline where you most struggle and need Christ's help?
- How are you teaching discipline to your children?
- Have you considered seeking Christian counsel for your weak areas?

DON'T ACCUSE

Do not accuse anyone for no reason — when they have done you no harm.

PROVERBS 3:30

Many people have a built-in accusatory nature. It may come from their heritage or it could have been just recently developed. Regardless, it's a destructive force inside a home.

To accuse others falsely can bring no good to a home. When speaking of others — whether or not they have harmed you — do so with positive speech. The old saying "If you can't say something good, don't speak" is a good motto to live by.

The reasons to keep your family disciplined in this area are many. First, accusations create a negative tone in your home, and that negativity will filter into the rest of your conversations. Second, you don't really know the other person's life and circumstances, so to make assumptions is dangerous and can lead to false accusation. Their lives are for God to deal with, and it would be much more helpful to pray for them than to accuse them. Third, not accusing others falsely is God's command for us to follow. That responsibility is heavy enough for us to shoulder. ❖

PARENTING PRINCIPLE

If you hang with people who falsely accuse others, you can bet they'll eventually accuse you.

POINTS TO PONDER

- Is your home one where people are falsely accused?
- Why is it easy to fall into this pattern?
- How will you set a better tone in this area?

SLEEP TIGHT

When you lie down, you will not be afraid; when you lie down, your sleep will be sweet.
PROVERBS 3:24

Have you had sleepless nights? Have you ever awakened in the middle of the night and not been able to get back to sleep because of stress or worry? If so, you're normal! It's part of the parenting plague.

But it doesn't have to be that way. There are ways to end the sleep-deprivation cycle. The key is to continue to mature and develop in your understanding that God sees what you are dealing with and will provide. Make a list of those things that keep you from sleeping and one by one give them to the Lord. Picture yourself putting them in God's hands. Do not be afraid—do not fear. Greater is he who is in you than Satan, who is of this world.

As you lie down to rest, think pleasant thoughts and of sweet memories. Seek to relax and enjoy those blessings of God. ✤

PARENTING PRINCIPLE

Give your worries to the Lord and sweeten your sleep.

POINTS TO PONDER

- What keeps you from relaxing and sleeping?
- What are the things that should make you feel relaxed? How often do you focus on these?
- Have you considered counseling if you cannot achieve this on your own? Do not be afraid of counsel.

NO FEAR

Have no fear of sudden disaster.   PROVERBS 3:25

Especially when your children are little, you may find yourself conjuring up thoughts of disaster. It is normal to think of the "what if's." What if they are in an accident? What if this or that happens? Though it's always possible something could happen, you can't let this fear overwhelm you. You must keep it in proper perspective.

The reality is that some events will happen in your children's lives that you don't like or don't want to deal with—perhaps even a tragedy. Bad occurrences are part of the human experience. But a parent who accepts this reality and depends on the Lord will be well prepared in the event of any actual accident or tragedy. Nobody wants to prepare for disaster, but they are wise to do so.

Consider how our sovereign God has worked through the so-called "disasters" you experienced and how they actually deepened your relationship with him. The same process will happen in your children if they trust the Lord while experiencing trials. ✤

PARENTING PRINCIPLE

No event surprises God. Depend on him to manage them!

POINTS TO PONDER

- What disaster do you fear?
- Is your personality prone to worry about disasters?
- How could you tone it down a little in terms of worry?

LISTEN UP

Now then, my children, listen to me; blessed are those who keep my ways.

PROVERBS 8:32

This verse tells us to listen.

Most Christians have the discipline of praying and reading the Bible, but this idea of listening to God can be a fairly new concept even to a seasoned follower of Christ. Yet, when we take time to listen to him, we are not only equipped to keep his ways, we also receive his blessings.

If you think about it, Proverbs 8:32 reflects every parent's desire that their children will listen to them. You want them to stop being distracted, focus on what you are saying and then do what you say. You only want the best for them.

The same is true in your relationship with Christ. You need to put aside all the busyness of life and just sit quietly in his presence. Listening to him is an art few are committed to learning. When you sit with him, jot down the thoughts and ideas that come to you. You might be surprised how he speaks when you take the time to listen. Then you can do what he says and receive his blessings. ❖

PARENTING PRINCIPLE

Before we ask our children to listen, let's learn to listen ourselves.

POINTS TO PONDER

- Is listening to God a new concept to you?
- Why do you think this kind of listening is difficult?
- How could listening benefit you and your family?

HIDE-AND-SEEK

For those who find me find life and receive favor from the LORD. PROVERBS 8:35

How long has it been since you played a game of hide-and-seek? If you have young children, you have probably played recently. Depending on the age of your children, this can be a fairly easy or very frustrating game.

For many of us, finding God is often difficult, perhaps because we look for him where we want him to be versus where he might be leading us. No one wants to look in the scary places. We want him to be out in the open where there are no dangers or challenging circumstances.

But even though parenting is filled with difficulty, God is not hiding. He may be in some of the least obvious places or in some of the most terrifying places, but he is not hiding. If we seek him, we will not only find him, we will receive his favor. So keep looking! ✤

PARENTING PRINCIPLE

For those seeking God, hide-and-seek needs to include the tagline "find and receive."

POINTS TO PONDER

- Where are you seeking God right now?
- What keeps you seeking? Why don't you give up?
- What are some of the blessings you have received as a result of seeking?

DON'T MOCK

Whoever corrects a mocker invites insults.   PROVERBS 9:7

One of the lessons life has taught us is that mockers—people who make fun of or slander others—are not easy to deal with. Some children will find it very difficult to deal with offences. Here are a couple of ways to help your children cope with insulting language.

First, help your children understand that people who insult others are struggling with issues about themselves. These are people who may be insecure or dealing with challenges of which nobody is aware. Make sure you help your children understand that hurting people often hurt other people. Second, explain to them that their own identity should not be found in what other people say about them; rather they should find it in what God thinks about them. Encourage them to live to honor God, not other people.

Teaching these principles to your children will help prepare them for the insults that are coming. ❖

PARENTING PRINCIPLE

If someone is mocking you, don't listen to them but to the Lord.

POINTS TO PONDER

- Why are insults tough to take?
- Have your children faced insults?
- How do you handle insults?

SEEK THE WISE

Instruct the wise and they will be wiser still.   PROVERBS 9:9

Who in your life speaks truth to you? Is there someone you will listen to and not get defensive but rather welcome their comments as beneficial for you as a parent? If you can name someone, and you accept their observations as positive, then you are a very confident and mature individual.

Frankly, most of us turn away from those who challenge us, especially if it's our spouse. But parents who have wisdom usually have others who speak into their life. They recognize their deficiencies and welcome the wisdom and experience of others that will benefit them.

When you are able to receive this type of counsel, you will move into the upper tier of parenting, where you can see life from a more God-like view and understand that your purpose on earth is not to make yourself happy but to please God. ✤

PARENTING PRINCIPLE

You can be as wise as you want to be, but you can't accomplish anything alone.

POINTS TO PONDER

- How are you at receiving correction/instruction from others?
- Why do you think this is difficult?
- Are you giving your children a good example to follow in this area?

FULL OF FOLLY

Folly is an unruly woman; she is simple and knows nothing.   PROVERBS 9:13

Folly is in every child. Their heart is full of it. It is the way we are born! But Proverbs 9:13 teaches that unchecked folly leads to a life of foolishness and nothingness. Parents are responsible to wean their children off their natural folly over the years. You can do so through discipline and character lessons.

Again, don't worry if your child has folly, because they come by it naturally. Don't think you will rid them of it all in a moment's time, either. It's a process. Many adults still deal with folly. It's all around us. To claim that folly is dead would be foolish.

As parents, watch for folly in your children and address it when it occurs. Talk about what it leads to and show your children examples of unchecked folly. Let them see those who continue to make unwise decisions and how their lives are hard and often destroyed. Be a patient teacher, because getting rid of folly is a lifelong job. ✤

PARENTING PRINCIPLE

Folly is bound up in the heart of a child, but unchecked it turns into foolishness.

POINTS TO PONDER

- What does folly look like today?
- Where do you see your child struggling with folly?
- How have you grown over the years in this area?

HIGHLIGHTS AND LOWLIGHTS

A wise son brings joy to his father, but a foolish son brings grief to his mother.

PROVERBS 10:1

There is no greater joy for a parent than when their children love Christ and make good decisions. But there is no greater pain for a parent than when their children are not following Christ and choose to live in disobedience.

As a parent, you will likely experience both this joy and pain. Unfortunately, you will remember the pain of your child's disobedience much quicker than the joy you feel when they're following the Lord. It seems to be built into our DNA to do so.

The best thing about Proverbs 10:1 is that it reminds us that we are not alone. Many parents have gone through similar ups and downs. They made it and so will you. This path may not be the one you would have chosen for yourself, but God will sustain you.

Celebrate how your wise and discerning children are honoring God, but don't despair over the children who are not honoring God. God will strengthen you and always remind you he is there. ✤

PARENTING PRINCIPLE

Parenting will be filled with highlights and lowlights—be faithful in both.

POINTS TO PONDER

- How wise were you as a son or daughter?
- Does grief keep you from being a focused parent?
- What is something you should celebrate today?

LEARN TO EARN

Ill-gotten treasures have no lasting value. PROVERBS 10:2

If you think about it from the perspective of a three-year-old, how he got something doesn't really matter to him. Whether a parent bought it or he took it from a playmate, the end result is the same: It's his now!

But to allow the three-year-old mentality that makes it okay to take from a playmate to develop into adult behavior would convey that stealing is okay. You must teach your children that what you have is the result of hard work, not taking from others. An additional caution is that if society promotes the principle that everyone should "have equally" then our children may not only develop poor work skills but resort to theft to make their world "even."

Be insistent on teaching at a very young age that stealing will lead to emptiness and dissatisfaction. And if this verse rings true, then the opposite thought will ring true as well: Treasures attained through hard work will be long lasting and valuable. ❖

PARENTING PRINCIPLE

Treasures of life are not things; they are things learned.

POINTS TO PONDER

- Think of someone who tried to get ahead by stealing and tell that story to your children.
- Are your children learning the value of working for what they want?
- What are some ways you are teaching them the value of work?

WORK FOR IT

Lazy hands make for poverty, but diligent hands bring wealth.   PROVERBS 10:4

The Bible is very clear about the difference between someone who is poor and someone who is merely lazy. Many people have nothing because they make no effort to help themselves. This is unacceptable. Yet, there are a lot of lazy people in our society.

This issue often becomes political when it's actually a Biblical issue. God expects us to work with all of our skills to provide for our family. Then we are to teach our family to provide for themselves, and that should continue into future generations. To instill this value in our children and help them appreciate the difference between laziness and hard work, it's a good idea to work together as a family to accomplish chores and other projects around the house.

Getting your children involved may slow down a task a bit or mean that something isn't done exactly as you would have liked it. But remember, that's okay because in the long run you are teaching them how to work. Focus on the big picture. That's most important. ❖

PARENTING PRINCIPLE

Give a child everything, and they will never stop taking. Teach a child to work, and they will never stop giving.

POINTS TO PONDER

- How do you define a hard worker?
- What age-appropriate chores are your children learning?
- What is a way that you could work together more as a family?

day30

NAME GAME

The name of the righteous is used in blessings, but the name of the wicked will rot.

PROVERBS 10:7

Have you ever met anyone who would do anything to keep their name held high, even if it meant turning their back on their child? When you see it, you want to make sure you never do it!

Your family name might go through the wringer a time or two as you raise your children—that's expected. But if you live a righteous life, please understand that your child who is not living a righteous life cannot block the blessings God will continue to give you. Think of it in the context of the old saying, "Don't throw the baby out with the bathwater." The name of the righteous will be blessed.

In other words, be righteous even if your child isn't. Your family will actually gain a higher place of respect if you continue to live a God-honoring life while you deal with your child's difficulties. Your name will be blessed even as people who do not honor God will have a name that rots. ✤

PARENTING PRINCIPLE

Your family name doesn't determine your reputation, your life does.

POINTS TO PONDER

- What reputation do you have among people?
- Have you ever been embarrassed of your family's name? Why or why not?
- What are some of your family blessings?

STRAIGHTEN UP

Whoever walks in integrity walks securely, but whoever takes crooked paths will be found out.   PROVERBS 10:9

It's fairly easy to sum up Proverbs 10:9: If you lie, you won't get by. Throughout history people have thought they could get away with the crooked path of life and be okay in the end. But you can tell your children no one has been okay to date. Unfortunately, humanity simply refuses to accept that the path of evil and crookedness doesn't work.

There is a good chance your child will decide to test this path too. It looks fun. It looks different. It looks like the path to plenty. And it is—the path to plenty of trouble!

As a parent, there will come a time when your words will not be enough to change or turn your child's heart. They will have to do it on their own. That's when the lessons of integrity you have taught them will hopefully take hold, and the principles and values of your home will overcome the temptation of the crooked path. ❖

PARENTING PRINCIPLE

Integrity is often the path less traveled. Make sure your children see you walk it.

POINTS TO PONDER

- What have been some of your crooked paths and the resulting consequences?
- Will you be patient as your child walks down a crooked path or two?
- By what examples are you showing your children to walk with integrity?

# day**32**

FILL THEM UP

The mouth of the righteous is a fountain of life, but the mouth of the wicked conceals violence.   PROVERBS 10:11

When people open their mouths, they usually have an opinion to express. This is especially true for the people who live in your home. When you think about it, would you say their words bring a fountain of life? For many of us, I'm guessing that's unlikely. However, it must be the goal.

Bringing life to your family involves speaking words of encouragement to your children. This means you are giving them hope through tough times. For example, you remind them of their talents when their report card knocks their self-confidence off the charts. When they miss a crucial shot on the basketball court or get a lesser grade on a homework assignment, you try to speak with comforting tones and offer uplifting encouragement versus attacking them or being confrontational.

How are you doing so far? Take time today to reflect on the past two weeks to see where you could have been more of a fountain of life. Accept your weaknesses in this area and grow. It's never too late to change the way you speak to your family. In some cases it may take a while, but it's possible to re-establish your reputation and be proud of your work in this area. ❖

PARENTING PRINCIPLE

Before you speak it, tweak it!

POINTS TO PONDER

- What would your family say about what comes out of your mouth?
- How could you take one step that would improve your language tone?
- What do you see your children imitating from you?

LOVE CONQUERS ALL

Hatred stirs up conflict, but love covers over all wrongs.　　　　PROVERBS 10:12

Hatred is a strong word. No one wants to admit to hatred in their heart. But hatred does exist, and sometimes it can be present in our families.

What eradicates it? Love! Love is the single greatest gift we can give to our family. Christ gave it to us by dying on the cross for our sins. Now we must follow his example and love those who don't always deserve it.

What does that look like? Simple. Don't return wrong for wrong. Don't speak evil of those who have done evil to you. Instead, spread forgiveness and love in the rows others have plowed against you. It might be contrary to how most people respond, but it's how God expects us to react. He tells us to love our enemies.

Your children will actually watch in shock and awe as you exhibit love where there should naturally be hate. This is the opportunity you long for—to tell them where this kind of love comes from and how Christ has instilled it into your life. ✤

PARENTING PRINCIPLE

Spread seeds of forgiveness and love into the rows others have plowed against you.

POINTS TO PONDER

- Who has been a great example of love for you?
- Are you replicating that example?
- When have you taught your children this principle?

day**34**

STAY FOCUSED

Let your eyes look straight ahead; fix your gaze directly before you.   Proverbs 4:25

Distractions are a major concern for parents. Many times we focus on completing one goal with our children, only to get sidetracked and accomplish nothing.

The key to keeping your paths straight and accomplishing your goals is to fix your eyes on the end goal. That commitment to completing the task will help you.

Distractions for parents can come in many forms. It might be issues you struggle with, outside forces, complications at work or with your children—the possibilities are numerous. Add to this all the times you have been distracted in the past, and it can seem pointless to think you could ever fix your gaze on what is directly before you.

Remember Proverbs 4:25—keep your eyes looking straight ahead or, in other words, focused. If you stay focused, you will be able to carry out the tasks before you. Once you win a time or two, you will begin to see hope for achieving even more accomplishments. ❖

PARENTING PRINCIPLE

Distractions are a part of life. Parting from distractions is a life choice.

POINTS TO PONDER

- What are some of the distractions that prevent you from keeping your eyes fixed on the goals you set?
- What distractions are you avoiding?
- What are some of the goals you have set for your family—long-term and short-term?

day35

EXERCISE GOOD JUDGMENT

Teach me knowledge and good judgment. PSALM 119:66

Exercising good judgment takes lots of discernment and expertise. When you think of wise judges who are able to listen to all sides of a case and then make knowledgeable decisions, you tend to respect them for their "good judgment."

As parents, we would like to earn long-term respect from our children for our ability to make wise decisions. When your kids are three years old and want a lollipop before dinner, of course you say no. If they want to eat all their Halloween candy in one sitting, you use good judgment to remind them that nutritionally it's not a good idea. They may not understand your decision in the moment when they're 16 and want to spend the night at a friend's house whose behavior you think is questionable, but they will one day. You say no because you're using good judgment.

Although they might not joyfully receive that decision and others, as a parent you are not interested in developing a present buddy/buddy relationship but rather a long-term relationship founded on wisdom and respect. That's why you need to make smart, informed and discerning decisions that will benefit your family. ❖

PARENTING PRINCIPLE

As you make judgments on behalf of your family, remember to align your decisions with what will matter on God's judgment day.

POINTS TO PONDER

- Where have you used good judgment with your children and where have you failed to use good judgment?
- How is your child doing at their age of responsibility in making wise decisions?
- How can you get your children involved in making decisions and wise judgment calls?

day36

BE HONEST

My mouth speaks what is true, for my lips detest wickedness. PROVERBS 8:7

Speaking the truth is of utmost importance in a parent-child relationship. A parent who lies to their child loses all credibility when asking for truthfulness in return. Notice that Proverbs 8:7 calls untruths wickedness. As parents, we are seeking to rid our homes of all wickedness. Truth is an important step in that process.

Take a simple test with your family. Put a jar on the kitchen counter and challenge every family member—including you—to put a nickel in the jar whenever they don't tell the truth. Include little "white lies." You will probably be surprised at how quickly the jar will fill up because, though we don't intend to, we stretch the truth a lot. This little family experiment will be a great way to push the idea of telling the truth to the forefront of your family life.

As you do this, talk with each other about what you are learning and how telling the truth has helped Proverbs 8:7 come alive. ✣

PARENTING PRINCIPLE

The family that tells lies together dies as a family together.

POINTS TO PONDER

- Why do you fudge on the truth?
- How does this harm your family?
- What would be the result if everyone in your family practiced the principle in Proverbs 8:7?

day37

THE TRUE CREATOR

Remember your Creator in the days of your youth, before the days of trouble come.

ECCLESIASTES 12:1

Our children are growing up in a time when they are told something other than that it was God who created them. If you ask a child who grew up in the last ten years how often they heard that God made them other than from people at church, they will tell you that it was not very often.

Children today are told they were formed some other way than by God. That's why it's important to remind them through your daily actions that God is their creator. You might have the only voice that's whispering that into their ear.

The reason it is so crucial is that if our children understand that God made them, they will also understand that he has a purpose for their life. Without that purpose, life becomes pointless fairly quickly, and through the teen years that mindset can show up in some rebellious and uncomfortable ways. So teach your children that God made them, that he formed them and created them for a purpose. ✤

PARENTING PRINCIPLE

Teach your children about the ultimate Creator.

POINTS TO PONDER

- Have you talked to your children about the Creator?
- How would you handle objections or doubts from your children about the Creator?
- How can you help your children discover their life's purpose?

day38 february 7

GET SMART

My son, do not let wisdom and understanding out of your sight.　　Proverbs 3:21

The theme of wisdom and understanding runs rampant throughout all of Psalms and Proverbs, making it obvious that it's a key factor for getting through life. It doesn't take new parents very long to figure out how much wisdom and understanding are needed. When your child isn't sleeping and you've gone sleepless as well, it takes wisdom to know how to keep it all together. It takes understanding to realize this stage will pass.

When your children are teens, there may be times when it appears they are devoid of wisdom and understanding. It requires mature parents to know that gaining wisdom and understanding is a part of their children's maturing. The process of growing in wisdom and understanding is one that is repeated throughout Scripture, and it's one that is repeated throughout the life of a parent.

A practical way to gain wisdom and understanding as a parent is to simply admit there are areas where you need assistance. Seeing a counselor or having a conversation with a pastor might be a good idea to help strengthen your position as a parent in a difficult situation.

Get smart about how invaluable wisdom and understanding are in the parenting process. ❖

PARENTING PRINCIPLE

Wisdom and understanding are repeated a lot in Scripture because they are needed repeatedly in our lives.

POINTS TO PONDER

- Why do you think God put the theme of wisdom and understanding in Scripture so many times?
- How often do you find yourself seeking godly wisdom, and how often do you try to wing it on your own?
- What are some practical ways you can continue to apply wisdom to your own life?

day39

MORE IS LESS

Do not withhold good from those to whom it is due, when it is in your power to act.

PROVERBS 3:27

It's so easy to point out the flaws in our children. They seem obvious, especially when they're little or they're teens. When they become adults, they still seem obvious. It's always been true that focusing on the negative is easier than the positive. If you don't believe me, just watch the evening news.

Our challenge as parents is to focus on the positives in our children and to give credit where it's due as we recognize those positives and realize it's in our power to act. Even if you have a child who is disobedient most of the time, point out, celebrate and reward those times when they do obey and their attitude is positive.

Every home needs a little bit of celebration. If your natural tendency is to focus on the negative, your children will react accordingly. Taking time to remind them that you will also key in on their positive actions will go a long way in unlocking tension in the relationship. Celebrate more and focus on negatives less. ❖

PARENTING PRINCIPLE

Maintain a healthy balance between celebrating the positive and needing to point out the negative when it's helpful.

POINTS TO PONDER

- How do you acknowledge negative behavior without building animosity?
- How do you celebrate positive behavior?
- How could you do a better job of celebrating accomplishments?

# day40   february 9

AVOID WICKED

The LORD's curse is on the house of the wicked.   PROVERBS 3:33

No one would ever want to classify their home as wicked or not God-honoring. Most people would do anything to protect their home from being called a place of wickedness. But in reality, many homes across our nation are wicked. Your children will probably enter homes where those who live inside practice wicked ways. That's why it's important to educate your children about what Scripture refers to as wicked and explain why you haven't chosen that lifestyle.

Don't be afraid to talk to your children about how wickedness may look fun and enticing, but in the end it leads toward death. Don't protect your children from knowing that wicked things exist. It's safer for your children, when it's age-appropriate, to talk about the schemes and wicked devices that are out there and available to everyone. Talk about it, and help them understand that God's desire is for us to make sure that we turn away from those types of homes and behaviors.

If one of your children is practicing wicked ways, it's important that you set boundaries for them and insist they follow your God-honoring expectations. ❖

PARENTING PRINCIPLE

God is the God of boundaries who will protect and guide you as you seek to honor and please him.

POINTS TO PONDER

- When have you seen wicked ways ruin someone's life? Tell your kids about it.
- How have you protected your home from wickedness entering in?
- With what kind of protection or boundaries can you surround your home?

MANY BLESSINGS

The LORD ... blesses the home of the righteous. PROVERBS 3:33

We read about how the Lord curses the home of the wicked, and now we see that he also blesses the home of the righteous. It's natural to wonder what those blessings look like, especially when you are going through a trial and not feeling blessed at all. You think there must be something wrong with you or that you did something to cause the adversity. But trials are just part of living on this earth, not God's way of removing blessings.

Therefore, when you evaluate the blessings in your life, you have to consider the big picture. Don't look at the momentary, day-to-day things. Look at your family overall. Blessings come in a variety of ways and can include longer-working appliances and cars that run smoothly, as well as good health and positive experiences. Your blessings may not be what you thought they would be, but God blesses those who honor and please him.

Throughout Scripture you can see that the house of those who followed after the Lord had a special touch on it, and that is true for us today. God is good to those who choose to follow after him. ❖

PARENTING PRINCIPLE

If you made a list of all your blessings, they would be as numerous as the stars.

POINTS TO PONDER

- What are the simple blessings in your life this week that have encouraged you?
- Do your children see you recognizing God's blessings and giving him thanks?
- How are you helping your children recognize the blessings that are part of your family?

day42 february 11

JUST LISTEN

Listen ... to a father's instruction. PROVERBS 4:1

This verse sounds awesome, but the reality is that its principle can be difficult to carry out in family life. If you as a parent aren't obeying your heavenly Father's instructions, then it's difficult to ask your children to listen to you. Asking your child to listen to and obey you when you aren't living a life that respects and honors God is foolishness.

Take a moment today and reflect on what it would take for your children to listen to you. It takes the ability to see that discipline doesn't always work the way you would like. It takes the ability to see that the path you would choose isn't always the path your children choose. Even though your children listen, their actions may differ from what you had hoped.

A practical way you as a parent can share this verse with your children is to show them how you seek to listen to God. Hopefully, your example will make their desire to listen grow. Incorporate thoughts about how you listened to your parents.

Being a parent is multi-faceted. Continue to grow in your understanding of God's love so you can pass that understanding on to your children. ❖

PARENTING PRINCIPLE

We should be fascinated at how God loves us and pass that fascination on to our children.

POINTS TO PONDER

- Did your parents model God's love for you?
- Where do your children see Christ in your actions and where do they struggle most with your actions?
- Pray for wisdom and guidance in knowing how to be a parent who teaches with patience and understanding.

PUSH PRIDE ASIDE

When pride comes, then comes disgrace.   Proverbs 11:2

Pride is difficult to manage in a family. For example, you want your child to be proud of the excellent grades he or she is achieving, but you don't want them to flaunt their intelligence in the classroom. Keeping a balance between healthy self-confidence and arrogance is challenging.

One of the best ways to teach your children this balance is to always remind them of how their talents and abilities come from God. Praises can easily go to a teenager's head. Help them remember that they need to keep their feet firmly planted in that knowledge to mature in this area.

Another key for parents is to believe in your children but don't "over believe" in them. What? I'm talking about how many parents tell their children they are or can be unbelievably good at everything. It's usually unrealistic, and all that does is set them up for a big fall when they get out in the real world.

It's good for anyone to be confident in who they are, and it's good to instill this confidence in your children. But you should never forget that, apart from Christ, you can do nothing. With him, you can do all things he would have you do, but then you need to give him the glory. ❖

PARENTING PRINCIPLE

Pride builds unhealthy arrogance while confidence builds healthy self-esteem.

POINTS TO PONDER

- Where do you see pride in your family life?
- How have you seen pride affect other families?
- Do your children have a healthy self-confidence? Why or why not?

 # day44

february 13

LIVING UPRIGHT

The integrity of the upright guides them.   PROVERBS 11:3

When a family member has integrity, it is a gift to the rest of the home. Remove that integrity, and the feelings toward that family member will be changed.

Families that thrive are full of upright individuals who seek each other's guidance and prosper together. What do you do to expose any areas in your family that lack integrity? In a healthy family, a lack of integrity will surface more quickly because the lack is not the norm. In an unhealthy family, it won't be exposed as easily because it will be hidden among other issues. You need to look closely at each family member's life and address areas where integrity is lacking. This effort may be uncomfortable, but it's necessary to maintain integrity in the home.

If your child shows signs of lacking integrity, you need to confront this issue quickly and remind them of Proverbs 11:3. Help them to instill more integrity in their life. ❖

PARENTING PRINCIPLE

Always live with integrity and you will always experience the guidance of God.

POINTS TO PONDER

- Is your family high in integrity? Are you?
- Where does your family need help with integrity? How can you help?
- Are you building barriers of protection around your family in this area? How?

FAMILY SECRETS

A trustworthy person keeps a secret. PROVERBS 11:13

A family has many secrets — or rather information or situations that shouldn't be shared outside the family. How those confidences are handled and which ones should be kept private is open for debate. Obviously, illegal or abusive actions should never be kept secret, but the type of secrets most families have should be held close to the heart. Building trust among family members is crucial to having a close-knit family. It doesn't take much for disunity to occur when trust is broken.

Wise parents help themselves and their children by having discussions about what is to be held within the family and what is regarded as open information. Allow yourself and your children some grace as mistakes are made, but then make sure you learn from those mistakes. Your children will learn to respect you more as you respect them more in this area.

Trust is a learned behavior and one that you can teach your children. ✤

PARENTING PRINCIPLE

Building trust in your family is critical to building unity.

POINTS TO PONDER

- Are you good at keeping secrets and confidences?
- Do you and your children have a good understanding of each other in this area?
- Are your children trustworthy in this area?

# day46 february 15

BE KIND

Those who are kind benefit themselves.   PROVERBS 11:17

We all love to be around kind people. They do something nice for you and you love them even more. Kind people also seem content. They may go through tough times, but even then, as you watch their life, you wish you could be more like them. In other words, kindness wins no matter how you look at it.

We need to teach our children the principles of kindness and help them develop this character trait. Kindness sees after needs. Kindness doesn't laugh at those less privileged. Kindness reaches the destitute. Kindness submits appropriately. And as Proverbs 11:17 says, those who are kind benefit themselves.

Talk with your children about how they view kind people and what they are learning from those acts of kindness. As they learn to read the Bible or hear the stories within, they will begin to see a pattern of kindness woven throughout Scripture. ✤

PARENTING PRINCIPLE

Be a family of kindness in your neighborhood and you will be a family of influence.

POINTS TO PONDER

- How have you shown kindness as a person and parent?
- What are some of the benefits you have seen as a result of your kindness?
- How are your children learning to be kind?

day47

BEAUTY AND THE BEAST

Like a gold ring in a pig's snout is a beautiful woman who shows no discretion.

PROVERBS 11:22

A gold ring in a pig's snout—what a comment! A comparable statement is when politicians say, "You can put lipstick on a pig, but it's still a pig." This verse teaches us that our beauty—and who we are—is not determined by the bling on our body but rather the character we have in our lives.

This is a message our children will not hear through any of their social media networks. It is a message we must teach at home because it will be greatly tested. Just expect it, and don't be surprised when your children try to express who they are through their clothing styles and body adornment.

You have taught them that their true value is in the Lord, so hopefully that knowledge will be the end result of their journey in defining themselves. Their outer appearance may differ from you or others, but internally they should strive to be like Christ in their words and deeds. ✤

PARENTING PRINCIPLE

A ring in a snout and bling in the belly button will pass, but a discerning heart will last.

POINTS TO PONDER

- Does your family make too much of looks? Be honest!
- Where do you see your main values coming from?
- Are your children finding their value in Christ?

AGAINST THE WIND

Whoever brings ruin on their family will inherit only wind.   PROVERBS 11:29

Deciding how to pass on heirlooms and split the family pot has been a source of contention for ages. One of the reasons is often because a child in the family has been a squanderer of the resources already given to them, and no one wants them to be included in the inheritance. Seems fair when you consider all the disappointment and possible ruin they brought on the family.

It's a challenging time when a father and mother have to make these decisions. That's why every child needs to know how their lifestyle and behavioral choices affect that determination. It could be the deciding factor for whether they end up with any inheritance at all.

Proverbs 11:29 seems to indicate that it's a parent's discernment that ultimately determines what happens to the family treasures. Use wisdom and seek godly counsel as you make this crucial decision for your family. And most important, teach your children that ruin brings ruin. ✤

PARENTING PRINCIPLE

If you ruin your family, you ruin your life.

POINTS TO PONDER

- Are you living to deserve the inheritance you might receive?
- What has the potential to ruin your family?
- Are your children bringing joy to your home?

GET OVER IT

Fools show their annoyance at once, but the prudent overlook an insult.

PROVERBS 12:16

Family life will include times of annoyance. It's just a fact of life that if you spend any amount of time together you will be bothered by something someone says or does.

Healthy families know how to deal with annoying moments. The most obvious way to be prudent is to get away from each other for a while. Usually that distance gives time for things to smooth out a bit, and then maybe a follow-up conversation can offer some additional healing for whatever has transpired.

Another way to improve in this area is to observe what, where and when these annoying times seem to occur in the family and seek to deal with the root causes. So often we endure the symptoms instead of dealing with the source of the trouble. Don't be afraid to explore the origin of these annoyances so you can experience them less. Never stop looking for ways to grow together as you endure flaws that are all part of typical family life. ❖

PARENTING PRINCIPLE

Instead of adding insult to injury, practice prudence and find peace.

POINTS TO PONDER

- How are you sometimes annoying to others?
- How do you handle annoyance in your family?
- How do you see your children dealing with personal annoyances?

# day50 february 19

STRESS LESS

Anxiety weighs down the heart, but a kind word cheers it up. PROVERBS 12:25

If you are prone to worry, you are all too familiar with the weight of anxiety. When your family goes through stressful times, you will feel a heaviness that could possibly lead to depression. Families will often experience this during holidays. There are a number of reasons that this type of stress could occur. It may start with one family member but then eventually extend to others.

Kind words exchanged among family members during this time will provide a great sense of relief, especially to the one who is dealing with the stress. Being aware of what is happening around you and the interpersonal issues that might exist will be crucial in helping your family through these seasons.

If someone in your family is more prone to stress than others, be sensitive to them and speak kind words and phrases. Then try to follow up with actions that will help them cope more easily. ✣

PARENTING PRINCIPLE

Lift the weight of a worried heart with the love of cheerful lips.

POINTS TO PONDER

- What makes you anxious or stressed?
- What ways have you developed in your family to cope with anxiety?
- Where do you see anxiety in your children that needs to be addressed?

day51

PREVENTING FOOLISHNESS

The way of fools seems right to them, but the wise listen to advice.   PROVERBS 12:15

No one plans to become a fool. But it happens. A teenager can get to a place where foolishness is masked as truth, and any advice offered other than what they want to hear falls on deaf ears. Teach your children at a young age to listen to people they trust, and then let them make their own decisions.

As an example, when in their early teens their friends are going to see a certain movie and they ask you if it's okay to see it, throw the decision back on them. Ask them if it's okay by their standards. They will learn to live by the personal values they have for themselves because you are helping them develop the ability to make sensible decisions.

Obviously, if they are listening to and following the advice of fools, you need to get involved. But typically, if children are empowered to make decisions when they are young, they will make better decisions as they age. This is not foolproof, but it is a general pattern. Continue to be wise as a parent and model this character trait for your children. ✤

PARENTING PRINCIPLE

Fools' names and fools' faces always lead to unhappy places.

POINTS TO PONDER

- What is a great piece of advice you have received recently?
- How did it help your family?
- How are your children wise? How are they not?

day52

TRUSTING TRUTHFULNESS

Truthful lips endure forever, but a lying tongue lasts only a moment. PROVERBS 12:19

Have you ever been around someone who told the truth sometimes and also lied at times? Is there anything more frustrating? Was it a family member?

Teaching our children the importance of telling the truth is a central part of parenting. Telling our children the truth is crucial. Liars last for only a moment. This means that those who lie will not have the reputation of someone who is reliable, and thus they have the potential to be a destructive force in any family. If you have ever watched this destruction occur within a family, you will never want lying anywhere close to yours. It's important to teach truthfulness early on to avoid this.

Make sure you discipline your children for lying when they are young; otherwise, their lying tongue will lead to disastrous results. Remember that the pain of punishment will lead to the trust of truthfulness. Such discipline is worth the price in the long run. Proverbs 12:19 implies that truth telling will last forever. ❖

PARENTING PRINCIPLE

The cost of punishing your children for lying will be worth the price when it leads to the trust of truthfulness.

POINTS TO PONDER

- What has been a destructive force in your past because of lies?
- What did you learn from it?
- Are you dealing appropriately with your children in this area?

day53

CHOOSING FRIENDS

The righteous choose their friends carefully, but the way of the wicked leads them astray.
PROVERBS 12:26

Do you remember how you chose friends in high school? I'm guessing righteousness wasn't on your checklist or the first thing you considered. So be patient as you see your children begin to choose their friends. They will definitely become like the people they hang out with, so help them see the pitfalls of having friends who don't make wise choices.

However, don't beat yourself up if they make some poor decisions. It's part of the maturation process and a natural function of growing up. Our goal as parents is to expose our children to as many nuggets of truth as they can receive and accept. Then pray they will own these beliefs as they align their lives with God's Word and God's will.

The key words in that last sentence are "God's will." We can often set our agenda and goals for our children ahead of God's will even in this area of friendship. Be careful not to judge your children's choices based on the choices you made at their age. This is an easy pitfall for parents—so be careful! ✤

PARENTING PRINCIPLE

Choose good friends and your children will benefit from your example.

POINTS TO PONDER

- What have you learned about making good choices in friends?
- What type of choices in friends are your children making?
- What are some things you can do to continue to guide your children in this area?

SHARING CREATION

Your hands made me and formed me.   PSALM 119:73

Our children are being raised in a society where many no longer recognize the Judeo-Christian heritage of our nation. To assume they will know that God is their creator would be foolish.

Teach your children that they are made by God and that he has a purpose for their life. Once they understand this, they will begin to grasp their purpose. Here are a few activities that will help them learn more about their creator.

Walk through a nature trail and discuss all you see. Talk about how the environmental system works and why it's delicate. Discuss the intricacies of plants and animals. Do this in a way that is understandable for their age. Talk about how God put it all together.

Find a dark place on a starlit night and talk about the massive universe. Show them the constellations and ask them how they think they all stay in place. Let them develop an awareness of God the Creator as they observe his creation. Share Scripture that matches what you talked about. ✤

PARENTING PRINCIPLE

The best way to discover the Creator is to look at his creations.

POINTS TO PONDER

- In what way can you better influence your child's beliefs?
- What else can you teach your children about God the Creator?
- How do you discuss theories out there about creation?

MAD GAB

Sin is not ended by multiplying words, but the prudent hold their tongues.

PROVERBS 10:19

Have you ever had anyone say you talk too much? Probably not! But perhaps they have wanted to. You can be assured as a parent that your child might not say it, but they will think it! When they are in the teen years, your voice will be like a metronome that won't stop ticking in their heads.

Don't lose heart in these times. They are normal. The key to a great and healthy relationship is not whether or not they want to hear you; it's that what comes from your mouth should not be gibberish, or a steady stream of words, or things you don't mean. Say what you mean and mean what you say, without multiplying words unnecessarily. And at times, it will be prudent to hold your tongue.

When you mess up—and you will—tell them you're sorry and press on. Parenting is a never-ending opportunity to grow. See your mistakes as growth spurts. ❖

PARENTING PRINCIPLE

Say what you mean and mean what you say. Live to parent another day.

POINTS TO PONDER

- Do you talk too much or say what you don't mean?
- If so, how could you use this challenge as an opportunity to grow?
- Are your children already multiplying words? How can you help them?

# day56

UNCOMMON SENSE

Fools die for lack of sense. PROVERBS 10:21

Common sense is a great gift from God. If you have plenty of it, be thankful.

Parents with common sense are much further ahead than others because they know how to discern what are big issues and little issues. They make their points and move on. They are easy to work with because they understand and remember what it was like to be a child.

Common sense will keep you from lots of pitfalls. Parents who use common sense are living life lessons in front of their children without even realizing it. That's beneficial, because common sense is developed through the natural process of maturing.

Children will develop their own common sense by the example you set. There will no doubt be periods when they will appear to have lost common sense, but their roots run deep and hopefully they will pass common sense on to your grandchildren. ❖

PARENTING PRINCIPLE

Common sense is not as common as you think. It needs to be taught and developed.

POINTS TO PONDER

- How did you develop your own common sense?
- Where could you use common sense more?
- How can you help your children develop common sense?

TREE STANDS

When the storm has swept by, the wicked are gone, but the righteous stand firm forever.
PROVERBS 10:25

There is a tree that stands by a body of water near my home. I have sat near that tree in the heat of summer. I have watched out the window during a storm and seen the branches twist around like a kite tail. I have also sat in my car near that tree in the dead of winter when the winds were howling and the snowflakes were flying, but the tree never wavered. After any and every storm the tree stands like nothing ever happened.

That is the picture I believe Christ wants us to show our children through all we face in life. We need to learn to be steady in an unsteady society. We need to be strong when everything around us is weak.

How do we do that? We do it by standing firm in our righteousness. By being holy as God is holy. God's Word and righteousness will stand the test and trials of time. ❖

PARENTING PRINCIPLE

The firmness and steadiness of a tree makes it a secure home for many of God's creations.

POINTS TO PONDER

- How are you like a steady tree?
- What could you do to be more righteous and steady?
- Are your children developing age-appropriate steadiness with their issues?

day58

february 27

SCALES OF JUSTICE

The LORD detests dishonest scales.   PROVERBS 11:1

One thing you will be accused of during your years of parenting is being unfair. If you have more than one child, you can count on one of them telling you how you like their sibling more than them and that their sibling gets away with more. It goes with the turf.

You have to be able to discern if there is any truth to what they're saying. It's true that each child requires different parenting to a degree, but determine if what your child is saying is fact. It might be, and nothing frustrates a kid more than unfairness.

Be sure you weigh issues with each child with "honest scales" and as much fairness as you can, and don't be afraid to seek outside counsel if necessary. Then move on as a parent. If you spend too much time dwelling on wrong decisions made in the past, it will hamper your future. Just accept that you will do some things that are unfair, but if overall you are continuing to work at keeping fairness at the forefront of your family, bless you and keep it up. ❖

PARENTING PRINCIPLE

There is no such thing as perfect parenting. Instead, be perfectly willing to practice fairness and diligence, and you will leave a great impression.

POINTS TO PONDER

- Have you ever felt like people were unfair with you, dishonestly evaluating you?
- Do you see fairness in your children?
- How do you practice fairness in your parenting?

STICKS AND STONES

The words of the reckless pierce like swords, but the tongue of the wise brings healing.
                                                                    PROVERBS 12:18

In your family of origin, did a parent or guardian's words bring hurt or healing? Children are affected by the words their parents or caregivers speak. They later influence the way we talk in our own homes. We either copy what our parents taught us or we do the exact opposite.

That's why it's important to recognize that your children are now analyzing your words. They are thinking about them and noting how they make them feel. They will decide if your talk is what they will want in their homes in the future.

Reckless words, which are all too often the norm in most families, are destructive. It's the wise parent who recognizes what some of their habitual reckless words are and seeks to remove them from their vocabulary. If they don't, they will earn a reputation for having a reckless tongue.

Healing words are essential to every family. When times of dissention and struggle come, the single act of speaking peace into those situations will be more helpful than we know. Speak peace into the life of your family. ❖

PARENTING PRINCIPLE

Sticks and stones only break bones, but piercing words destroy the heart and soul.

POINTS TO PONDER

- What was your home of origin like in this area?
- How often do your words pierce your family? What will you do to change that?
- Are your children developing the ability to offer healing words?

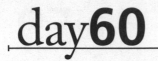

day60

PEACEMAKERS

Deceit is in the hearts of those who plot evil, but those who promote peace have joy.

PROVERBS 12:20

As a parent, you will be perplexed at times. You will see that despite all you do, the world brings a lot of evil and deceit to your family. No one is immune from it. What will frustrate you is that initially it will appear that people who regularly practice dishonesty or maliciousness are getting away with it. You will wonder whether God sees any of it, and many times you will feel like he doesn't.

But remember, those are feelings and not truth. History's lessons remind us that evil and deceit don't win in the end. What looks like someone living a life free of consequences is nothing more than a broken vessel.

This is why we must continue to live with peace in our hearts and integrity in our actions, regardless of what is happening around us. We must do all we can to promote a home of peace. We must not look at the initial short-term consequences of any situation but focus more on long-term joy for our families. Parenting doesn't happen all in one day. Peace doesn't always come in a day. But over time, freeing our homes and lives of deceit and promoting peace brings the ultimate desire: joy! ❖

PARENTING PRINCIPLE

The peacemakers will inherit joyful homes.

POINTS TO PONDER

- Where does deceit most often creep into your family life?
- What do you do in your family to promote peace and experience joy?
- How do your children join in the peace process?

DELAY IS OKAY

The prudent keep their knowledge to themselves, but a fool's heart blurts out folly.

PROVERBS 12:23

As you age, you learn that sometimes the best response is a delayed response. You've probably learned this when you've opened your mouth too quickly a few times and the results weren't helpful to a person or in a situation.

As a young parent, you will feel sure you know the exact thing to do in a certain situation, and then later you will discover that surety perhaps wasn't as certain as you thought. Life has a way of unraveling perfectionists and those living with absolute certainty.

Parenting is a much more reflective process. We learn by our mistakes, and we apply what we learn to avoid looking foolish the next time. If you are a quick-answer, always-right person and parent, you will be wise to memorize Proverbs 12:23. When this verse refers to keeping your knowledge to yourself, that doesn't mean you never share it. What it means is that you should discover wise and clever ways to reveal to your children what they need to know. You'll realize that often it's not your words but your life experiences that are the better teacher. ✤

PARENTING PRINCIPLE

A parent who ponders is often a great responder.

POINTS TO PONDER

- Are you a quick responder or do you ponder before you reply?
- Who do you know who is a great responder? What is it about that person you admire?
- What practical ideas do you have to improve in this area?

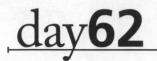# day**62**

STOPPING THE MOCKING

A mocker does not respond to rebukes.   PROVERBS 13:1

No one enjoys being rebuked, and most people don't want to be called a mocker, either. Mockers ridicule and divide others. They frustrate the hope of others and disappoint them.

But if you have a child who becomes a mocker, you will find it to be one of the most frustrating of all parenting moments. It will feel more like a lifetime than a moment. Often, mockers don't see (or won't see) what they are like. If you were to put on their shoes, it would appear as though everything that's wrong is someone else's fault. They will scorn your rebuke — and blame you!

What's a parent to do? First, be a parent of prayer. God will honor your cry for help and will be your hope for redemption. Second, continue to reprimand your child appropriately. Don't yell and scream, but simply continue to say and do the things that are right. Third, if you struggle knowing what is right, seek the help of a professional counselor or pastor.

Last, remember these things take time. That's not what we want to hear, but it's the truth. ❖

PARENTING PRINCIPLE

Mockers are talkers, but God can silence their nonsense.

POINTS TO PONDER

- Have you ever been a mocker? If so, how did you overcome that stage of life?
- How would you deal with a mocker in your home?
- What are you doing to guard your home from a mocking attitude?

day63

FINANCIAL PEACE

Dishonest money dwindles away, but whoever gathers money little by little makes it grow. PROVERBS 13:11

Just explaining financial principles to your children won't be enough. They are tough enough for adults to grasp, so young children will need more than just words. Start by getting your children a piggy bank. Teach them to save their coins and show them the result in six months. If you save, you have.

A recent study by Crown Financial revealed that in America the average person spends $1.22 for every $1.00 they earn. It doesn't take a genius to see where this is headed. When you live in a nation that spends more than it has, or in a home that spends more than it earns, it's easy for a child to fall into financial trouble even at a young age. Teaching your children the importance of money is huge. Giving them incentives to save and add to their account will help to increase their financial savvy. Just do all you can to promote healthy financial habits; your children are going to need them.

Be smart with your own coins too. It all adds up, and you don't want to leave a financial burden on your children as you get older. ❖

PARENTING PRINCIPLE

Waste not and want not!

POINTS TO PONDER

- What has been your pattern for spending and saving?
- What are the ways you are teaching your children to save?
- Are you doing a good job preparing for your own financial future?

# day64

WHERE PRIDE RESIDES

Where there is strife, there is pride. PROVERBS 13:10

If you experience strife and conflict in your home, look around and you will most likely find someone who is prideful. Inappropriate pride might be in one person, two people or everybody, but it's there.

Parents need to rid themselves of inappropriate pride if that's where it first exists in the family. What might this pride look like? It can come in all shapes and sizes. It might be in an arrogant parent who always thinks they're right and discourages anyone from questioning their decisions. It could be in someone's cunning deceitfulness that is subtle and crafty. However it is disguised, it's there!

Admit it. Own it. Confess it. Rebuke it. Get it out. The message is clear: Rid yourself of it because it will bring destruction to your family.

Then, after cleansing the parent realm, you can look at areas in your children's lives where inappropriate pride might reside. You can't remove their pride, but you can talk about how eliminating pridefulness in your life helped you. Show them how addressing pride will benefit them and the family as a whole. But be sure to deal with it so there can be long-term peace where constant strife cannot penetrate. ✤

PARENTING PRINCIPLE

Just as strife is a symptom of pride, family destruction is a symptom of uncontrolled strife.

POINTS TO PONDER

- Are you prideful? Can you admit it?
- How could making changes in this area help your family?
- What are you doing to keep your children's pride in check?

day65

THE POWER OF HOPE

Hope deferred makes the heart sick, but a longing fulfilled is a tree of life.

PROVERBS 13:12

If you have ever had a rebellious child, you will understand Proverbs 13:12 on a whole new level.

Hope that your child will overcome the issues they are facing is what keeps a parent going. Remove that hope and they are dealt a severe blow that seems overwhelming. Many have endured this very situation. When you are in it, you have to rely on the Lord and press on. There is no quick word or answer. You can't just snap your fingers and have it all go away. It is only in the strength of the Lord that we are sustained.

But if you let that hope return until a breakthrough—a longing fulfilled—occurs, you will feel like a parent who could leap tall buildings. The joy and restoration that return to a heart that has been hopeless are almost unimaginable. When the prodigal son or daughter returns, you'll not only kill the fatted calf, you could eat the whole thing at one sitting. This is the cycle of parenting. It will happen to most parents. Be forewarned and be prepared. ✣

PARENTING PRINCIPLE

You will discover in parenting that you will do as well as your child is doing.

POINTS TO PONDER

- What has occurred in your family life that Proverbs 13:12 addresses?
- Are you experiencing hopelessness today?
- How are you seeking Christ for strength in these circumstances?

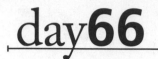 **day66**

RULES RULE!

Whoever scorns instruction will pay for it, but whoever respects a command is rewarded.

PROVERBS 13:13

You must teach your children to respect your parenting rules and guidelines. If they don't care to, remind them of Proverbs 13:13. Those who receive these instructions will find great joy and purpose in life and be a great family member. Those who don't will frankly be difficult to live with.

How does this apply to you? First, you need to look at yourself and determine if you are one who receives instruction or one who does not. Second, look at your children, who will also be one kind of person or the other. Third, develop some basic rules of the home—commands, if you will, to live by. Last, require that everyone in the family receive and respect instruction—and then reward them when they do.

Pray for wisdom as you establish these basic guidelines. If these expectations are set early on, they will be guiding lights for your family. This technique will also help keep you from changing the rules all the time if you keep the rules simple—a rule, for example, like "respect yourself and respect others." This simple little command will be crucial as your child passes through the early stage of life and into adulthood. After all, everybody answers to somebody. ❖

PARENTING PRINCIPLE

Commands or guidelines are usually viewed as negative or restrictive when they are in reality freeing.

POINTS TO PONDER

- What are some commands or rules your parents had that were helpful? Were any harmful?
- What are some rules you can develop for your family that will guide you as you grow together?
- How well do your children listen when you instruct?

WISE WORDS

The teaching of the wise is a fountain of life.   PROVERBS 13:14

One of the wisest individuals I've ever had the privilege of meeting was the late Coach John Wooden, the famous NCAA basketball coach of the UCLA Bruins. His fame, however, didn't come just from the action on the hardwood floor. It also came from the wisdom of his words.

Once, I had the privilege of spending several hours with him during which I asked many questions. One of the questions I asked was, "Coach Wooden, when you have departed from this world and ESPN is broadcasting a special about your life, what do you hope they will say?" As he always did, he pondered a moment before answering, and then gave this spellbinding reply: "I hope they don't mention basketball. I hope they focus more on how I loved my Lord, my wife, Nellie, and my family."

That's it! When it's all said and done, that's wisdom of the highest regard, that those who are around you know you love them with all your heart. I learned from a wise man, and I want to pass that same wisdom on to my children. Let us all be faithful to the great calling God has placed on our lives. ♣

PARENTING PRINCIPLE

Get and give wisdom—whatever you do, get and give wisdom.

POINTS TO PONDER

- What story could you tell your children about a wise person you have known? Tell it.
- How are you attaining wisdom?
- How can you seek God for wisdom for your home?

LET THEM DECIDE

Good judgment wins favor.   PROVERBS 13:15

Teach your children that as they make good decisions they earn more trust and win your favor. Of course, conversely, bad decisions destroy trust and cause them to lose favor.

When parents make too many decisions for their children, they actually delay the maturing process for them. And if you are with your child and someone asks them a question, don't answer for them. If you do, you only curtail their independence and hinder their social skills.

As they decide on hobbies and careers, don't tell them what they like; let them tell you. This is how they learn to make decisions, though you can guide them along the way and help cultivate their good judgment.

Get them to see the value of making decisions by letting them make decisions. Give them age-appropriate choices. Of course, if they are heading in the wrong direction, use wisdom to guide them. But help them to see the benefit of making good decisions on their own, including winning favor. ✤

PARENTING PRINCIPLE

You can lead a horse to water. But if you shove their head in it, it doesn't taste nearly as good.

POINTS TO PONDER

- Do you have and use good judgment?
- How could you improve in this area?
- Are your children being allowed to develop their judgment? If not, what will you change to let this happen?

day69

THE BENEFITS OF DISCIPLINE

Whoever disregards discipline comes to poverty and shame, but whoever heeds correction is honored.   PROVERBS 13:18

Discipline is the way to life.

Does this sound like an ironic statement? Most people think of discipline as a burden that is placed upon an individual. No child celebrates discipline. Yet it's the hope for everyone. It teaches us the right way to live and how to overcome challenges. It guides us when our self-will would choose a lesser way. It challenges us to be all we can be.

But to both discipline your children and teach them self-discipline is to give them hope for the future. Physical discipline, spiritual discipline, mental discipline—the list could go on and on. Reflect on these disciplines and consider which ones could be effective and helpful to guide your home. Be an example of living a disciplined life for your children so they will see the importance of it for their lives. Celebrate and embrace discipline with your children and cite examples of how it has helped everyone from the president of the United States to the athlete or the engineer.

Discipline is central to your child's health and welfare. And though your children may at times fail in discipline and in fact need to be disciplined, teach them that heeding correction brings them honor. ❖

PARENTING PRINCIPLE

Discipline may seem difficult; yet it makes the difficult easier.

POINTS TO PONDER

- How do you practice discipline in your life?
- What are the benefits of discipline in your life?
- How are you instilling in your children an appreciation for discipline— both being a disciplined person and accepting correction?

REGARD THE RIGHTEOUS

Trouble pursues the sinner, but the righteous are rewarded with good things.

PROVERBS 13:21

If you notice, those who live in sin and make bad choices always seem to be dealing with trouble. In addition, sinners always think their trouble is somebody else's fault. Troublemakers and troubled people can't seem to "own it." They can't admit when trouble is their fault.

Try to find examples of this behavior in our society and then let your children observe it. Don't wait until they are older. Teach them early on in their adolescence. Let them see the consequences of bad decisions.

In contrast, show them examples of people who live righteous lives that have obviously resulted in their having good things. Teach them that although those people also deal with tough issues, they don't blame others and make it through because of their righteousness.

If your children ever find themselves in that "trouble" zone, you can hope and pray those examples they observed will provide direction for their long-term growth! Be faithful with your instruction. God determines the outcome. ❖

PARENTING PRINCIPLE

Pursue righteousness and you will handle trouble gracefully and be rewarded.

POINTS TO PONDER

- Who are some examples of troublemakers? Who are examples of righteous people who come to mind?
- What are some of the rewards God has blessed you with in your life?
- How are your children seeing and learning about God's blessings?

BUILDING BLOCKS

The wise woman builds her house, but with her own hands the foolish one tears hers down.   PROVERBS 14:1

A wife who builds a home is filled with character. She knows how to encourage those around her and fill their lives with good things. A mom who builds a home will have life-long support and love. As she ages, her needs will be met by those who have been the recipients of her goodness.

The opposite will be true for a wife or mom who squanders her opportunity to build a home and loving family. She will be mocked and turned away from. Her days will be lonely, and foolishness will follow her all the days of her life. That doesn't sound good for anyone.

The obvious question for a wife or mom is this: What will you do? Think about your home and determine if you are building it up or tearing it down. Be honest with yourself. Ask your family to give you input. Be prepared for whatever feedback you receive. If it's less than positive, accept this truth and be willing to change. Learn to grow in wisdom, and instead of becoming defensive, let it help you become all the wiser and wonderful for your family. ❖

PARENTING PRINCIPLE

A wise mom is a great builder and an incredible gift to her home.

POINTS TO PONDER

- What are you doing to become all you can be for your family?
- What areas of foolishness are there in your life?
- How would your children answer questions like the above about you?

DETECTING DEVIANTS

Whoever fears the LORD walks uprightly, but those who despise him are devious in their ways.   PROVERBS 14:2

Have you ever known a devious person? What did you see happen in and to their life? How difficult was it to be around them? Do you want to be around them today? Did you think they were not honoring the Lord with their behavior?

We would probably all answer those questions the same way, especially if the devious person was someone in our family. Devious people in families are nothing more than home wreckers and troublemakers. That spirit needs to be purged from the family. To allow them to continue in their devious ways is to allow your home to be filled with strife. Pray for God to expose it if deviousness does reside in your family.

Be diligent, and watch for devious ways in your children before they become one of those troublemakers. Teach them how devious ways lead to more trouble ahead and do not honor God. While that's going on, don't forget to celebrate the uprightness that exists in your family. Too often we get blinded by the struggles of one child and take for granted our children who walk uprightly. We need to see those God-honoring children as a great blessing on a daily basis.

Stay involved. Be aware. Be on the lookout. These actions will be keys to maintaining an upright home. ❖

PARENTING PRINCIPLE

Diligent parents detect devious ways.

POINTS TO PONDER

- What have you learned from recognizing your own devious ways or the devious ways of others?
- Why does uprightness matter to God?
- How do you detect devious ways in your children?

PURITY TEST

To humans belong the plans of the heart, but from the LORD comes the proper answer of the tongue.   PROVERBS 16:1

It won't be long into the life of parenting before you will see manipulation that can be generated by the plans of an impure heart. By the time your child is a toddler, they'll be gifted at it. Teens could make a living at it. It's just part of the deal. Being able to discern if your child's motives are pure will be crucial in your family's development.

Parents can be guilty too. It's easy to project a pure heart in some parenting situations, knowing all the time that manipulation is part of your plan. Being honest with yourself is important. If your home is filled with manipulation, there will be a tipping point when the whole family will topple over and suffer irreparable damage.

Begin with yourself. Check the motives behind your plans to make sure they honor God and then move to an examination time for each member of the family. When the motives fail the purity test, address them, and seek to change the direction taken. By talking about it and dealing appropriately with it, manipulation can be avoided so that everyone wins. ❖

PARENTING PRINCIPLE

If the path you walk is pure, then your ways will be pure.

POINTS TO PONDER

- Do you have questionable motives at times?
- How do you protect yourself from letting this become your mode of operation?
- Do you see and correct manipulative behavior in your children?

# day74

HOPE VS. PLANS

Commit to the LORD whatever you do, and he will establish your plans. PROVERBS 16:3

Most parents have a plan laid out for their family. We dream dreams as our kids grow, and sometimes they come true.

But other times, they don't. The problem is that we forget that it is God who establishes the plans. By committing our lives to God, we don't get to decide the outcomes of our lives or our children's lives. Too often we respond with disbelief when life is not working out as we had hoped. We don't understand that God's ways are not our ways. His plans for us may not even be on the road we are traveling or had hoped to travel.

The process of accepting this is called maturity. It's the level of spiritual maturity Job dealt with. Jesus exemplified it. Now we must trust that God's plan is the best—even if it doesn't look like it. Our goal is to commit whatever we do to God. At that point, we find complete surrender and complete joy. Yes—joy! ✤

PARENTING PRINCIPLE

If you parent with a "my way or the highway" mentality, God might take you to a dead end.

POINTS TO PONDER

- How do you commit you and your family to the Lord?
- How do you react when something doesn't work out the way you planned?
- How can you help your children discover God's plan for them?

KNOW THE WORD

Through love and faithfulness sin is atoned for; through the fear of the LORD evil is avoided.
PROVERBS 16:6

Jesus is the author of love and faithfulness. He has atoned for our sins, our children's sins and the sins of any others who will follow in our lineage. Our families have hope today because our Savior has paid for all the sins we will ever commit. Make sure your children know this powerful truth. Jesus gave us an awesome gift that we should be grateful for every day, and we should help our children understand its power.

What does God ask from us in return for this gift? He wants us to turn away from and avoid evil through the fear of the Lord. We must teach our children the consequences of evil so they will understand how important this is. Now, that doesn't give us immunity from evil existing in our family. But if they know about his gift our children can act upon it when they recognize their own need for atonement. They will see their own path to avoid evil.

Be faithful to teach God's Word and plan to avoid evil—for today and for the generations to come. ✤

PARENTING PRINCIPLE

The best way to avoid evil is to know God's Word.

POINTS TO PONDER

- What has Christ's atoning power done for you?
- How do you show that you have proper fear of the Lord?
- How are you teaching your children Biblical concepts?

day76

LESS IS MORE

Better a little with righteousness than much gain with injustice. PROVERBS 16:8

Much gain is a tempting thought. Who wouldn't like to have more stuff? What teen wouldn't like a new car and all the trimmings that go with it? Many times a quick gain comes through illegal and unjust practices. It's happening daily all around us. And because our children live in this world, we need to teach them that gain through unjust practice is wrong.

As a parent, the process of teaching our children how to attain money honestly and then save little by little so their savings will grow is essential in helping them to develop healthy financial skills. Each child will understand this in different ways, so seek to develop tools and ideas that guide them with their unique perspective.

Raising responsible children who appreciate a little and not always yearn for more—especially by unjust means—will be no easy task. But teaching these concepts early on in their life will give you a good foundation to build on. As they attain more and mature, they will be able to become good stewards of all their blessings—and realize the validity of Proverbs 16:8 along the way. ❧

PARENTING PRINCIPLE

Little by little, bit by bit, with perseverance and effort, you will win the race.

POINTS TO PONDER

- How have you been a good example of righteous gain and not unjust gain?
- What do you do to make sure your family is grateful for all you possess?
- What have your children learned about earning and saving money?

MUST TRUST

Whoever gives heed to instruction prospers, and blessed is the one who trusts in the LORD.

PROVERBS 16:20

To listen to good instruction is to learn from others who are wiser than you. To accept this instruction doesn't just mean you are open and willing to grow. God says you will prosper.

To prosper means to succeed at an activity or to become strong and flourish. This is the dream of every parent for their child. When we see our children succeed or flourish, they are some of the most joyous and successful moments we'll experience. Proverbs 16:20 teaches us that the willingness of a child or individual to listen and grow is a tremendous key to their success.

Often our children think we do what we do, especially in the area of instruction, because we like to hear ourselves talk! Make sure they know the idea of teaching and instructing is Biblical. We didn't just come up with it for their annoyance.

The latter part of the verse is for us as parents. We must trust the Lord with what we have taught our children and pray it takes root and grows as they develop into adulthood. It will be their own beliefs that finally help them to also trust fully in the Lord. ❖

PARENTING PRINCIPLE

Listen and learn, prosper in turn.

POINTS TO PONDER

- Are you good at receiving and giving instruction?
- What is the last instruction you received that you greatly benefitted from?
- As a family, how could you all win in this area?

ROAD LESS TRAVELED

There is a way that appears to be right, but in the end it leads to death. PROVERBS 16:25

Have you ever been on track toward a goal, but when you reached the goal it wasn't what you expected? That's the road the world is taking. It looks right. It feels right. Everybody else is traveling that way. But in the end—surprise!

Our children will be tempted to take this much-traveled road, just as we are sometimes tempted. They will think they're the one who will finally get the end result everyone else has missed. Satan is cunning and knows how to make wrong look right and right look wrong.

But we know different. We know to watch for any fake detours that are all too often available to us. Talk to your children about these detours that lead to dead ends. As they experience pitfalls, even early on in life, use those pitfalls as teaching moments. Just yelling at children and telling them how "stupid" they are is not parenting. It's confusing. Patience and wisdom will be your comrades as you walk this road with your family. ❖

PARENTING PRINCIPLE

The road less traveled will seem lonely but it leads to life.

POINTS TO PONDER

- What have you done that appears right but was wrong?
- What did you learn through that experience?
- What roads are your children traveling, and are they heading toward a dead end?

day79

GRAY IS GOOD

Gray hair is a crown of splendor.   PROVERBS 16:31

Our society doesn't see gray hair the same way the cultures in Bible times did. In those times, gray hair was a beautiful representation of a wise, elderly and much-respected person.

In our day, it is more of a representation of someone who just slows us down. People don't listen to the wisdom those with gray hair have attained. Our children will be influenced by our culture to think that same way unless we do something about it. I propose that you expose your children to those who are elderly by putting them in a place where they can hang out together. Older people love to be around children and vice versa. Just their being together will help your child build respect for the elderly. Allowing your child to hear them tell their stories and other incredible life experiences will develop in your child an appreciation for them.

In a world that's trying to figure out how to make euthanasia legal, let's help our family develop a healthy understanding of God's love for the elderly, and make sure we invest in their lives. ❖

PARENTING PRINCIPLE

Respect the elderly. You will be there one day.

POINTS TO PONDER

- What elderly person do you spend time with who has given you wisdom?
- How could you develop more relationships with the elderly?
- Are your children learning to respect and appreciate the elderly?

TEACH THEM EARLY

A prudent servant will rule over a disgraceful son and will share the inheritance as one of the family. PROVERBS 17:2

Rebellious adults and children who make poor decisions sometimes don't get it. They want to blame everyone else in the family for their poor choices. Then if the family reaches out to or cares for another—a friend, a neighbor or even an employee—they sometimes assume the family is trying to replace them or doesn't love them anymore. They just don't own their decisions and their consequences.

We hope this never happens in our home, but we need to be prepared. Your children need to hear you talk about the fact that poor decisions will lead them to trouble, and that trouble will make them feel separated from those who love them most and possibly feel jealous of others. You can't imagine it could happen when they're toddlers, running around all cute and pliant. But they don't stay that young forever. As they age, you'll see changes in their behavior, and some behaviors will be quite shocking.

So be prepared. Have conversations with your children now about how you will stand your ground as they get older and test you. It will help you as you cope with a child who feels left out and estranged when you do stand your ground. Make sure they learn to own their decisions and not blame others for the consequences of bad choices. ❖

PARENTING PRINCIPLE

You will want to blame yourself for an estranged child, but they are responsible for their decisions.

POINTS TO PONDER

- How will you prepare yourself to deal with this if it happens in your family?
- Have you observed it in other families? With what results?
- Have you taught your children your expectations as they age?

THE PERILS OF PARENTING

A wicked person listens to deceitful lips; a liar pays attention to a destructive tongue.

PROVERBS 17:4

No one ever sets out to become wicked. We all think we'll never be deceived. Then, if and when we are deceived, we might refuse to accept it. But if wickedness has entered into our lives, then we are vulnerable to more deceit and destructive tongues.

The key for parents is to watch for front doors wide open or back doors slightly cracked open where deceit has the opportunity to barge in boldly or sneak through quietly in the first place. Watch with diligence and fervor. Observe your own life too. Remember, Satan is subtle. Deceit tends to creep in over time. It is often disguised in the form of beauty, leaving those who are unprepared shocked by the ugliness underneath. Wisdom and maturity are needed to have a discerning eye. If your child is prone to listen to those who lie, they will fall prey to the temptation to lie. You may need to have some strong boundaries around the other family members to protect them from the destruction your child's lies can lead to.

No one wants to face these circumstances, but they often come with the perils of parenting. So simply be prepared. ✤

PARENTING PRINCIPLE

Keep the doors to deceit shut and locked.

POINTS TO PONDER

- What guards have you put in place to protect your family from deceitful lips?
- How have lies harmed you in the past? What did you learn?
- How have you handled it when your children lied?

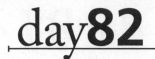

day82

REACH OUT

Whoever mocks the poor shows contempt for their Maker.　　　　PROVERBS 17:5

One of the principles every parent wants to teach their children is to care for the poor. Ironically, what is taught often ends up as mostly lip service because we rarely get our families involved in actually helping the poor. It can be inconvenient and uncomfortable. It's a lot easier to tell the kids that you sent a sum of money to an organization that provides services to the economically disadvantaged than to help them show care in person.

Instead of the easy way out, consider the difference it might make to actually go out, meet and get to know someone who is in need. Invite them and their possibly unkempt lifestyle into your home. Eat with them. Talk to them. Help them. Put a face on the world of the poor. Get your children's hands involved in actually touching their lives. Who knows, helping the poor might be their life's calling. What a joy to know your child might actually do something with their life that Jesus commands us to do.

Most parents want to teach their children to truly care for the poor, but to actually help them do it involves effort and perhaps risk. ✤

PARENTING PRINCIPLE

If the poor will inherit the earth, then be sensitive to that part of God's heart.

POINTS TO PONDER

- What do you do to impact the lives of the poor?
- How do you get involved in personally touching their lives?
- How can you get your children more involved in helping the poor?

FOSTER LOVE

Whoever would foster love covers over an offense, but whoever repeats the matter separates close friends. PROVERBS 17:9

Love sometimes feels like more than a four-letter word. It will rock you, break you, cause you to submit and teach you more about yourself than you ever hoped to know. If you love "Jesus style," you will die to yourself more times than you would have ever imagined.

But God's Word teaches that this kind of love and its consequences are wonderful for your family to experience because they will foster amazing relationships. It won't always feel so wonderful, however, because God is faithful to teach us in all our offensive ways.

But there is a limit to what God asks of us. A family member or friend can cross a line that separates us. Our goal is to foster love in such a way that it isn't taken advantage of but is used to overcome all the challenges that family life can face.

Be willing to be Christ-like so God can do his work among your family, even when an offense separates you. ✤

PARENTING PRINCIPLE

Of all the four-letter words your family experiences, keep *love* at the forefront!

POINTS TO PONDER

- How do you foster love through different circumstances?
- What has caused you separation in the past?
- What are you doing to keep your children close in love?

day84 march 25

BE A BLESSING TO GRANDPARENTS

Children's children are a crown to the aged. PROVERBS 17:6

Grandchildren are supposed to be a great blessing to grandparents. Almost every grandparent would agree. But when grandchildren are defiant and disrespectful, that golden crown Proverbs 17:6 speaks of turns to a thorny one.

Teach your children that they are a joy for their grandparents to be around. Encourage them to be respectful and loving by letting them assist their grandparents with chores and listening to their stories from years gone by (even when those stories are repeated). In other words, to be a blessing. Grandparents are irreplaceable. Just ask anyone whose grandparents have passed away. They will tell you they wish they had one more day with them to let them know how thankful they were to have them around. So if that window is still open for your children, help them through it and benefit from the experience. Someday they will be glad they did.

Grandparents also need us. It may be especially frustrating to be around older grandparents sometimes, but without them none of us would be here. Be thankful and show that thanks by being involved and having the children involved in their lives. ✤

PARENTING PRINCIPLE

Celebrate your parents and you'll have a better chance of being celebrated as parents.

POINTS TO PONDER

- Do you have a good relationship with your parents? Why or why not?
- Do your children understand how special they are to your parents?
- What do your children do to celebrate their grandparents?

day85

RESPOND WITH LOVE

Do not repay anyone evil for evil. Be careful to do what is right in the eyes of everyone.
ROMANS 12:17

Are you a revenge seeker? Do you feel like you win when you pay someone back? Romans 12:17 commands us to not return evil for evil, but to do the right thing and forgive those who offend us.

This is contrary to what is practiced in our society. Do you have a neighbor who's tough to get along with? Do your children see how you act or react when you're around that neighbor? Are you happy with how your child sees you respond? God is expecting us to show kindness to everyone, even those who make us miserable.

There is a country song about a dad who hears his child use a four-letter word. Then he asks the child where he learned that word. The child responds by saying, "I've been watching you, Dad. Ain't that cool!" Our children will learn how to react to those who aren't easy to deal with by watching us respond to it.

Don't build a foundation that includes repaying evil because of your unwillingness to forgive those individuals who make your life tough. ✤

PARENTING PRINCIPLE

Forgive when you can—all you can and keep your home clean and free!

POINTS TO PONDER

- How do you handle evil people?
- Do you exact revenge when you get a chance?
- How could you improve in the area of forgiveness?

THE BENEFITS OF SIBLINGS

A brother is born for a time of adversity.   PROVERBS 17:17

How cool is it to raise our children to see that they are a gift to each other? They have been born to help and care for each other, especially in difficult times. Sadly, in too many families, the brothers and sisters actually become adversaries of each other. What can a parent do to prevent this from happening?

Parents can only do so much. You can teach your children to respect and value each other when they are young, but as they age and become adults, they will decide how deep their sibling friendships will grow.

We can, however, do our part by treating each child fairly and making sure we help them understand the gifts they have and how they might be helpful to the family at large. Maybe one child is good with numbers, and another is creative. Blended together, they can hopefully complete each other rather than compete with each other.

Help your children develop as individuals, and then see how their own gifts and skills can benefit their siblings and eventually foster healthy relationships. ✤

PARENTING PRINCIPLE

Don't force your children to be best friends but help them foster healthy relationships.

POINTS TO PONDER

- Do your children understand how they could be a blessing to each other?
- How were you in understanding how to build healthy relationships with your siblings?
- How could you help your children appreciate each other more?

NO FIGHTING ZONE

Whoever loves a quarrel loves sin. PROVERBS 17:19

As parents of siblings, you have seen how children squabble. As a parent, nothing can wear you out more than two kids who just can't learn to share a toy or refuse to get along. It happens. It's part of a family's life. What's important for every parent to note is that it can't go unchecked. You can't allow the children to start quarrels and run over each other all day long, because the result will be children who believe they win and get what they want by fighting. That leads to sinful behaviors that will bring long-term destruction on them and the family.

The process of monitoring these quarrels on a daily basis is one of the most energy-draining, thankless, pooping-you-out parts of parenting. You will want to pull out your hair. In fact, you will actually utter that very thought!

It's our responsibility, however, to press on and teach our children not to quarrel endlessly for the simple fact that it keeps them from moving into a selfish and sinful lifestyle. ❖

PARENTING PRINCIPLE

Stop the fight and see the light.

POINTS TO PONDER

- Who in your family instigates a lot of quarrels?
- What are you doing to change his/her unhealthy behaviors?
- What are you doing to encourage your children to be self-aware in this area?

day88

STAY, NOT STRAY

To have a fool for a child brings grief; there is no joy for the parent of a godless fool.

PROVERBS 17:21

Nothing scares a parent more than the prospect of having a child grow up and make their life hell! Many parents are just hoping their child does not make the same mistakes they did.

At all times, we have to keep perspective. A godless, foolish child will most likely never be in our homes. They might make foolish decisions, but seldom do they literally renounce God and all we have taught them. Even then, God's spirit has a way of prodding them and walking with them through the dark days.

Our children need to know that if they break the family rules and make bad choices, it's incredibly disappointing to their parents. It causes sleepless nights and long days. It can create a dreadful atmosphere in the home. Don't be afraid to tell them these facts. Let them know when they disappoint you. You don't ever want to know the enormous pain and grief that comes with having a godless child. Keep praying that this day never comes for you and your family. ✣

PARENTING PRINCIPLE

Pray your children will never stray from God. Simply pray.

POINTS TO PONDER

- Do you know of a family whose child has walked away from God? Do you pray for them?
- What will you do to protect your family as much as you can from Satan's deception?
- What do you do when one of your children breaks the family's rules?

day89

A DOSE OF CHEER

A cheerful heart is good medicine.   PROVERBS 17:22

What makes a cheerful heart? Ask a parent, and they will say what makes a cheerful heart is a home filled with laughter where the people are getting along and love each other. That's a single sentence to read and write, but oh how challenging it is to live out.

First, a home filled with laughter. Someone has to keep a light-hearted spirit in the midst of various family styles. A tone must be established that keeps a home a fun place to be. People have to practice loving and be engaging to keep a family cheerful and fun. It takes effort. Second, a place where people get along. As personalities develop and differences arise, it will be more difficult to get along. Find the commonalities among the family members and spend time there. It will encourage people getting along and enjoying each other. Third, simply love each other. Love is patient and kind. Love does not keep a record of wrongs. Love is willing to see views other than its own.

These are the ingredients that will keep the home cheerful, and the verse says a cheerful heart is good medicine. In other words, we all get sick and need these remedies. Let's practice them at home. ✤

PARENTING PRINCIPLE

Kids like to take medication if it tastes sweet. Cheerfulness is that kind of good medicine.

POINTS TO PONDER

- Is your home full of cheer?
- What could you do to improve the tone in your house?
- Do your children respond favorably to laughter in the home? What can you do to generate more?

FORGET, DON'T REGRET

The one who has knowledge uses words with restraint.   Proverbs 17:27

As a parent, there will come a day when you will want to "let it fly." By that I mean you will want to let some words rush out of your mouth that you might regret later.

When your child is having a temper tantrum and calls you the "meanest parent in the world," your mind will think of a quick but perhaps not loving retort. It will take much patience and wisdom to keep it all together. If your teen stands toe-to-toe with you and says, "You are an idiot," it will be hard to keep from saying, "It takes one to know one." But you will have to do so. The reason is because of your knowledge of where they are and your recollection of going there those times yourself.

Parenting is really all about maturity. It's realizing you may be able to talk with your child, but they may not be able to fully understand all you are saying. Their responses might trigger reactions of anger and brutal words. Be careful—they will recall those words and phrases the rest of their life. Be the adult. It will be difficult, but with Christ you can muster the restraint you need. ✤

PARENTING PRINCIPLE

Think before you speak or you might regret what's spoken.

POINTS TO PONDER

- Do you have good self-control when responding to your children?
- How could you improve in this area?
- When you are discussing issues with your child, can you remember what you were like at their age?

IN THE MOOD

Whoever has understanding is even-tempered. PROVERBS 17:27

If you have more than one child, there is a good chance you will have one who is moody. They will not be prone to exhibiting even-tempered behavior as often as your other child or children. You will probably have to intervene many times between them and their siblings to squelch a difficult situation. Speaking frankly, that one child who is more moody and whiney will most likely be the initiator of the problems most of the time.

It's easy to become more frustrated with this child and say things that only exacerbate the situation. But notice that Proverbs 17:27 indicates that with this child in particular, it will take understanding on their part to become even-tempered. It will not be natural. It doesn't mean something is wrong with them. Never say that. Teach them that it's how they have been created. It will take patience and understanding on your and their part to initiate methods that help them deal with their moodiness and temperamental swings.

Wise parents are involved in this process and become great cheerleaders for their child when they grow in this area. ❖

PARENTING PRINCIPLE

Tempers must be tempered.

POINTS TO PONDER

- Who is the most even-tempered and least even-tempered person in your family?
- Do you help the least even-tempered or make it tough for them?
- What methods can you come up with to assist them in this area?

MIGHTY TOWER

The name of the LORD is a fortified tower; the righteous run to it and are safe.

PROVERBS 18:10

Teaching your children the value of the name of the Lord has many benefits. He can be prayed to. He can be confided in. He is a good listener. And when you need it, he is a comforting, protecting fortress that we can run to.

When we run to God, we receive his protection and his love and mercy. There will be times you will not be able to comfort your child no matter what you do. When that happens, you can give them the knowledge that they should and can run to Christ. Tell them stories of how he has comforted you in your times of great trial or distress. Tell them how you have not been able to find that comfort in any individual or even your parents. Share with them that you can try other things, but nothing will replace that strong and fortified tower. It has stood for centuries and will remain sturdy when your family has gone.

So boldly proclaim his name and rest assured that he will not fail you or your family as you run to him. ✤

PARENTING PRINCIPLE

Teach your children where to run for comfort by running there yourself.

POINTS TO PONDER

- Have you been a good example of running to Christ?
- Do your children have an understanding of what this looks like?
- What does a fortified tower mean to you?

FALSE SECURITY

The wealth of the rich is their fortified city; they imagine it a wall too high to scale.

PROVERBS 18:11

It's easy to surround ourselves with stuff and think that we have great protection. We might believe a 401K has us all covered. We think having the right limit on our insurance policy is all we need. We might not verbally say those things, but subconsciously we think we are protected.

Job was in an incredibly protected spot—if belongings counted. But as we see, no wall could stop Satan's attacks. Let us learn from others who have faced incredible trials no matter how much they had.

We never find, as a family, our protection in what we do or have—it ultimately comes from God. Teach your children that their protection comes from the Lord. Don't give them a false sense of security by allowing them to trust in things or teaching them by your example that you trust in things. God is our final guardian, and he may allow us to be exposed to some trials for our own growth and good. ❖

PARENTING PRINCIPLE

Our protection comes from the Lord; not in what we have.

POINTS TO PONDER

- What do you sometimes put your faith in other than the Lord?
- How have you grown by being tested?
- Do your children put their trust in things or people?

# day**94**

LEARN TO LISTEN

To answer before listening—that is folly and shame.   PROVERBS 18:13

Do you ever prepare a response before the person you are talking with has finished their sentence? Do other family members think of you as an interrupter? If so, this devotional is for you.

Even when we don't agree with what another person is saying, we should listen in case there is a nugget of truth offered that would benefit us and help us become stronger as parents. Your child might have the wrong perspective on an issue, but they may have made an observation that would be helpful if you're open to hearing it.

Today, consider changing the way you approach conversations where there is a difference of opinion. Set a good example for your child by listening attentively to others. And open your heart to the possibility that you could improve your dialogue with your child by being attentive to what they say and using language that illustrates that attentiveness. ✤

PARENTING PRINCIPLE

Learn to listen. Listen to learn.

POINTS TO PONDER

- Are you a good listener or an interrupter?
- What could you do to enhance your listening skills?
- Is your child developing good listening skills?

day95

PREVENT SPIRIT CRUSHERS

The human spirit can endure in sickness, but a crushed spirit who can bear?

PROVERBS 18:14

Sickness is a part of family life. Sometimes sickness is a temporary thing, but many families deal with lifelong health issues. We have all witnessed the resolve of a family enduring some devastating health issues.

Crushed spirits on the other hand cause relational sickness that can rip a family apart. While physical sickness can sometimes draw a family even closer, this spirit-crushing sickness will only alienate family members. It comes from trust being broken, lies all around, deceit, and intentional harm aimed at a sibling or parent or child. Soon the person who is being attacked seemingly gives up and slips into a deprived state of mind and being.

Parents must guard themselves from spirit-crushing comments, tones and actions and also guard their children from spirit-crushing actions. Watch for it and keep it out of your family life. ❖

PARENTING PRINCIPLE

The most destructive sickness in your family might be the unseen.

POINTS TO PONDER

- Do you deal with a lot of sickness? The physical or crushed-spirit type?
- How does your family cope with it? In a healthy way?
- How are you protecting your home from the crushed-spirit variety?

GIVER OF GIFTS

A gift opens the way and ushers the giver into the presence of the great. PROVERBS 18:16

A child's first instinct will not be to give. In fact, one of the first words we are likely to hear from a child is "Mine!" Teaching them to develop giving habits will be instrumental in their understanding of how much God has given them.

How do you develop these giving qualities? First teach them to share. Most parents seek to do this right from the start, and it's the first step in learning to give. A second and most important step is to get them to not only share but actually give something they consider valuable to another child. Soon they will discover they are fine without whatever they gave and that it isn't the end of the world. Don't force your child to do it, but if it's age-appropriate, talk to them about how fun it would be to bless another child. Again, let it come from their understanding and development and not by force.

These types of actions will have a natural reward and they will feel a sense of fulfillment through their act of kindness. As they age and understand God's love for them, it will actually make it easier for them to receive. ❖

PARENTING PRINCIPLE

The act of giving is actually the act of receiving.

POINTS TO PONDER

- What have you done to set an example of giving for your children?
- How have your children developed the act of giving?
- What can you do as a family to grow in this area?

WORK IT OUT

A brother wronged is more unyielding than a fortified city. PROVERBS 18:19

If we take this verse literally and apply it to family life, we can see the importance of teaching our children to love each other and be understanding. We can mandate this behavior for the first few years, but there comes a point when they will have to make their own decision to be careful and not wrong each other. To be absolutely conflict-free would be almost unthinkable. But to expect your children to forgive each other and not allow disagreements to ruin their relationship is a fair ask.

When they are young, help them settle their disputes. As they age, give them the skills to handle them on their own. Help them understand each other's personalities—a biggie! Don't label your children with descriptive terms that put them in a box and make this reconciliation process difficult! If you see walls being built up against each other, be sure to help or ask if they want your help in leveling these walls.

Life will give siblings plenty of opportunity to disagree. Your goal is to teach them resolution skills, and then as they become adults you must let them work it out on their own. ❖

PARENTING PRINCIPLE

Help your children work it out and work yourself out of it.

POINTS TO PONDER

- How capable are you at resolving conflict between siblings?
- How did you learn the skills you have?
- Are there differences now that you need to resolve?

 # day98

BITTER IS NOT BETTER

Each heart knows its own bitterness. PROVERBS 14:10

Reflect a little on what can cause bitterness in a family. No one sets out on a course to bring bitterness to their family or life; it's just part of what can happen. A wrong word spoken. A lie that is never addressed. Hurtful actions by a family member. Soon a wall is built and the offended moves into a stage of unforgiveness that results in bitterness. It claims the lives of many families.

So the obvious thing we have to do is avoid letting things happen. But when they do, learn to address these incidents so they don't result in bringing this long-term harm on the family. Teach the children how to resolve conflict in healthy ways. Help them see how easy it is not to confront issues and the build-up that occurs. Be faithful to instruct even though it is tiring.

Life will have its moments of bitterness, but healthy families know to work through it. ✤

PARENTING PRINCIPLE

Turn the bitterness into betterness by forgiving and keeping your life "grudge free."

POINTS TO PONDER

- Where have you held on to bitterness in your life?
- How have you learned to let it go?
- Do your children work through bitterness effectively?

THE POWER OF WORDS

The tongue has the power of life and death. PROVERBS 18:21

Take a moment to recall some of the words you heard your parents say that you will never forget. Were they good words that encouraged you or words that still sting just as they did many years ago?

Our words matter. As Proverbs 18:21 says, our tongues have the "power of life and death."

Our control of the words that escape our mouths is incredibly important. When dealing with frustrating family situations, do you easily get angered and end up verbally assaulting everyone around you? If so, this behavior has to change. Your children will remember your hurtful words and one-liners like a memory stick recalls information from your computer. They will replay them in their heads over and over.

Your words of encouragement, however, might be what turn them away from the temptations that are so persuasive in their lives. They might recall them through a time of depression, discontent or discouragement. Just as we absorbed our parent's words, our children are now soaking up our words. That's why it's important that your words bring life to your child and breathe hope into them. ❖

PARENTING PRINCIPLE

A parent's words may not be seen, but they are felt by the soul.

POINTS TO PONDER

- Are you able to articulate how your own parent's words affected you?
- What are your children hearing from you now?
- How will you work to make sure the words in your home are positive?

LETTING GO

For if you forgive other people when they sin against you, your heavenly Father will also forgive you.
MATTHEW 6:14

Knowing how to forgive someone and then letting the offense go is instrumental for building strong families. If we don't do this, God can't forgive us and our family can't grow in love.

Do you have a family member who regularly holds on to a grudge after they claim to have forgiven you? You talk about the problem with them and think you have it finally resolved, and then one day they bring it up again! That's tiring.

Don't be guilty of offering forgiveness but then holding the offense over their head. Teach your children the proper method for letting things go, which is practicing true forgiveness. When you forgive, really forgive! You can encourage this with your children when they are at a very young age. When you hear them say they forgive someone, but then later hear them bring up that issue again, confront them. By doing this, you will help them develop healthy habits in the area of forgiveness. This will be pleasing to God and of great value to them. ❧

PARENTING PRINCIPLE

Teach your children that forgiveness means not holding on but letting go.

POINTS TO PONDER

- What offense have you recently overlooked and how did you do it?
- What good habits have you taught your children in this area?
- What offense should you let go right now in order to help your family?

NOT MY CHILD

A foolish child is a father's ruin.   PROVERBS 19:13

Children don't understand why their choices should affect their parents. After all, children think, it's their life, so why do their parents care? Proverbs 19:13 is a great reminder that you aren't out of your mind for being affected by their actions, despite what your children say. It's normal for a parent to hurt—even feel "ruined"—when their child makes poor choices or walks away from faith in Christ.

In those moments, parents can find comfort in the knowledge that God created their child and has a plan for their life. You might learn that your dreams for your child, however, are not God's plan for them. This might be difficult to accept, but it is with acceptance that you'll find a depth in trusting Christ you previously didn't know existed.

It's important to remind yourself daily that although *you* are the person God gave this child to, it is only for a season on this earth. Remember, God is their heavenly Father, and your child will only find their peace and contentment when they truly find him. ✤

PARENTING PRINCIPLE

My dreams for my child might not mirror God's plan for my child.

POINTS TO PONDER

- How have you handled disappointments in your child's choices?
- Where do you find your peace in these difficult situations?
- How can you specifically pray for your child to stay close to God?

# day102

TALK ABOUT SPIRITS

Wine is a mocker and beer a brawler; whoever is led astray by them is not wise.

PROVERBS 20:1

Teaching your children the dangers of alcohol is wise. If your children were to learn about the effects of alcohol only through television commercials, they'd believe alcohol leads to "the good life." Those who counsel with individuals who have been influenced by alcohol's destructive force will tell you that's not reality. This devotional is not an attempt to change your behavior as it relates to alcohol, but to make you think about the effect it's having or could have on your family.

Alcohol will be a temptation at some point in your child's life. The most important thing you can do is teach your children, before they ever take a sip, how alcohol can influence their thinking, behavior and perceptions. Of course, this should be done when it is age-appropriate. You can find plenty of help with a simple Internet search. Add the Biblical teachings of Proverbs 20:1, and you will give your child a well-rounded view of this common but often overlooked intoxicant. ✤

PARENTING PRINCIPLE

Teach your children a general rule that too much alcohol will make them a fool!

POINTS TO PONDER

- What struggles might you have with alcohol in your own life?
- Have you discussed alcohol with your children at the appropriate age?
- If not, what plan can you make now to inform your children of the dangers of alcohol?

IT'S UP TO THE LORD

There is no wisdom, no insight, no plan that can succeed against the LORD.

PROVERBS 21:30

Our children need to know that the Lord will do what he wants to do. He is almighty. He is sovereign. Proverbs 21:30 tells us that no plan of ours will succeed against God—even if we think we are right and he is wrong, even if we don't understand his motives.

We don't always fully grasp this thought because we cannot reconcile the bad things that happen with our knowledge that God is good. We want to ask why. It's worth noting that after all of Job's trials and even with the lessons God taught him about life, God never told him *why* he was suffering. It's enough to say that God doesn't have to answer to us or explain anything.

As you accept this eternal principle, you must also teach it to your children. They will work to understand these concepts as they mature and grow, but you can assist them in the process by setting the example of complete submission to God. You will sometimes have to say, "I can't explain that." What you do know and can explain is that the will of God will always prevail. We can pray to him for understanding and guidance through all the "what ifs" and "whys" of life.

But in the end, his way is not our way. Accepting this truth will be to the benefit of your family. ✜

PARENTING PRINCIPLE

God is God and I am not!

POINTS TO PONDER

- What examples of submission to God do your children see in your life?
- What plan have you created that you now see was not necessarily God's plan?
- How can you learn to accept God's plan more readily in the future and to teach your children this skill?

PURE THOUGHTS

But whose delight is in the law of the LORD, and who meditates on his law day and night.

PSALM 1:2

This verse presents a delicate situation for parents when it comes to living out your faith at home. If you talk about Jesus night and day there will come a point when your children will be turned off to that constant bombardment of all things "faith." The better approach is to create a healthy environment where Christianity and the love of Christ are contagious, not just preached.

To meditate on his law day and night is equivalent to the concept of "pray without ceasing." It positions us to always be available to God. We can make that happen by maintaining a clean and pure relationship with him and avoiding whatever keeps us from that instantaneous connection.

Psalm 1:2 challenges us as families to be pure in thought, honest in action and open to his Spirit. Talk about these things with your children and keep that delight of knowing the Lord a joyous and continual process. But do not let your talk become mundane, ritualistic—or a bombardment! ✤

PARENTING PRINCIPLE

Keep the Lord in your sight and serve him out of delight.

POINTS TO PONDER

- How do you meditate on the Lord in your home in a way that is contagious?
- What are some things you can do to enhance all you do to delight in Christ?
- When have you seen your children enjoy their faith?

STAND TALL

That person is like a tree planted by streams of water, which yields its fruit in season.

PSALM 1:3

Locate a tree near your home that has stood strong over many years. Think about all the different weather conditions it has endured. Consider how it rejuvenates itself in the spring. Marvel at how deep its roots go and how they are interconnected.

Now use that tree as a life lesson for your children. Share your observations with them, and help them to see these unseen things about this tree. As you talk with your children about the tree, transition into how all of this correlates with life. There are storms and there is sunshine. There are cold seasons and warm seasons. Talk about the fruits of the spirit such as peace, love and joy. Help your children understand how individuals can be sturdy like a tree and that by living that way they can set an example for others.

Parents, we are that sturdy tree right now for our children. They crawl through our branches and observe our lives. Help them establish their own strong roots by living a faithful, God-fearing life. ❖

PARENTING PRINCIPLE

Be sturdy like a tree and help your children grow their roots in thee.

POINTS TO PONDER

- How have you worked to grow deeper roots in Christ?
- How are your children learning from you in this area?
- What are you doing as a family that could be a deterrent to deep spiritual growth?

EVERY BREATH YOU TAKE

I lie down and sleep; I wake again, because the LORD *sustains me.*   PSALM 3:5

Most of us live life in such a routine that we often forget that without God we would not take another breath. God also gives us each of our abilities, and, without him, we would not even be able to understand the next word we read. Again, because we do so much effortlessly we take it for granted.

Your children will take God's provision for granted as well. We must remind them that every ability, every breath and every new morning are gifts from God. We have it all because the Lord sustains us. In other words, he renews us each day to make us capable of performing daily human routines.

That's why it's important to be thankful for each day and each provision and to teach your children to live with an attitude of gratitude. Pay attention to your own often ungrateful attitude and clean it up, especially when your children are around. It will be much easier to teach your children a spirit of thankfulness if you model it yourself. ❖

PARENTING PRINCIPLE

Today is not a right — it's a privilege.

POINTS TO PONDER

- What kind of appreciation do you show for your daily sustained provisions?
- How could you be more aware of this daily sustaining power?
- What daily activity could you incorporate that would help your family appreciate their blessings?

day107

STARRY, STARRY NIGHT

What is mankind that you are mindful of them ...? PSALM 8:4

We live in an unbelievable universe. Take your children out on a clear night to a dark environment and observe the starry sky. Do some research so you can show them the different constellations and planets that are visible to the naked eye.

Stand in silence at first, take it all in and then let them share their thoughts. Listen to their perspective of how God created all this wonder. They might say things that you would never have imagined.

After you share this awesome time, ask them why they think God made man and woman. What would he want us to do for him on this earth? Enjoy their comments, and if they say something that doesn't fit exactly with the way you think, don't overreact, just logically and calmly talk about it. You don't want to squelch their curiosity or stifle their imagination. Give them the freedom to share their own deeper thoughts. Close your time out by talking about how much God must love us to give us the ability to observe all he has created and to enjoy it. ❖

PARENTING PRINCIPLE

Teach your children to be mindful of the immensity of God's love and his glorious creation.

POINTS TO PONDER

- What makes you mindful of your own humanity?
- Why do you think God loves you so much?
- How can you help your children get a sense of their own worth?

A SPIRIT OF THANKSGIVING

I will give thanks to you, LORD, with all my heart; I will tell of all your wonderful deeds.
PSALM 9:1

We are to live with an attitude of thanks in our home. Notice Psalm 9:1 doesn't say to give thanks when everything is going well. Instead, it implies that we should be thankful even when circumstances are challenging.

It's all about perspective. God has blessed us more than we deserve and so we need to be thankful. If your family has food, be thankful. If you can fill the gas tank in your car, give thanks. If you lay your head on a comfortable pillow at night, give thanks.

There will always be a temptation to focus on what we don't have instead of what we do possess. Every television commercial tries to convince us that we are missing something. They draw our attention away from gratefulness and toward neediness—or merely want.

A spirit of thanksgiving is a choice we can make. As your children watch that steady gratitude emerge from our lives, it will be easier for them to keep their eyes off themselves and develop a thankful heart of their own! ✤

PARENTING PRINCIPLE

It is better to give than to receive, and better to thank than to want.

POINTS TO PONDER

- Is there a spirit of thankfulness in your home?
- How do you help foster this spirit? What distracts you?
- How do you tell of his wonderful deeds in your home?

day109

RIGHTING THE WRONGS

He rules the world in righteousness and judges the peoples with equity.   PSALM 9:8

There will be times when your kids will think you are not being fair. For instance, they may accuse you of liking one of their siblings better than you like them. But there is great news for you in Psalm 9:8.

Explain that you are doing your best to be fair, but that even your best will never be perfect because you are not God. Share with them that during those times, you will both need to be reminded there is a righteous and equitable God. He is perfect and he will never falter in his judgments. We may be wronged on this earth, but there is a day coming when all wrongs will be righted.

This knowledge will give your children hope for the eternal and take the pressure off you to always manage to be fair. Through your ongoing experiences you can all gain insight into the holiness of God because of his righteous and equitable judgment. ✤

PARENTING PRINCIPLE

When your children feel wronged, remind them that someday God will make it right.

POINTS TO PONDER

- In what areas of your family life do you need to try to restore righteousness and equity?
- How does knowing God's righteous equity give you peace?
- What can you do to help your children put their trust in this righteous God even when they feel they have been wronged?

day110

WISDOM VERSUS KNOWLEDGE

My goal is that they may be encouraged in heart and united in love, so that they may have the full riches of complete understanding, in order that they may know the mystery of God, namely Christ, in whom are hidden all the treasures of wisdom and knowledge.

COLOSSIANS 2:2–3

In our society there has been a shift away from viewing wisdom as a top priority. We have replaced it with education—get all you can! But intellect and wisdom are two different things.

This wisdom is not based on our IQ or our social status. It is not based on our church affiliation or what we own. Wisdom is a gift from God, and he will provide it to us all if we ask. Every parent will need wisdom to build a godly home.

Wisdom comes from reading God's Word and spending time with him. It can come from wise counsel and pastors. It can come from those who have made it through the tests and trials of everyday life. The point is, it's available and all you have to do is ask God for it. ✣

PARENTING PRINCIPLE

The wisest home builders are those who seek God as their foundation.

POINTS TO PONDER

- Where do you get the advice you use to build your home?
- In what ways are you seeking God regularly?
- How could you improve in your daily walk with Christ and in seeking him for advice?

day111

NUGGETS OF KNOWLEDGE

Through knowledge its rooms are filled with rare and beautiful treasures.

PROVERBS 24:4

Proverbs 24:4 doesn't say parents fill the rooms of their homes with knowledge. It simply says knowledge fills the rooms of the house. It's what we learn from our life experiences — nuggets of knowledge — that will help us grow.

That knowledge can come in all shapes and sizes and from any family member. In fact, some of the best knowledge we will ever gain will come from our children. Their untainted view of how the world should be will often add refreshment to family life.

Let knowledge come. Don't fight it. When you learn something from another family member, embrace it. When you see knowledge in action, speak about it. Thank the child who makes an insightful comment. Be open to a suggestion that might not be your own or even representative of how you think. Listen and learn. These are keys to cultivating wisdom.

In the end, the result of your willing spirit to receive knowledge will yield rare and beautiful treasure: a home filled with God's love and joy. ❖

PARENTING PRINCIPLE

The road map to knowledge will lead to rare and beautiful treasures.

POINTS TO PONDER

- What are some recent knowledge nuggets you have learned in your home?
- How have you encouraged your whole family to share knowledge in your home?
- What is another source of knowledge you are aware of that you haven't tapped into?

DO NOT FALTER

If you falter in a time of trouble, how small is your strength!　　　PROVERBS 24:10

Think back to the last time you were tested as a parent. How did you handle it? How small is your strength?

All these questions will apply at some point during your parenting years. You might answer them easily today but there may come a day when these questions will pop off the page and bring you to tears. That's why our strength must be found in the Lord. When it is tested, we have the opportunity to go deeper with God.

If you feel yourself faltering, gain strength from knowing other faithful followers of Christ have made it through tougher times than you will ever face. Remember, God knows how much you can handle, despite how overwhelming it seems. When you feel like giving up, Christ will be there to sustain you. When you pass the test, you will be stronger and your children will learn from your example.

Let your children see your faithfulness now so they will hopefully be more faithful later. ❖

PARENTING PRINCIPLE

Pass the test of putting your faith in the strength of the Lord and you won't fail to pass a test.

POINTS TO PONDER

- How have you faltered in the past? What did you learn through that experience?
- What trial are you currently being tested in?
- What can you do to deepen your faith for these moments?

day113

MAKE A DIFFERENCE

Rescue those being led away to death; hold back those staggering toward slaughter.

PROVERBS 24:11

If Jesus came to your home, one of the things he would ask you about is what you are doing to reach "the least" of our society. Reaching this population was his mission on earth, and it flew in the face of every self-absorbed religious group.

Things haven't changed. Christians still like their comfortable religious groups. Jesus doesn't mind you being in one of those groups, but he does want to know if you are making a difference.

If you and your family aren't aware of the modern-day slavery happening around the world now just as it was occurring when Proverbs 24:11 was written, do research on the Internet to educate yourself about this great tragedy. Just make sure that what you share with your children is age-appropriate for them. Talk as a family about how you could get involved in helping to stop this horror. Find an organization making a difference and ask them what your family can do to help the effort of rescuing or preventing victims, half of whom are children. ❖

PARENTING PRINCIPLE

Decide as a family to make a difference—and you will!

POINTS TO PONDER

- How are you reaching out to the least of these?
- If you have not been reaching out, what's been stopping you?
- How will you move forward to find the best way for your family to get involved in a cause?

SWEET WISDOM

Know also that wisdom is like honey for you: If you find it, there is a future hope for you, and your hope will not be cut off.   PROVERBS 24:14

Wisdom is a drum we need to virtually beat. Our children will always have hope if they have wisdom. As Proverbs 24:14 says, wisdom is like honey. To our soul, it is a sweet reminder that God is aware of where we are and what we need at all times.

It's hard to think of our children facing difficult times, but it's likely to happen. When their own lives are in turmoil, however, they will recall the golden nuggets of wisdom they heard from you, the sweet wisdom from God that has been passed on. The godly wisdom you instill in your children will go with them even when you can't.

Specifically, Proverbs 24:14 focuses on future hope, such as the legacy of wisdom and hope we will leave for our children after we pass on. If you have been given that gift of wisdom and hope by a parent or stepparent, be thankful and don't allow the generational chain to be broken. ❖

PARENTING PRINCIPLE

Pass on your wisdom before you pass on.

POINTS TO PONDER

- What is some of the wisdom you learned from your parents or grandparents? How has that given you hope?
- What do your children see in you that relates to wisdom?
- How are your children showing some measure of wisdom?

IT'S NOT FAIR

To show partiality in judging is not good.   PROVERBS 24:23

It's challenging as a parent to always be impartial. If you have more than one child, they will accuse you at some time of being unfair in your judgments.

Always remember that *you* are the parent. You see the bigger picture and your children's view is narrow. It's the same in our relationship with God. If you try to explain all your seemingly unfair decisions, you will typically get nowhere because there are things that are beyond your children's comprehension. They will often argue with you about it, but remember they would eat their Halloween candy all at once if you let them. Their brains are simply not developed enough to understand all that is involved in managing a family.

But you don't have to answer to your children for the judgments you make; you have only to answer to God. Pray for wisdom in your decisions and give them considerable thought. Let your children know that you are seeking God and godly advisors in your actions. Press on. Be as impartial and as confident as you can. ❖

PARENTING PRINCIPLE

All your children can ask is that you try to be fair—and that's fair!

POINTS TO PONDER

- How do you seek fairness in your judgments?
- Where do you struggle in your judgments?
- How do you seek God for wisdom in your weak areas? Who could you ask to help guide you in those areas?

day116 april 26

DON'T GLOAT

Do not gloat when your enemy falls. PROVERBS 24:17

Every parent knows what it is to have an enemy. People—and Satan himself—will try to defeat us. And when someone who has wronged us has to pay for what they have done, it feels pretty good. But we need to set an example for our children when this happens. In fact, if you have an opportunity to do good to those who hurt you, do it!

Your children will experience being wronged soon enough. A neighbor kid will probably put your child through something difficult. And then your child will want to shout out a big cheer when that other child pays a price for their bad behavior. You probably will too, but that's in opposition to what God requires.

Justice is a good thing, but justice should not include gloating. God teaches us that it's not healthy for you or your children because of the sense of domination you would feel over that person. That's not our place. God is the final judge of all, and gloating can lead to judging. Don't fall into this trap. You can teach your children to expect justice but refrain from celebrating another's shortcomings. ✤

PARENTING PRINCIPLE

Instead of gloating when your enemy falls, help them up.

POINTS TO PONDER

- Why is it so easy to gloat?
- How do you celebrate justice but refrain from gloating?
- What could you do to grow in this area and set a good example?

day117

DON'T BE A BURDEN

The righteous lead blameless lives; blessed are their children after them. PROVERBS 20:7

Your children probably have no idea how blessed they are to have a parent who reads devotionals in an effort to be a better mom or dad. Too many parents around the world don't care about the long-term health and welfare of their children because they are so consumed by their own selfish ways.

Being a godly parent is a challenging lifestyle. But it is of utmost importance, because God wants our children to reap the rewards of our righteous lives—to be, as Proverbs 20:7 tells us, blessed after us. It is worth noting that the opposite is no doubt true. Parents who live to please only themselves will be a burden on their children, not a blessing.

Choose today to be righteous and seek God's direction in all you do. If you are doing what displeases God, change today and begin to walk a pure and holy path of life. God calls us to be holy because he is holy! So be holy in all you do. ❖

PARENTING PRINCIPLE

Don't live to please yourself but to please God, and your children will reap the rewards.

POINTS TO PONDER

- How are you living in a way that will bless your children?
- Are there any areas of your life that you need to clean up?
- What are some of the blessings you have already enjoyed?

day118

LIVE ABOVE REPROACH

Even small children are known by their actions.   PROVERBS 20:11

How we act is usually who we are! Have you ever known a child who earned the moniker "brat"? Of course, we shouldn't think of a child that way, but unless we know the child is acting out of some sort of neglect, abuse or emotional problem rather than simply misbehaving, we do.

Do you want a teen in your house who has no respect for others? It's difficult to trust and respect them! But consider a teen you've met who cares for others and invests energy and effort into the lives of younger teens and children. They have become known for their actions too, but in a good way.

It's important for your children to understand that they will be known for what they do. Teach them how to make good choices. Let them know people are watching and making assessments regarding their actions. Show them that if they live in such a way that they respect themselves, then others will too. Teach them how to live above reproach. ❧

PARENTING PRINCIPLE

A parent's actions will speak louder than their words.

POINTS TO PONDER

- What would be your moniker based on how you act?
- What monikers would you give your children to match their actions?
- What do you want to be known for in the long run? What might you need to change in your own life?

THE MANY PARTS

Ears that hear and eyes that see—the LORD has made them both.   PROVERBS 20:12

Most people are more grateful for something after it is gone. A person who had good health but now suffers with sickness understands this principle.

Our ears and eyes and the rest of our body parts exist for one simple reason—the Lord has made them. Though a person may not have ears and eyes that function just as well as ours do, the Lord has allowed that part of their life so that their journey can be enhanced in some way. To help your children understand how people with disabilities are not blessed less but blessed differently, try this experiment. Blindfold them and then have them move about the house, noticing things they may not have with their eyes. Have them sit quietly inside or outside and reflect on how their sense of smell, hearing and touch help them appreciate God's world just as much as sight does.

Reflect on how different does not equal less. God has given us five senses, all of which are capable of helping us appreciate the blessings in our lives. ❖

PARENTING PRINCIPLE

You will fail to notice everyday blessings if you fail to look for them, especially if you feel God has not blessed you.

POINTS TO PONDER

- Why do we tend to overlook everyday blessings God has given us?
- How can we develop a better attitude for recognizing blessings, especially in times of trial?
- How will you help your children develop a thankful heart for all the people God has made?

day120

COME CLEAN

"It's no good, it's no good!" says the buyer—then goes off and boasts about the purchase.
PROVERBS 20:14

Scammers are people who knowingly take advantage of others and act the whole time like they don't know what they are doing. And the person in Proverbs 20:14 who buys at less than a fair price while pretending his purchase is no good is an example of a cheater from long ago.

The Internet has made it even easier for scammers to operate in our society. Since our children's lives will in many ways revolve around internet use, we need to teach them about these evils and how to guard against becoming scammers themselves. They need to understand that scammers are usually found out and then become people others want to avoid when it comes to business dealings. But if we live by the Golden Rule—treating others as we would like to be treated—others will respect and trust us.

Our children could easily be lured by scammers into hurting others to make a quick buck. Hopefully, they will turn away from those opportunities to cheat and conduct their business with integrity just as you taught them. ✤

PARENTING PRINCIPLE

If you cheat others you are actually cheating yourself.

POINTS TO PONDER

- Where, if ever, have you struggled with integrity in your family's business dealings?
- How do you guard against any temptation to cheat others?
- How will you convey these principles of integrity to your children?

WATCH THE TALK

A gossip betrays a confidence; so avoid anyone who talks too much.   PROVERBS 20:19

Whose name came to mind when you read Proverbs 20:19? A better question might be: If someone else read this verse, would your name come to their mind? We do not want the reputation of a gossip, and we certainly don't want that for our children. As Proverbs 20:19 says, anyone who talks too much is better avoided.

Next time you are around your family, really listen to their conversations. You will discover that, unfortunately, it's a pretty common trend in family life to talk stink about others. Most people do it to make themselves feel better. Establish good policies early on in your home that help curb a gossiping spirit. Make your home a place where people are talked about positively.

Teach your children by example the principle of only saying positive things about others and keeping silent about what others have told you in confidence. It will make it less likely that you and your family will be avoided for "talking too much." Try it, and see if you don't get immediate results. ✤

PARENTING PRINCIPLE

Teach your children that instead of talking negatively about others, we should talk to the Lord about how to be more positive.

POINTS TO PONDER

- How have you seen gossip hurt you or others?
- How would you rate your skills in talking about others?
- How can this Biblical teaching about those who gossip help your family?

day122

SEEK ADVICE

Plans are established by seeking advice.   PROVERBS 20:18

We can't build a strong family by acting on our own! Going to God for advice and then seeking others to come alongside us as we follow that advice is a recipe for a good, healthy family.

Here is some advice for building a strong family: Establish some guidelines that everyone in the family can follow. You need to communicate these early on in your children's lives so they have a clear understanding of your expectations. This should help eliminate surprises or claims by your children that you are inconsistent or that rules are constantly changing. By setting these unswerving, basic rules from the very beginning, you have laid a foundation that can be built upon. Remind your children of this when they try to dodge compliance by asserting unfairness. That won't happen if you are reliable in your application.

Needless to say, the advice you seek for creating these guidelines is critical. Seek wise people and wise principles that are supported by the Bible, not opinions. It's not necessary to reinvent the wheel when solid instruction is already available. The most respected parents are the ones who stick to their standards when the going gets tough. ❖

PARENTING PRINCIPLE

Plan today to prevent issues tomorrow!

POINTS TO PONDER

- How do you go about seeking advice?
- Who can help you establish a good family plan?
- How and when will you communicate this plan to your children?

day123

WAIT ON THE LORD

Do not say, "I'll pay you back for this wrong!" Wait for the LORD, and he will avenge you.
PROVERBS 20:22

Patience doesn't rate high on the scale of a child and it's even lower for a teen. So to help your child understand they need to be patient and allow the Lord to avenge any wrongs seems nearly impossible.

Teens are known for quick reactions. They get it all figured out and decide they don't need to wait because they can solve the issue immediately. That's why Proverbs 20:22 presents not only a challenging principle for us to live out personally but also to teach to our children.

One of the best ways for our children to learn this patience is to talk to someone older, like a grandparent. They may have experienced how continuing acts of revenge will only lead to regret and digging deeper holes into which they can fall.

So teach the wisdom of this verse and help your children learn these life lessons. Don't simply tell them what to do but help them figure out what to do based on this insight and understanding. ❖

PARENTING PRINCIPLE

When you pay back evil, you will get short changed out of a blessing by God.

POINTS TO PONDER

- What have been the results when you have paid back wrongs?
- How can you become more like Christ in this area?
- What examples can you use to teach your children this principle of waiting on the Lord?

FOLLOW THE LEADER

A person's steps are directed by the LORD. How then can anyone understand their own way?   PROVERBS 20:24

At some point your child will say, "I've got this, I don't need you." They might be right. But if that phrase is symbolic of an attitude that is defiant, and they continually think they don't need help, trouble may be right around the corner.

Gaining independence is a normal part of becoming an adult. Do not panic or overreact. Instead, talk with them about how you felt at their age and how you learned from your mistakes. You need to understand that they may need to make their own mistakes in order to "get it." If they don't listen and instead insist on following their own way, continue to pray that their heart will soften and heed your instruction.

It's important for your children to know Scripture like Proverbs 20:24 that will give them direction. They may seem ungrateful today, but remember tomorrow is coming. Because we have walked with the Lord through times like these, we know he is the one to direct them through it! ✤

PARENTING PRINCIPLE

If all you understand is from you, then you don't understand at all.

POINTS TO PONDER

- What are the results when you attempt to do things on your own?
- When have you seen your children fall into this trap?
- What is the best way for them to learn principles like the one in Proverbs 20:24?

HEART CONDITION

The human spirit is the lamp of the LORD that sheds light on one's inmost being.

PROVERBS 20:27

It's pretty easy to tell when your child is not emotionally well. They might mope around or stay in bed all day. They might avoid eating or overeat. Teens might also tend to exclude themselves from family activities. The problem could be a physical ailment, but most likely your child has a "down spirit" reflective of what is going on in their life and their heart.

The light is being shed on something going on in your child's life. Whatever it is, pray for discernment and wisdom to understand how to help your child express what is happening in their life.

It's also important to celebrate when they exhibit a positive, upbeat spirit. A teen will appreciate having you point out their optimistic spirit, instead of only focusing on the negative.

Lastly, examine your own spirit. Determine whether you are a boost to your family's overall spirit or a drag to it. Stay on top of your heart condition and hopefully you will continue to reflect an encouraging, nourishing spirit that will lift up your family. ❧

PARENTING PRINCIPLE

The human spirit is delicate, but God's light shines strong.

POINTS TO PONDER

- What do you do to keep a positive spirit in your home?
- What is the current condition of your children's spirit?
- How can you help your child regain or maintain a positive spirit?

day126

THE GLORY OF STRENGTH

The glory of young men is their strength.   PROVERBS 20:29

Our culture has changed. When Proverbs 20:29 was written there was a much greater respect for the wisdom and maturity of the gray. We have not, however, lost our glory of young people — though today that glory isn't necessarily based on strength or maturity, but rather sex appeal.

It will be a challenge to help your sons and daughters understand that appearance is not the central factor in their life just because the media constantly throws lies at them and says it is. Appearance is fleeting and is not what will bring them glory.

The lesson of this verse for young people is that their strength is their glory. And the most important strength is not physical but found when they learn who they are in Christ. When they match their outward strength as an individual with an inward strength that comes from depth in Christ, they will understand the glory that counts. ❖

PARENTING PRINCIPLE

Physical strength can be depleted, but inner strength from the Lord is what's really needed.

POINTS TO PONDER

- Where are you in this shift from strength to splendor? Define how this principle plays out in your own life.
- What are you doing to help your children know and learn from those with gray hair?
- How can you continue to develop your family in understanding glory?

day**127**

MORE OBEDIENCE, FEWER APOLOGIES

To do what is right and just is more acceptable to the LORD than sacrifice.

PROVERBS 21:3

It seems that humanity chooses penance over obedience. Obedience requires righteous living and doing things we don't always want to do. Seeking forgiveness and not permission seems like today's mantra.

This will be the case for our children. At all ages and stages of development, they will sneak around and possibly do something they know they shouldn't. When they get caught, they will usually offer an apology or offer a sacrifice to make up for their wrong. As parents, we want fewer sacrifices and more obedience.

Teaching our children to simply do what is just and right is challenging. While we could easily focus on this daily and bombard them with rules, our homes would soon turn into burdensome chambers of mandates.

Instead, we want the desire to do the right thing to spring from their heart. That can happen by blessing and encouraging them when you see them doing something right. This will take patience because they will have to go through the same stages of development you did as you learned these principles. ❖

PARENTING PRINCIPLE

Do what's good for goodness' sake!

POINTS TO PONDER

- What does right and just mean to you?
- What have you taught your children about the meaning of right and just?
- What will you do to build your family toward doing what is right and just?

# day128

UP ON THE ROOFTOP

Better to live on a corner of the roof than share a house with a quarrelsome wife.

PROVERBS 21:9

This verse could just as easily say it's better to live on the roof than to share a house with a quarrelsome husband, teen or child. The intended spirit is this: If anyone in the house is inclined toward quarreling, the whole house suffers.

What do you do with a quarrelsome child? There are no perfect answers, but here are a few suggestions. Make sure you have consequences for squabbling children. Take something away they really enjoy. Initially that may cause more arguments, but hopefully it will teach them a lesson. Give them more responsibility. When children aren't busy, they are prone to think of themselves more. When that happens, they become quarrelsome. So don't let their minds be idle. After trying these suggestions, if the situation doesn't improve, seek counseling or pastoral advice. You might be too close to the situation to see it clearly. Listen to godly advice, and hopefully it will lead you to enjoying more of your home rather than just the corner of the roof. ❖

PARENTING PRINCIPLE

Choose peace over quarreling and live in the house, not on the corner of the roof.

POINTS TO PONDER

- What might bring on a quarrelsome attitude for you?
- When do your children seem to quarrel more?
- Besides the ideas above, how can you help your family in this area?

DECK OF CARDS

The Righteous One takes note of the house of the wicked and brings the wicked to ruin.
PROVERBS 21:12

Do you ever feel like the wicked seem to thrive? It's like they spit in the face of God, mock his ways and get all the media attention for their uniqueness. Based on how they see the wicked in today's world, your children may consider your Biblical value system foolish.

Have confidence in your beliefs! God is not blind. He sees it all. Teach your children that it might look like the godly are losing but with God this will never be true. There will be a day of reconciliation when it all makes sense.

The house of the wicked will fall like a deck of cards—scattered and ruined—but the righteous will stand. Your children need to hear and know this truth. They may not believe it at some point, but we must continue to teach it.

Hold fast to your desire to serve the righteous One. Be true to what you know and not just what you see. In the end, God will bless your righteous home. ✤

PARENTING PRINCIPLE

Be relieved because our God sees!

POINTS TO PONDER

- How do you resolve the conflict in your spirit when you see that the wicked seem to get away with evil?
- How do you respond to your children when they notice the same thing?
- How can you focus more on building a righteous home?

THE PRODIGAL CHILD

Start children off on the way they should go, and even when they are old they will not turn from it.   PROVERBS 22:6

This verse is probably one of the most quoted and well-known proverbs for parents. It's also one that is confusing to those parents whose children have wandered from their family and faith despite a righteous upbringing.

The key to the principle in Proverbs 22:6 are the words *starting off*. Your child is on a journey. You only get to participate in an in-depth way in stage one. In that phase, the truths and Biblical principles you instill in them will eventually come back to their minds when they are older.

In the parable of the prodigal son in Luke 15, Jesus said the boy "came to his senses." This indicates a child can temporarily lose their common sense. Most likely it's because physically the front part of their brain, which controls reason and decision-making, is not fully developed.

As parents we must trust that those concepts we instilled early on will call them back to their senses. Be confidant that Christ knows where you are and where your children are as well. ❖

PARENTING PRINCIPLE

Sow seeds of righteousness in your child and their roots will remain strong.

POINTS TO PONDER

- What godly principles have you instilled in your children?
- How can you continue teaching them godly principles?
- Where do you need to trust God for your children today?

day131

PURE HEART

One who loves a pure heart and who speaks with grace will have the king for a friend.

PROVERBS 22:11

Let's focus on helping our children have pure hearts and speak words of grace. To accomplish this, you have to experience purity yourself. Teens have built-in lie detectors. If you live with impure motives, it's unlikely your discerning child will listen to what you have to say.

One way to help your child grow in this area is to confess to them an impure area you are facing. Maybe you did something with the wrong motive or you haven't been completely honest about something. As you confess and grow, you will inspire your children to do the same.

Speaking with grace is a character development trait born out of a pure heart. It's about learning to hold your tongue and give people second chances. If your children see you growing in these areas, they will be encouraged to grow at their own level of maturity.

Proverbs are not mandates but teachings that, if followed, will bless you and help you grow closer to Christ. ❖

PARENTING PRINCIPLE

If my motives are pure and my words speak grace—my friends will be abundant!

POINTS TO PONDER

- What benefits are there to adhering to this teaching in Proverbs 22:11?
- What kind of example have you set for your children in the area of friendships?
- How do you see your children growing in grace?

day132

START EARLY

Folly is bound up in the heart of a child, but the rod of discipline will drive it far away.
PROVERBS 22:15

We are all born selfish, which means folly and disobedient behavior start early. When parents—or others—read Proverbs 22:15, their immediate reaction is to debate about whether or not it's okay to spank your child. You can Google this question and get a variety of answers plus add your own opinion.

The meaning behind Proverbs 22:15, however, is that you better discipline your children or there will be hell to pay! Yes—I said hell!

First, establish the method of discipline that will work best for you and your child, and then be sure to stick with it and discipline consistently. The idea that you will discipline one time and laugh at that same behavior the next time is dangerous turf.

If you have difficulty settling on a type of discipline, seek wise counsel from a mentor, pastor or counselor. There are many great strategies available for parents, so educate yourself! But don't fail to discipline your child. ✤

PARENTING PRINCIPLE

How you discipline your children is your choice but whether you should discipline your children has already been answered by God.

POINTS TO PONDER

- What is your method of discipline and do you as parents agree on it?
- If not, what can you do to make sure you are on the same page?
- How is your children's folly decreasing as they age?

COOL DOWN

Do not make friends with a hot-tempered person, do not associate with one easily angered, or you may learn their ways and get yourself ensnared. PROVERBS 22:24–25

Your children will be exposed to hotheads everywhere. They will be with them in the classrooms, on the playing field and at the local hangouts. Be sure you are not one of them. The more they are around hotheads, the more potential there is to become one.

Teaching your children that they can become like who they hang out with is an important lesson. If your child hangs out with a kid who lies, odds are pretty good they will begin lying. This is also true if they hang out with someone who is easily angered. If your children start to exhibit this same behavior, they might try to justify that behavior by saying, "I'm not as bad as so and so." But they need to know you don't compare them to other kids; you measure them against Biblical standards.

Parents shouldn't compare themselves to other parents either. Our standard is what God expects of us. Live and teach that truth, and your children will have a good reason to hang out with people who are good influences. ✿

PARENTING PRINCIPLE

If you are losing it, everyone is losing.

POINTS TO PONDER

- How do you keep good control of your anger?
- What friend choices are your children making?
- How can you continue to monitor your children's choice of friends?

day134

FIGHT GLUTTONY

When you sit to dine with a ruler, note well what is before you, and put a knife to your throat if you are given to gluttony.　　　　　　　　PROVERBS 23:1–2

The Bible has verses, like Proverbs 23:1–2, that seem extreme. Your children will read it and wonder about the sanity of the writer who suggests taking a knife to your own throat! This is why it's important to be discerning about teaching the concepts of Scripture.

This is a verse from Solomon, to whom God gave incredible wisdom. Solomon is teaching that when you get around the incredible bounty of the wealthy, you might fall into the temptation of thinking that having a lot of stuff will make you happy. Solomon had it all, and yet he understood how quickly an abundance of wealth could ruin someone's life. He's telling us to be careful not to give ourselves over to the pleasures of this world because it could cost greatly.

It's a deep teaching that your children need to know. Think of a way to communicate this lesson about gluttony — or the dangers of excess — using a modern-day example, like how many lottery winners end up unhappy and sometimes bankrupt. ✤

PARENTING PRINCIPLE

The only excess in your life should be an excess of faith.

POINTS TO PONDER

- What is the thing that most tempts you to go after it?
- What tempts your children?
- How do you protect yourself from falling into the trap of "gluttony," or excess?

day135

RICH IN SPIRIT

Do not wear yourself out to get rich; do not trust your own cleverness. PROVERBS 23:4

Being able to buy what you want or let your children go to events or on expensive trips is nice, but none of it is necessary.

Be thankful if you're in a place where you can provide in this way but teach your children that temporary pleasures will never fully satisfy them. The temptation to spend all our energy on making money so we can have more to spend is always present. Your children will love getting their first paycheck. It will motivate some children to work more to earn more. That's not wrong, unless they start to trust their own cleverness in attaining stuff instead of trusting God.

Those who desire more wealth in order to do more for others have figured it out. They don't seek riches for their own personal gain, but to help further God's kingdom.

Help your child understand that being able to earn money is a gift, and not to let that God-given gift become their destruction. It's clear in Proverbs 23:4 that greed can be a stumbling block. Take note and protect yourself and your family. ❧

PARENTING PRINCIPLE

If you are prone to chase riches, you may find yourself spiritually bankrupt.

POINTS TO PONDER

- What example have you set in regard to riches?
- What potential do your children have for making good money?
- How will you help them develop these skills in a healthy way?

CHOSEN BY GOD

As you come to him, the living Stone—rejected by humans but chosen by God and precious to him. 1 PETER 2:4

Your children will have a difficult lesson to learn when they aren't welcome somewhere. Children are innocent and can't imagine that someone would not want them around. But life has a way of teaching hard lessons in this area.

Explaining to your children that they may not always be welcomed everywhere will be critical when it actually happens to them. It's also important they understand that rejection might be the result of something they did, but more likely it will be the other person deciding to reject for some issue of their own. This is a delicate conversation. Some children will handle rejection better than others, but for some it could jump-start low self-esteem issues.

The bottom line is that you want your child to be secure in who they are and in those moments when they sense rejection, not to take it personally. That ability is accomplished by having our confidence in who we are in Christ. ✤

PARENTING PRINCIPLE

Remember, if you are rejected, it is not by God.

POINTS TO PONDER

- When have you felt a time of rejection and how did you handle it?
- When have you ever made others feel like you were rejecting them?
- How can you continue to help your children prepare for the moments of rejection that are a common part of life?

APPLY YOURSELF

Apply your heart to instruction and your ears to words of knowledge.   PROVERBS 23:12

You will use the phrase "apply yourself" a lot while your children are in school. You want them to be dedicated to hard work and to focus on the stuff that's important.

That's the spirit of Proverbs 23:12. When we apply ourselves to learning, especially learning from God, we grow. If your child isn't open to this teaching, you need to show them its benefits. Perhaps tell them about a time when your boss gave you instructions to help you learn a new task or how God recently gave you an instruction through his Word and it's making a difference in your life.

We naturally shy away from instruction because it could mean we have to change. But if we embrace it, we open ourselves up to new levels of growth. That may not make sense to your child, so apply instruction in a way that fits their age like through a game or getting them involved in an activity they enjoy. Whatever the method, as they open their hearts and ears, the whole family will win. ❖

PARENTING PRINCIPLE

Open your heart and your ears so God's instruction can fill you through the years.

POINTS TO PONDER

- How open are you to instruction? How can you grow in being more open to instruction?
- Can you receive instruction from your children? How?
- What have you done to make receiving instruction fun for your children?

WISE CHOICES

My son, if your heart is wise, then my heart will be glad indeed.   PROVERBS 23:15

As a parent, you will usually be doing as well as your child is doing. It's a simple fact that how our children choose to live affects us. There may be different levels of how this plays out, but we will rejoice when our children make wise choices.

Your children will not understand why their decisions are such a big deal to you. Only when someone has a child does their understanding of the parent-child relationship change. Don't waste your time trying to get your child to understand what it's like to have a child. Instead, spend your energy on helping them build a foundation that is wise. It may be a few years before you see those good and godly decisions kick in, but when they do, you will experience a great gladness.

Just as Christ rejoices and all heaven rejoices when a child of God decides to fully follow him, we also rejoice because it's what parents love too. If you aren't there yet, press on. God will provide you with the strength to keep pushing toward gladness with your children. ❖

PARENTING PRINCIPLE

Gladness of heart starts with wisdom.

POINTS TO PONDER

- When have you seen the truth of this verse?
- What are you doing to guide your children in making the right decisions?
- How can you pray for the Lord's continued touch on your home in maturing your children?

SPEAK TRUTH

My inmost being will rejoice when your lips speak what is right.　　PROVERBS 23:16

When your children's lips speak what is right — the truth — and only what is right, you have reason to celebrate. Teaching your children how to speak the truth and what is right is challenging. One child might be as honest as the day is long while another child is prone to stretch the truth.

Too often we wait until our children speak a mistruth to say anything to them about the importance of honesty. Then it looks like we only focus on the negative. If you have a child who is faithful with their lips, praise and reward them now. It will inspire them to continue and your positive words will benefit your relationship with them.

If you have a child who is causing you sleepless nights because you can't trust what comes from their lips, talk about it with them. Ask them how it would feel if they couldn't trust you. Ask them why they sometimes lie and how they think it's beneficial in the long run. Your goal is to give them something to think about that will hopefully change their behavior. ❖

PARENTING PRINCIPLE

If you always tell the truth, your sincerity will not be questioned.

POINTS TO PONDER

- What is your track record for speaking what is true, what is right?
- How are you doing as a family in the area of honesty?
- How can you seek to improve?

day140

REAL ZEAL

Do not let your heart envy sinners, but always be zealous for the fear of the LORD.
PROVERBS 23:17

To always be zealous for the fear of the Lord is challenging. Zeal can be as fickle as the weather. The reality is that your circumstances will affect your zeal and therefore be different each day unless you are intentional about maintaining it.

To always be zealous might seem more attainable if we think of it as being aware of God's power and sovereignty. To help our children achieve this state of mind, we need to teach them to serve and seek God every day, not just on one day of worship. And to honor God in our home all the time, not just when people are over. Zeal for the fear of the Lord must become a lifestyle.

Things of this world like envy, greed and pride will constantly pull at our children. Many famous people live evil lifestyles that look good on the outside, which will appeal to some children. When they are tempted, your godly teaching to be zealous for the fear of the Lord will be a barrier to Satan's attacks. ❖

PARENTING PRINCIPLE

Parents who maintain their zeal help their children see God's appeal.

POINTS TO PONDER

- What do you do to keep yourself fresh—zealous for God?
- Is there someone in your life who is an example for your children of what spiritual zeal looks like?
- How do you help your children keep their zeal?

DEDICATED PARENTS

Listen to your father, who gave you life.   PROVERBS 23:22

This verse assumes dads are talking to their children. The only way children can listen to our guidance is if we're involved in their lives and understand what connects with them.

If you struggle with communicating with your children, here are some easy steps.

First, stop thinking you have to be a perfect parent. If you are afraid of making mistakes, you will shut down. Own your mistakes and use them to help your children in the future. As you build a relationship with them, have conversations about the things you have learned through your struggles.

Second, see your child as a sponge. They are looking to absorb whatever comes their way. You have the unique ability to put things in their life that no one else can. They long for your security and love. They long to be wanted. As you bring what they need into their life, they will feel valued.

Third, stay involved. Don't check out. Be there for them as they go through all the stages of life. Live in such a way that you will be the first person they want to go to when they are facing issues. ❖

PARENTING PRINCIPLE

A dedicated parent will open the ears of a child.

POINTS TO PONDER

- How are you staying involved in your children's lives?
- What could you do to be more involved?
- How do you think your children would answer these questions about you?

OVERBEARING

Do not despise your mother when she is old.   PROVERBS 23:22

What could cause a child to despise a parent—if not during childhood then as an adult child? It could be related to neglect or abuse, but it could be an overbearing attitude. When this is the case, parents must work hard to restore the relationship to the best of their ability.

This overbearing behavior emerges from a genuinely good heart, but it gets in the way of children becoming who God wants them to be. Overbearing parents are too eager to share their opinion with their kids instead of letting them seek out their advice. Once their children are ready to leave home, these parents need to get out of the way and let their child experience becoming an adult.

The best way you can know if you're overbearing is to ask your children! If they say yes, don't give excuses. First be sure their complaints are valid (asking a spouse or another close adult will give you a good picture). Just apologize and learn from it. You won't want to hear it, but you need to because you don't want to be despised. ✤

PARENTING PRINCIPLE

Learn to discern when it's appropriate to put your nose in your children's business.

POINTS TO PONDER

- In what areas do you think you are too involved in the life of your adult children?
- If your children are not adults, are there any areas where you see yourself being overbearing?
- Are you willing to ask your children about these thoughts?

THE LEAST OF THESE

Whoever is kind to the poor lends to the LORD, and he will reward them for what they have done.
PROVERBS 19:17

Most of us believe that we should care for those who are less privileged than we are. We talk about it. Our pastors preach sermons about it. We know missions groups that meet this need.

But why should families do it? According to this wise verse, anyone should do it because when they do, they are lending to the Lord himself. He came to help the poor, the blind and the lost. When we as individuals and then collectively as a family do something for the least of these, we are doing the work of Christ.

Teach your children to help the poor, not out of abundance but because it's what Jesus would do. The most beautiful part is that the Lord will reward us for joining forces with him. That reward might come in a way we aren't expecting, but it will come. Our eternal reward will outlast any temporal reward we might receive in doing the work of Christ. ❖

PARENTING PRINCIPLE

Children have a natural heart for the poor. Copy it, don't cure it.

POINTS TO PONDER

- What are you as a family doing to copy Christ's example?
- Do you see it as a duty or an opportunity to get involved in Christ's work?
- How have you learned from your children in this area of giving?

# day144

PAYING THE PENALTY

A hot-tempered person must pay the penalty; rescue them, and you will have to do it again.   PROVERBS 19:19

If you are a parent who makes excuses for your children's bad attitudes and actions, you are only hurting them. There's always room for grace and second chances, but let them pay the consequences for their poor choices. It's called "paying the penalty," and it is how your children learn.

If you know a parent who always covers for their child, then you've witnessed an enabling parent. The sooner you let children pay the price for their bad choices the better. A two-year-old who has been told they can't have something will try to figure out how to get it anyway. Don't let them get away with it no matter how many times they try, because you will be the one to pay the penalty by having to deal with continued misbehavior. Knowing this up front will give you the perseverance you need to stick with your plan when you're about ready to throw in the towel.

Remember, let your children take responsibility for their actions and there will be fewer penalties to pay. ✤

PARENTING PRINCIPLE

Fool me once, shame on you. Fool me twice, and I enable you!

POINTS TO PONDER

- Do you cover for your children? If so, why?
- How could you improve in letting them continue to grow in being responsible for their actions?
- What have your children learned from paying the penalty for their bad choices?

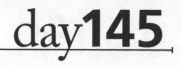

BE COUNTED AMONG THE WISE

Listen to advice and accept discipline, and at the end you will be counted among the wise.
PROVERBS 19:20

If there is one verse every parent could benefit from hearing, Proverbs 19:20 is the one! Wisdom comes from being teachable and listening. If our children see us practice this principle they will count us among the wise, and our home will continue to be a blessing to them.

Of all the aspects of parenting children, discipline won't always feel good. Your children may count you more among the irritants in their life, not necessarily the wise. That's why you don't parent to achieve a buddy-buddy relationship, but for the long-term development of the child. Your consistent focus on listening and disciplining will help in forming a healthy parent-child relationship early on and an adult-adult relationship in the future.

Don't sacrifice the long-term just for a temporary "feel better about yourself" relationship. Your child should never consider you their best buddy in the way they do someone their own age. They should revere you as an authority figure who loves them with an unconditional and unyielding love. A mutual respect and appropriate friendship will naturally form. ❖

PARENTING PRINCIPLE

When the final count is tallied, parent to be counted among the wise.

POINTS TO PONDER

- How are you consistent in listening and disciplining?
- Where do you sometimes "drop the ball" in this area?
- In what way do your children see you as a respected authority figure?

day146   may 26

UNFAILING LOVE

What a person desires is unfailing love.   PROVERBS 19:22

Regardless of our age, we all like to feel secure. A child's security comes from a parent in the form of unfailing love. It means that through their failures you will never abandon the parental love that is God-given. As adults, we crave that same unfailing love.

God has this unfailing love for all his children and this is the example we must seek to emulate. Have you ever considered how we must frustrate God beyond belief? There have to be times when he looks at our muckiness and just wants to be done with it all. It's the same for us with our children. When they seem to have crossed the proverbial line one too many times, we have to be responsible parents and deal with it by showing them unfailing love.

There will be occasions when you might not want to be their parent and you might wish they weren't your kids, but that isn't what unfailing love is all about. It's about loving them when their behavior is unlovable. Be faithful to this duty with great joy, and God will give you the grace you need. ✤

PARENTING PRINCIPLE

"I love you to death" is just a phrase, but it should also be a lifestyle.

POINTS TO PONDER

- How is your home one of unfailing love?
- When are you hard to love as a parent?
- When is showing love to your children hard for you?

FEAR THE LORD

The fear of the LORD leads to life; then one rests content, untouched by trouble.

PROVERBS 19:23

The idea of being untouched by trouble is appealing to a parent. However, Proverbs 19:23 doesn't say we won't have trouble, it says we will be untouched by it. In other words, trouble will not affect who we are in Christ.

When we hear the phrase "fear the Lord" we might retreat with almost a hand up for protection from his wrath. That's a misunderstanding of the concept. God should be feared out of respect for his encompassing power. Use this analogy: If I told you I fear lawn mowers, it would mean I don't stick my hand underneath one while it's running. But I don't cringe every time I see a lawn mower. I just respect its power.

When we have a healthy fear of God and teach what that looks like to our children, we help them have a good life—a life that may include trials but that recognizes God's power even in the midst of those trials. Our children can rest content knowing God is God. Period! ✣

PARENTING PRINCIPLE

Fear the Lord and rest content for that is God's intent.

POINTS TO PONDER

- How have you come through a time of trouble, yet are untouched by trouble in the long-term?
- Are your children learning to rest content? How?
- What is one way you can help your children develop a proper fear for the Lord?

day148

SOAK IT UP!

A sluggard buries his hand in the dish; he will not even bring it back to his mouth!
PROVERBS 19:24

A child is like a sponge. Whatever you teach them in the early years will be what they soak up and remember later on.

For instance, if you always put away their toys for them and then allow them to create another mess the next time they play, you are teaching them to be a sluggard like the one in Proverbs 19:24. Eventually they will catch on and proceed to mess everything up just to watch you put it back in place again.

As every parent knows, some days it is easier just to do it yourself. But in general, teaching your children to clean up their own messes is the first step in teaching them to work. They seem so trivial, but those seemingly insignificant, everyday routines will form the bridge from lazy kids to responsible, hard-working individuals. If you take a look around at our society, you'll see that hard-working individuals are faring well. To teach a child to provide for themselves is to teach a child a lifelong lesson. ✤

PARENTING PRINCIPLE

If your hand is in the cookie jar, make sure you helped bake the cookies.

POINTS TO PONDER

- How often and why are you picking up after your children's messes?
- What rules do you have in place for them to follow in responsible cleaning?
- What can your children learn through their individual chores and responsibilities?

day149

GOD'S INSTRUCTION

Stop listening to instruction, my son, and you will stray from the words of knowledge.
PROVERBS 19:27

If you have a child who refuses to listen to you, their life will bring you pain. This is not just an idea or insight; it's taught in the Word of God. Teach your child that to defy you and ignore your words of instruction is not only disobeying you, it's disobeying God's teaching. All the more reason that our words of guidance should not just be fabricated ideas of what we think is best but instead should be grounded in godly wisdom and Biblical teaching!

Many parents come up with impractical rules that are often the result of their own struggles with rebellion. They think these rules will stop their children from behaving in the same wayward manner they did at their age. Unfortunately, this type of reactionary parenting has the potential to perhaps push them closer to the dangers you hoped they would avoid.

Show your children why they need to receive instruction and lay out realistic and reasonable expectations with God's Word and godly counsel as a starting point. All of this is in an effort to curb the stray. ✢

PARENTING PRINCIPLE

When a child is hell-bent to stray, pray that heaven will get in their way.

POINTS TO PONDER

- When was a time when you did not listen to instruction?
- What did you learn from those experiences?
- How can you effectively talk to your children about this?

day150

UNFAILING FRIENDSHIPS

Many claim to have unfailing love, but a faithful person who can find? PROVERBS 20:6

Finding a person who will never let you down is difficult. Many relationships start out good but may leave you burned in the end.

Not only is it important for parents to have unfailing love for their children, but they also need to help their children find that type of love in their friendships with others. This will be important because they will seek counsel from these others as they develop into an adult.

When your child is upset over a lost friendship, your instinct might be to get down and dirty with them and drag that person's name through the mud. Rise above that temptation. Instead, help them understand how resisting that urge develops character and is the kind of character they should seek out in friends — as well as in a future mate. Question them if they begin to develop unhealthy relationships and help them learn from their mistakes. Be sure they know that God's Word will always ring true and that they can know him as the truest of friends. ❖

PARENTING PRINCIPLE

A friendship lost comes at a great cost. To trust again takes a faithful friend.

POINTS TO PONDER

- With whom do you have an unfailing friendship? What has it taken to develop this friendship?
- What have you learned through lost and unfaithful love?
- How do you teach your children to guard their hearts against those who are not faithful?

DISCIPLINING FOR GOOD

Discipline your children, for in that there is hope; do not be a willing party to their death.
PROVERBS 19:18

At first glance Proverbs 19:18 might seem a bit extreme because it sounds as if a lack of discipline leads to death. But in its context of parenting, it simply reminds us that the daily energy we give to disciplining our children is worth it because it leads to hope.

As you seek to protect your child from making decisions and doing things that could be detrimental to their life, there are three things to consider when disciplining your child. First, each child is different and you will need to weigh and analyze the best way to approach each personality.

Second, consider what you were like at their age. Recall your own struggles and talk about them with your children. Letting them see you as a real person will be helpful.

Third, consider why you are disciplining your child. Don't just do it to do it. Explain your reasoning to them. These considerations will keep you focused on doing discipline properly and giving your children the guidance they need—for in that there is hope. ❖

PARENTING PRINCIPLE

Discipline is like discipling—it takes time and perseverance.

POINTS TO PONDER

- How do you normally discipline?
- How could these three considerations help you?
- What are some unique things you need to keep in mind when you are disciplining each of your children?

NOT FORSAKEN

Those who know your name trust in you, for you, LORD, have never forsaken those who seek you.
                                                                      PSALM 9:10

In family life, there will be times when someone feels forsaken. Parents feel forsaken when their children walk away from their faith and don't seem to care that their parent's heart is broken. Children feel forsaken when a parent spews out a hurtful comment that strikes at their core.

It is good to know that in those loneliest of times there is a friend who will never forsake us. He is our Lord. You might not be able to see him or feel him, but he is there. He fulfilled his promise that he would send the comforter (his Spirit) to help us in the moments we would feel forsaken so we would never feel alone.

When your children are struggling and you don't have the right words to say, remind them that the Lord is in them. Teach them to call out to him for peace. Let them see you seek him in all your lonely moments too. Our own patterns in life must reflect that we believe he is important and that we follow his divine wisdom. ❖

PARENTING PRINCIPLE

To seek is to find and to find is to never be forsaken.

POINTS TO PONDER

- When have you felt forsaken and God was there for you?
- How is your family seeking him?
- What is the best thing you do to keep trust in God?

ENJOY TODAY

Do not boast about tomorrow, for you do not know what a day may bring.

PROVERBS 27:1

Families need to enjoy today. This doesn't mean we stop planning as though tomorrow won't come, but in doing so we must not miss today! Parents often miss the present for two reasons. One is when we focus too much on future plans for our children, retirement or the next big vacation. We rush today in order to sneak a peek at tomorrow. Then when tomorrow comes, we look back with regret because we've missed enjoying what happened.

A second reason we want today to pass quickly is that we are experiencing frustration or heartache in our family. It might be related to our particular stage of parenting. We wish our kids were older and more independent and then in the next moment we wish they were little again.

We can learn from the elderly in this area. They have much to teach us about not rushing time, especially when life is challenging. They have weathered storms and given testimony to how those storms actually deepened their faith in Christ.

Choose to enjoy today, and celebrate every moment as you learn and grow with your family. It's possible that tomorrow will never come. ✤

PARENTING PRINCIPLE

Tomorrow may never come, so today deserves our full attention.

POINTS TO PONDER

- What keeps you from enjoying today?
- How could you be more focused on today?
- What happened today that you need to be thankful for?

day154

PRAISE GOD, NOT SELF

Let someone else praise you, and not your own mouth; an outsider, and not your own lips.
PROVERBS 27:2

Our lips should be reserved for praising God and others, not ourselves. Practice it, preach it, and teach it, so your family will find its identity in Christ, not in self!

Yes, we need to believe in our children. We need to find their areas of giftedness, seek to enhance them for their sake, and then celebrate them! But we also need to keep perspective. Sometimes parents give an abundance of accolades to their children to the point where the children become arrogant—and perhaps start to praise themselves. That's why it's important to seek balance in your admiration.

You can do that by teaching your children to be confident in who they are in Christ, and that their successes are because of his strength working through them. If others recognize those talents and compliment them, teach them to give all the glory to the Lord, rather than giving in to the temptation to praise themselves. Remind them to be thankful for the praise from others but not to focus on it or seek it out. ✤

PARENTING PRINCIPLE

When you focus on yourself, your self will lose focus.

POINTS TO PONDER

- In what ways might your family be self-consumed?
- What makes you lose perspective in this area?
- In what areas do you see your children seeking praise? Is it healthy?

SEEING GREEN

Anger is cruel and fury overwhelming, but who can stand before jealousy?

PROVERBS 27:4

Family gatherings can be challenging when siblings become jealous of each other. It may start with one sibling doing something that makes the other one angry but then it culminates with jealousy. It could happen because one child accuses a parent of playing favorites or maybe parents unknowingly do something that causes jealousy among their children. Many circumstances can result in these feelings of resentment.

The best way to deal with jealousy is to confront it head on. There's no guarantee it will simply evaporate, but it will expose the toxic condition and create an opportunity for growth. Perhaps there is one family member who is more problematic than others, and that truth needs to be exposed. It may magnify their jealousy, but you can't cater to only their feelings and allow it to destroy other relationships in the home.

Each family member is responsible to curb the jealousy in their own life. Don't worry your parenting life away trying to eliminate jealousy in your children. They have to see the green in themselves for their behavior to change. You can help show them where it's obvious, but more importantly, pray for their hearts to change. ✤

PARENTING PRINCIPLE

Jealousy is often just pride disguised.

POINTS TO PONDER

- Where might there be unresolved jealousy in your family?
- What circumstances might breed jealousy among your children?
- How can you help your children see the green in themselves?

day156

BE A STABILIZER

Better is open rebuke than hidden love.　　　　　　　　Proverbs 27:5

It's easy to understand that everyone needs open rebuke at one time or another. Hopefully as we grow and learn, rebuke becomes less needed. On the other hand, the meaning of hidden love is a bit more difficult to grasp.

Hidden love is knowing that something one of your children is doing could result in severe consequences down the road if it continues, but choosing not to correct it. This is because the confrontation will be difficult and might jeopardize your loving relationship with them. In essence, you are hiding your love from them, because it's actually more loving to confront the situation with open rebuke. It will be better to deal with a little pain now than what could be excessive agony later on if you allow the behavior to continue.

Open rebuke may sound like an opportunity to "blow them away" with some corrective teaching, but it's more about being open and honest with them and not beating around the bush about what they need to hear!

Parents must be willing to be stabilizers for their children even when enabling them seems easier. ✤

PARENTING PRINCIPLE

Expose hidden love and become a stabilizer for your children.

POINTS TO PONDER

- What are some areas of concern you need to confront with your child?
- Why is this difficult for you?
- How do you think your children will react to hearing the truth?

WOUNDS OF TRUTH

Wounds from a friend can be trusted, but an enemy multiplies kisses.   PROVERBS 27:6

Help your children find friends who will be honest with them—friends who are willing to go through some pain with them or even cause some pain to make them better people. At first your children might want to run from an individual who makes them face the truth and own up to their behavior, but in the end that is the person who will love them the most.

An enemy, as suggested in Proverbs 27:6, is someone who lets you get away with things and therefore seems easier to have as a friend. Unfortunately, while they are letting you slide in your behavior (only supplying you with "kisses") they are also setting you up and only multiplying your problems. Your children will not see this as clearly as you will. They might refuse to listen to you when you warn them and encourage them to end one of their friendships. But your words will eventually prove true, and after your children have experienced the true kiss of the enemy, your credibility will grow.

Hopefully in the end you will have also become a true friend to your child. ❖

PARENTING PRINCIPLE

The wounds of truth are better than the kisses of death.

POINTS TO PONDER

- What have you noticed in your child's friendship choices so far?
- How are you helping them develop good friendships?
- What are you doing to build a long-term friendship with your child?

day158

FLEEING ISN'T FREEING

Like a bird that flees its nest is anyone who flees from home. PROVERBS 27:8

If you have ever had the privilege of watching a mother bird hatch her eggs, you probably noticed her care and provision for that nest after the birds have hatched. God built an innate sense of caring for her young in that mother and often, depending on the kind of bird, the father bird too.

How much more, then, has God given human parents an innate love and nurturing mind-set toward their children? Yet, all across our nation and in the world we see parents fleeing their home. They run away. What is causing this mass exodus from home life? Selfishness! To feed, nurture and care for our young takes commitment, selflessness and dedication. Those three words are almost unheard of in our self-focused culture. Parents who cherish their responsibility for God's gift of children, however, will reap some tremendous benefits down the road.

Notice I said down the road. There will be some benefits today, but many of the rewards of good parenting are not experienced until the future. Sadly, many parents will miss out on those future rewards because they choose to give up their responsibilities to their children today. ✤

PARENTING PRINCIPLE

To flee will not make you free!

POINTS TO PONDER

- What circumstances have made you think about fleeing from your family?
- What has instead kept you focused on your family?
- How do you give your children a sense of security?

REACHING IN

Perfume and incense bring joy to the heart, and the pleasantness of a friend springs from their heartfelt advice.　　　　　　　　　　　　　　　　　PROVERBS 27:9

A good friend to a parent is like the sweet smell of perfume. A parent who has a friend they can talk to and get advice from is a blessed parent. If you have someone like that in your life today, be grateful and express that gratitude to your friend. If you do not have such a friend, consider these few thoughts about finding one and developing a trusting relationship.

A friend who gives you heartfelt advice is often someone who has gone through a similar situation. Seek out such a friend rather than dealing with issues in isolation.

You might find these potential friends through a small group at church or a community-organized event. Maybe you can start a parenting group in your own home. Doing so might not fit your personality, but as you reach out you will discover that you are really reaching in. Your life will be enhanced by these genuine friends. And as you share with other parents, you will discover that they also benefit from what you are learning through your experience. ❖

PARENTING PRINCIPLE

Reach out to reach in when it comes to friendship.

POINTS TO PONDER

- Who is your heartfelt parenting advisor?
- If you don't have one, how could you find one and develop trust in them?
- How would this type of relationship benefit your children?

day160

AN INVISIBLE SHIELD

Be wise, my son, and bring joy to my heart; then I can answer anyone who treats me with contempt.   PROVERBS 27:11

When our children are wise and learn to do the right thing in most situations, they bring joy to our hearts and, as a result, to other people in the family. They contribute to protecting the reputation of the family as a whole, and you can more easily defend your good name if others attack you.

If this invisible shield of protection is broken because of your child's negative behavior, however, your family is more vulnerable to outside attacks and slander and defending your good name will be more difficult.

You must stay true, then, to your desire to be a family that leads a Christ-centered life and not let your reputation unravel because of all that is going on around you. When your children don't do the right thing, it can be quite shocking to parents and throw them into a temporary tailspin.

But as you are faithful and as your child hopefully matures, you can again build that shield of protection around your family! ✤

PARENTING PRINCIPLE

The more wisdom your children gain, the less your family's reputation will be stained.

POINTS TO PONDER

- How have you established a good family reputation?
- How do you know if your children understand the importance of maintaining your family's reputation?
- How can you determine if your children care about reputation?

day161

AVOIDING DANGER

The prudent see danger and take refuge, but the simple keep going and pay the penalty.
PROVERBS 27:12

Our culture doesn't like consequences. We create programs for those who struggle so they can avoid the consequences of their destructive behavior rather than help them change their behavior. Those who receive this help feel they are entitled to it because of their perceived rights. They often continue on in their simple way without a care for consequences.

Although we do have the right to lead our life as we see fit that means we, and our children, can also be led across the line to danger where we cannot always escape consequences. Then we must pay the penalty for crossing the line, especially God's lines. As a parent, you can possibly prevent this from happening by correcting your children's behavior. That's your right!

Just as you would tell your child not to step in front of an oncoming car, you must tell them to be careful not to step into the flow of society's slide toward destruction. Help them to see dangerous situations ahead of them and steer clear of it. ✤

PARENTING PRINCIPLE

Don't be blind when you see the danger sign!

POINTS TO PONDER

- What dangers are you seeking to help your children avoid?
- How are you teaching them the consequences of bad choices?
- In what way might you be letting them avoid consequences and shielding them too much?

day162

A QUIET BLESSING

If anyone loudly blesses their neighbor early in the morning, it will be taken as a curse.

PROVERBS 27:14

Don't be a loudmouth. Teach your children by example how to have control of their tongue. Just because you want to hear yourself talk—even if what you intend is to "bless"—doesn't mean others want to listen to you. This concept seems so simple, but so often we experience a situation where a neighbor or friend doesn't know how to respect others by curbing their obnoxious behavior.

Do you have an obnoxious child? If so, do you blame their behavior on everything in the world and not correct it? Certainly your child may be experiencing a medical condition, like ADHD, but generally speaking those parents typically do all they can to assist their child through these difficulties.

Sadly, the most undisciplined and loudmouthed children are not those who have a reasonable excuse for their behavior. Usually it's the children who have an uninvolved and undisciplined parent. Therefore, be sure you are watching for these disruptive, selfish behaviors in yourself and your children. You do not want to be a curse to your family or your neighbors! ✤

PARENTING PRINCIPLE

A loud and proud family is a neighbor's nightmare!

POINTS TO PONDER

• What do you do to prevent being an obnoxious family?

• What obnoxious behavior might you be seeing in your children?

• What is a good balance between having fun and not annoying others?

day163

STOP THE LEAKS

A quarrelsome wife is like the dripping of a leaky roof in a rainstorm. PROVERBS 27:15

Though the message of Proverbs 27:15 speaks primarily to a husband and wife, it certainly speaks to parents as well. Perhaps you can recall feeling insecure as a child if your parents quarreled.

When you quarrel with your spouse, you cause anxiety in your children and that's a feeling they don't easily forget. The more you quarrel, the more you are like a continual drip on the canopy of their soul! This is not the kind of memory you want your children to have as they enter adulthood.

Instead, seek to eliminate the quarrelsome attitude that might be pervasive in your home. If it's there, acknowledge it and discuss with your spouse how you might begin to clear out this ongoing storm. It will take effort on both your parts, but hopefully you will see the importance of creating a "drip free" environment for your children. Your children might not immediately recognize your efforts, but someday those efforts will be appreciated when they reflect back on sweet childhood memories.

And remember, the best way to stop a leak is to never let it start. ❖

PARENTING PRINCIPLE

Repair the roof by plugging the holes and stopping the flow of quarreling.

POINTS TO PONDER

- Where might there be "leaks" in your home because of quarreling?
- How do you prevent or stop quarreling?
- How will you prevent your children from becoming quarrelsome?

day 164

SHARPEN YOUR SKILLS

As iron sharpens iron, so one person sharpens another.   PROVERBS 27:17

There is a national men's organization known as Iron Sharpens Iron. Their goal is to get together as men and challenge each other to grow in love for Christ, their wives and their children. Their sharpening includes holding each other accountable to areas of growth, such as getting more involved in activities that will help them grow with their family.

This concept is one that we need to adopt as families. We need to love each other, get together to challenge each other and hold each other accountable. This might prompt you to get a group of parents together in your home to discuss ways to sharpen your parenting skills. In doing so, you will naturally be more intentional about improving your family life.

Many parents will refuse this kind of accountability and turn away from this idea of being sharpened. They may believe their parenting is good enough or at least better than they received. Do not let that attitude represent you as a parent. Even if you do not think you are "dull," embrace the tools that will sharpen you and enhance your family! ❖

PARENTING PRINCIPLE

Razor-sharp parents can cut through the twine that tries to bind up their family.

POINTS TO PONDER

- What "dulls" you as parents?
- How can you better sharpen your parenting skills?
- Who are some people or what are some tools that could assist you in this area?

A MATTER OF THE HEART

As water reflects the face, so one's life reflects the heart. PROVERBS 27:19

There will be a stage in parenting when you will wonder what's going on with your child—good and bad. You may observe them doing something that is very caring and sensitive and you will be amazed wondering where it came from. Proverbs 27:19 tells you. It came from their heart. Those moments cause parents to smile in their souls.

It's also likely that a time will come when you can't believe your child's behavior. They will embarrass you and show no remorse. They will say and do things that you are sure you have told them to refrain from. You will wonder if everything you said went in one ear and out the other. This too is a reflection of their heart. What's inside will always come out.

This is why your children need to be strong in their own faith. Your faith won't transfer to them. Their heart needs to seek first God's kingdom so all the other things of life will fall into place, including their actions. Then life is exactly that—their life. It's our responsibility to do what we can to help them grow their heart toward God because one day they will be on their own. ✤

PARENTING PRINCIPLE

You can make your child look good, but only God can help them be good.

POINTS TO PONDER

- What does your own life reflect?
- What does your child's life reflect as an indication of what is in their heart?
- How can you pray for their heart?

CHASE NEEDS NOT WANTS

Death and Destruction are never satisfied, and neither are human eyes.

PROVERBS 27:20

Your child begins their life with hungry eyes and they don't even know it. Lying in their bassinet in a colorfully decorated nursery, your baby begins to see plush things and want them. Of course, they don't understand that desire, but eventually they'll catch up with everybody else in wanting all the things they see.

One trip to a shopping mall generates a hundred different wants for a five-year-old. Ten-year-olds are even more aware of what wants there are around them. By fifteen, your children have caught up on most of what the world has to offer and it's incredibly enticing. If you don't think so, then you are a parent with your head in the sand!

Remember, things won't satisfy people. They have not satisfied us and they will not satisfy your children. Many of us have tried to find satisfaction in material goods and our children might do the same. Show them the example by not chasing "wants." Be thankful for "haves" and seek to teach your children that only a life lived with Christ will satisfy them. ❖

PARENTING PRINCIPLE

Don't try to satisfy yourself with things, unless it's the things of Christ.

POINTS TO PONDER

- Why do we think "things" will satisfy us?
- Have you discovered the satisfaction of "what you have"? How?
- How can you teach good principles of gratitude to your children through your own lifestyle?

BE INVOLVED

Be sure you know the condition of your flocks, give careful attention to your herds.

PROVERBS 27:23

As a parent, you have two options. You can turn your head and hope things are going okay with your child or you can stay in the game and know the details of your child's life.

Consider this: If we saw a farmer ignoring his flock of sheep and letting them go off on their own, hoping they would be okay, wouldn't we tell him he shouldn't have sheep? But we don't raise sheep, we raise children—an even more important responsibility. We need to be involved and concerned about the details of their lives. Your children might accuse you of being too involved, but eventually they will learn to appreciate that involvement. This is a challenging element of parenting, but be faithful.

You can know what's going on in their lives by following their social networking sites, knowing their friends and knowing where they go. Be aware of behavioral and mood changes. This monitoring will require more energy than turning your head, and potentially you'll find out things you didn't want to know, but it's the best option to show you care. ❖

PARENTING PRINCIPLE

You have to be listening to hear the cries of your children.

POINTS TO PONDER

- How are you involved in your children's lives?
- How could you improve in this area?
- What could you say to help your children understand your involvement in their lives?

day168

THE GREAT OVERABUNDANCE

For riches do not endure forever, and a crown is not secure for all generations.

PROVERBS 27:24

We live in the most comfortable time in the history of civilization, a time that might be labeled "posh." Even a few generations back, most of our grandparents or great-grandparents, depending on our own age, barely had enough to rub two pennies together. But then the Great Depression gave way to the Great Overabundance. Even those who are considered to be living at poverty level in America today are wealthy compared to much of the world.

But riches do not endure forever. Our children need to understand that financial ruin can come to anyone. A child may squander every last cent of an inheritance without good financial advisors. Thinking that we will have security for ourselves and our children by having the most stuff is a myth. We do not know the future. The best we can do is plan for what might occur.

But don't let that be your security either. Find your security in your relationship with God and teach that to your children. It will last forever and will be all the security they need. ✤

PARENTING PRINCIPLE

Riches won't last forever but God's love will!

POINTS TO PONDER

- How might you have a false sense of security because of your riches?
- How can you plan ahead without letting that become your main focus?
- How can you help your children have good balance in the area of money and possessions?

GET TO WORK

When the hay is removed and new growth appears and the grass from the hills is gathered in, the lambs will provide you with clothing, and the goats with the price of a field.

PROVERBS 27:25–26

This verse speaks directly to the fact that when you work and do your work with diligence, you provide for your family. It suggests that we shouldn't look for handouts or get-rich-quick schemes.

By doing faithful work, which can seem routine and mundane, we will learn patience and commitment and the satisfaction of doing a job well. The return on our investment of work comes over time but the result is that we have what we need.

We need to teach this to our children. Take a simple chore like cleaning a room. If your children clean their own room, they probably will not let it get so dirty in the first place. If they sweep the floor, they might think to take off their shoes. In doing these little jobs, they can find fulfillment. Later in life that discipline and its rewards will help them provide for their family! ❖

PARENTING PRINCIPLE

If your children don't understand the value of work, they may always be out of work.

POINTS TO PONDER

- How can letting your children help around the house help them understand the value of work?
- How else can you show them the value of work?
- When and how have you seen your children benefit from work?

NO HIDING, MORE SEEKING

The wicked flee though no one pursues, but the righteous are as bold as a lion.

PROVERBS 28:1

When a child has something to hide, they hide. If your toddler is in the house, and it's been quiet for too long, you know something is up. But teens are of even more concern.

A teen will often avoid their family no matter what, but if there are things they are concealing, their avoidance can jump to a whole new level. Christian teens are notorious for hiding because of the guilt they feel in knowing God's commands and principles but choosing to ignore them.

Encouraging your children to talk to you, especially when they are doing things you have forbidden will be difficult, but not impossible. It will take patience and restraint because you will want to know the truth no matter how bad it might hurt. You need to boldly strive for that level of trust in order to keep your children from falling into more sin. If you can manage those conversations with control, you will have more of an opportunity to guide them toward a more righteous, open and honest life. ❖

PARENTING PRINCIPLE

Wise parents talk with their children about things that they don't really want to talk about.

POINTS TO PONDER

- Can you remember times when your children were hiding from you?
- How are you doing in talking openly and honestly with your children?
- What are you doing to be more open in your conversations?

FOLLOW THE RULER

When a country is rebellious, it has many rulers, but a ruler with discernment and knowledge maintains order.   PROVERBS 28:2

This verse is written for a nation, but certainly its principle applies to a home. A parent who has no control will have a rebellious home, but a parent who rules with discernment and knowledge will maintain order. It doesn't say you won't ever face disorder but order can be maintained with a system of checks and balances.

Analyze your parenting style to see if you are using discernment in those times of disagreement or in chaos. You must maintain your control even if everyone else is losing theirs. That will require extra effort and drain you of energy. But the alternative is if you lose control, all hell could break loose, and you will be living in a home that actually creates a rebellious attitude.

Again, understand that there will be rebellion in your home. How you handle it is what matters. You want to be the one sure "ruler" of your house. And if you are married, stay united in these times and your home will be a great place to live. ❖

PARENTING PRINCIPLE

To maintain order in your home, a good rule to follow is for your children to follow the ruler.

POINTS TO PONDER

- What is the tone in your home? Does it promote disorder?
- How do you keep control of yourself and thus the family in rebellious times?
- How could you improve in this area?

RESTLESS

A ruler who oppresses the poor is like a driving rain that leaves no crops. PROVERBS 28:3

A parent who oppresses their children will be viewed as Proverbs 28:3 suggests: one who simply doesn't care about the children in the home. It's hard to believe any parent just simply wouldn't care about their children, but it happens in ways that are not necessarily obvious.

Christian parents in particular can turn into oppressive parents out of misguided love. In an effort to protect our children from the "wilds of evil" we will justify our oppressive type of behavior. It is important to keep this in check. You can do that by discussing parenting issues and parenting styles with trusted friends and staying accountable to them. Parenting solo is like flying solo — if the mechanisms of your family life go bad, you can get yourself in big trouble. You may not always agree with your friends, but they will give you another perspective to consider.

Be willing to look at the areas of your life where you might be oppressive and consider adopting new behaviors that are more helpful and nurturing for your children. ✤

PARENTING PRINCIPLE

If you oppress, your child won't rest!

POINTS TO PONDER

- In what areas of your parenting might your behavior be considered oppressive?
- How could you be less oppressive and more of a help in getting your child to understand?
- Where can you find parenting help in this area of potential oppression?

PURPOSEFUL INSTRUCTION

Those who forsake instruction praise the wicked, but those who heed it resist them.

PROVERBS 28:4

If you asked your child if they praise the wicked, of course they would say no! You wouldn't ask them that, but understand that when they begin to stray from instruction, they are making a paradigm shift toward praising the wicked rather than resisting them. That can prompt a spirit of fear in the heart of a parent. But it shouldn't. Even though we cannot control all the circumstances surrounding our children, we must focus on what we *can* control.

We can instill godly truths in them every day even as they grow older. This instruction should be calculated and purposeful and not yelled out. It must correspond with the way we are living our lives with integrity. The truths of Scripture are the stones we should use when laying the spiritual foundation for our children to build on.

Continue constructing your home using Biblical wisdom, understanding and knowledge. Commit your ways to God and be a lifelong learner, and your children will hopefully do the same—resisting the wicked and earning rewards for the kingdom. ❖

PARENTING PRINCIPLE

The more your children learn, the more they'll earn rewards for the kingdom.

POINTS TO PONDER

- How do you generally share instruction with your children?
- How do you receive instruction from others?
- What are some improvements you can make in your family to help make these instructions inspiring to follow?

TEACH THE DIFFERENCE

Evildoers do not understand what is right, but those who seek the LORD *understand it fully.* PROVERBS 28:5

Have you ever gotten really frustrated watching someone make one bad choice after another and move toward ruining their life? In some cases, it's simply because a person chooses to live disobedient to God's teaching, thereby preventing them from seeing and thinking rightly.

We don't ever want to see our children develop this mind-set. We are to teach our children right from wrong so they will never have the excuse that they didn't know any better. They may hang around other people who don't know the difference between right and wrong, but hopefully these instilled truths will be a deterrent to them falling into the traps that may lie ahead.

Try to understand other children you may encounter who seem to struggle with making the right decisions. Perhaps you can invest a little time into their life to understand what they've been taught and how you might be able to influence their thinking. Our children may be a conduit for us in reaching other families. Be open to God using you for parenting beyond your own children. ✣

PARENTING PRINCIPLE

Teaching your children right from wrong will help everyone to get along!

POINTS TO PONDER

- How are you helping your children understand right from wrong?
- Who could you influence in this area beyond your own family?
- How can you pray for your family to be an influence on others?

LIVE WITH CONTENTMENT

Better the poor whose walk is blameless than the rich whose ways are perverse.

PROVERBS 28:6

In Proverbs 28:6 God is saying it is better to be poor and live with integrity than to be rich and be dishonest. In this material world, children tend to believe rich is better. They won't think walking blameless will look nearly as fun as walking in the ways of the rich, even if some of the rich have skewed values.

Teach your children how integrity is more valuable in this world than wealth. Instead of comparing bank accounts with others, help them to find their worth and contentment in Jesus Christ. That way their values and behavior remain the same regardless of their account balance. They will likely live more blameless and without wickedness.

Proverbs 28:6 is not promoting poverty in order to live with integrity, but to understand the temptation that comes with wealth: It can cause us to depend on ourselves and not God. Without dependence on God, we leave ourselves at risk to succumb to more perverse ways. ✤

PARENTING PRINCIPLE

If we depend on wealth for contentment, we can depend on falling short of God's glory.

POINTS TO PONDER

- What are some ways you can stumble in this area of poor versus rich?
- What do you do when your children get caught up focusing on what others have?
- How can you help your children develop an attitude of thankfulness for all their blessings?

JUDGES

A discerning son heeds instruction, but a companion of gluttons disgraces his father.

PROVERBS 28:7

To say that your child has discernment would bring much comfort to any parent. Unfortunately, discernment is not a single experience. It's a lifelong journey.

To have a child who still uses discernment when they are older will be a testimony to your effective teaching. You will be delighted knowing that discernment will also be taught to your grandchildren. Discernment simply defined means the ability to judge well. Though none of us will ever judge perfectly, over time and through all the experiences of life, our track record for judging will hopefully improve.

Be patient with your children as they go through similar stages of development in order to learn discernment. Learning to make good judgments takes time and experience and sometimes involves making a few mistakes. When your children make mistakes, you need to remind yourself that you've been at it much longer. You have learned through life situations and even your own foolish mistakes. If you spend as much time recalling your own development as you do talking to your child about it, you probably will have good balance in your own discernment with your children. ✤

PARENTING PRINCIPLE

Teach your children about discernment and then let them learn it through experience.

POINTS TO PONDER

- How would you describe your ability to discern?
- How do your children view your discernment ability?
- What will you talk about with your children regarding discernment?

EARS TO HEAR

If anyone turns a deaf ear to my instruction, even their prayers are detestable.

PROVERBS 28:9

The last thing we want to do is hinder the prayers we offer on behalf of our children. Notice that Proverbs 28:9 says God's receptiveness to our prayers depends on our willingness to listen to his instructions. And it's more than just about listening. We also need to be flexible and moldable to God's instruction. The more we submit to God, the more our prayers become as incense to God.

Parents feel this same way when their children are obedient. We want to reward them. How much more does God desire to give us good things? In the case of parenting, he grants us good things when we ask on behalf of our children.

In order to be a faithful prayer warrior for your children, you must first be a faithful warrior for Christ and never turn a deaf ear when he speaks. By following these ways, we help our kids understand someday how loving and faithful we have been to listen to the Lord's instruction and hold them up in prayer, expecting the Lord to hear. ❖

PARENTING PRINCIPLE

If you turn a deaf ear, then your children also will not hear!

POINTS TO PONDER

- How careful are you to listen to God's instruction?
- How often do you pray for your children?
- Is there anything that hinders your prayers, such as sometimes turning a deaf ear?

day178

AVOID THE TRAP

Whoever leads the upright along an evil path will fall into their own trap.

PROVERBS 28:10

It's human nature to want to hang around people who are like you. This is especially true for someone who is not making wise choices. They start to feel better about themselves when they connect with other people who are also making poor choices because it helps to justify their bad behavior.

A teen might also try to get other teens to follow their bad example just so they can tell you everyone else is doing it. But it's a trap. It's all part of Satan's plan to discourage and defeat us all. Your child might even fall victim to this deceitful activity of leading the upright along an evil path. In all honesty, adults do it too.

Parents first need to be careful not to participate in sinful activities themselves. Then they need to shield their children from the temptation to participate in them. Next, if your child is doing wrong, parents need to find ways to warn others—siblings, other parents, friends—not to be led astray. ❖

PARENTING PRINCIPLE

Teach your children that they too will fall prey when they cause others to stray.

POINTS TO PONDER

- When have you or someone you know been involved in these types of circumstances?
- What could you do to lead a more upright life?
- How can you continue to develop your children in leading an upright life and not leading others astray?

NOT IN CONTROL

When the righteous triumph, there is great elation; but when the wicked rise to power, people go into hiding.   PROVERBS 28:12

Show me a home where a parent uses power and domination to dictate everything that happens and I'll show you a home where the children learn to hide. Not hiding in the sense of a game, but hiding behind addictions, bad relationships, and other secretive behaviors to cope with the tyrannical leadership in the home. A belligerent parent will justify their actions by saying it has to be that way. They might even misuse Scripture to try to validate their point.

If this devotional makes you feel indignant in any way, then it's possible you are exercising too much control over your family. You might believe your children's silence on the issue equals approval, but more than likely they're afraid of you. Parenting through duress is not good parenting. You need help if you behave in this manner. At some point, your children will rebel against your style of parenting, which leads to hiding.

Misusing parental power will only bring harm to yourself and your children. It will not bring about obedience or a healthy home. ❧

PARENTING PRINCIPLE

Children who hide are not on your side.

POINTS TO PONDER

- In what ways might you be too domineering?
- In what way might your children be hiding because of your parenting style?
- What help do you need to be less tyrannical and more loving?

BE OBSERVANT

Whoever conceals their sins does not prosper, but the one who confesses and renounces them finds mercy.   Proverbs 28:13

It's important to be aware of how your child behaves in life situations and to make mental notes of the reactions you generally see. It's possible that patterns will emerge that will help you discover things that might have otherwise gone unnoticed. For example, if your child is concealing sin, they might act more irritably. Don't accuse them of suppressing something, just continue to observe their behavior and watch for further clues of a hidden agenda.

By paying attention to these details, you may eventually detect whether they are concealing sins. Be sure to share with them that sins should first be confessed to God before they confess them to you. Following this pattern will create a much more peaceful home because of God's mercy.

Be mindful of your behaviors too. Your children constantly watch you and they may sense any edginess caused by underlying sin. The best scenario for a family is living free and clean and enjoying the mercies of God. ✤

PARENTING PRINCIPLE

Concealing sin is like a thief with a concealed weapon. It holds plenty of danger.

POINTS TO PONDER

- In what areas of your life are you concealing sin?
- What patterns of behavior have you seen in your child that could be indications they might be hiding sins?
- How can you help yourself and your children stay clear and free of hiding sins?

KEEPING BALANCE

Blessed is the one who always trembles before God, but whoever hardens their heart falls into trouble.   PROVERBS 28:14

To tremble before God is to understand his awesomeness and power and to respect his supremacy. In our "grace" flowing society, we often forget the "fear and trembling" aspect of God's power. It's hard to think of a loving God who can also punish those who do evil—but he can!

That's why we need to help our children recognize that God provides our every breath. Embracing the truth of this power will hopefully keep them from shunning God and falling into the enemy's hands.

Guide your children through a study of this balance between "grace" and "fear." Even though we change, God doesn't change what has been his pattern since the beginning of time. He is just and will remind us that he is God and we are not.

Through the years, your children may lose respect for the one true God and harden their hearts toward him. You will need to walk along beside them during this period and pray they mature and experience God's grace until they return to him. ❖

PARENTING PRINCIPLE

Children who live with fear and trembling before God will live with grace.

POINTS TO PONDER

- What are signs that someone is hardening their heart?
- How do you keep the awesomeness of God in front of your family?
- How can you help your children continue to grow in "grace" but also in "fear and trembling"?

THE VALUE OF WORK

Those who work their land will have abundant food, but those who chase fantasies will have their fill of poverty.   PROVERBS 28:19

The Bible is full of wisdom regarding the importance of work, including Proverbs 28:19. We can easily make a correlation that when we complete a task we find value in who we are and what we have accomplished. Work provides us with food whether it's working to grow it or using our earnings from work to buy it.

These benefits alone should motivate us to teach our children the value of work and how it's better than the consequences of chasing fantasies that can lead to poverty. Through watching our habits and attitude toward work, our children can learn the importance of working until the day they "own" this value themselves! You can counter that by sharing examples of people who exhibited laziness and a lack of motivation and ended up with nothing to show for it. Assigning chores can also help them understand the benefits of hard work.

A working person, given the opportunity to work, will always be able to provide for themselves. ❖

PARENTING PRINCIPLE

Knowing the value of work will be of value to your child.

POINTS TO PONDER

- Have you seen a shift in society's view of work?
- If so, how has this shift affected your children's view of work?
- What are you doing to develop a good work ethic in your children?

day183

FAITHFUL FOUNDATION

A faithful person will be richly blessed. PROVERBS 28:20

Being a faithful parent will most probably come at a price. The price of being overworked, overtired, overstressed and underappreciated at times. The word *faithfulness* rolls off the tongue and is an eloquent-sounding word, but the actions of faithfulness take a strong work ethic.

Add to this how unfaithfulness is celebrated by our society, and you have an underlying current of potential clashes as you seek to swim upstream.

Faithfulness is a word we want used with our eulogy, but too often we don't live in such a way to deserve it. Our children will have the final say on this matter. They will either speak with great joy about how we lived or they won't want to speak about it at all.

Define yourself as a parent today and see if faithfulness is your foundation. If it isn't, make some changes in your life and be committed to the things that honor God. Stop seeking self-pleasure and personal gain. Develop a pattern of faithfulness in your life that earns you the opportunity to be richly blessed by God. ❖

PARENTING PRINCIPLE

Your faith should be as unmovable as a foundation.

POINTS TO PONDER

- What are some areas of growth for you to become more of a faithful parent?
- How do you begin to teach attributes of faithfulness to your children?
- How are you praying for God to bless your family's efforts in faithfulness to him?

BE FAIR

To show partiality is not good.   PROVERBS 28:21

We are all guilty of showing partiality. It's easy to do when that action will reap us some great rewards.

Our children will continually battle this temptation. Showing favoritism to one person could garner an invitation to a party or make them part of the "in group." They could get a better position on a sports team by showing favoritism to certain players. They might be able to lead their group by "playing the game" and doing what others want them to do. The temptation to show partiality is all around us all the time.

The first step in helping your children understand the importance of not playing favorites is to refrain from showing partiality in your home. Then, because it's possible your children may not see the problem with favoritism or even understand the consequences of it, take some time to explain partiality and give them some examples of how it can be harmful.

Follow it up by explaining how Christ is an impartial Savior to us all and why that is so important. Then celebrate the moments in your children when you see them being fair and not giving in to opportunities to show partiality. ✤

PARENTING PRINCIPLE

Showing partiality only shows you don't know the fullness of Christ.

POINTS TO PONDER

- In what areas could you be showing partiality?
- How can you improve?
- What can you share with your children to help them understand why partiality is not good?

THE BENEFITS OF REBUKE

Whoever rebukes a person will in the end gain favor rather than one who has a flattering tongue.   PROVERBS 28:23

We like people who tell us what we want to hear. Our children will inherit this trait. Too often, we surround ourselves with individuals who flatter us and give us a false sense of security. Our society witnessed this with the crash of the banking industry. Bank presidents were surrounded by vice presidents who protected the presidents by hiding their vices, which eventually corrupted the companies. In the end, they all lost favor.

In our families, we need people who will rebuke and challenge us when our behavior warrants it. You should do the same for your child. Don't turn away when you see them conducting themselves inappropriately. Step in and be the parent—rebuke, if you will. It will not always be easy. But in the long run, your children will be thankful for strong parents. The Lord has reasons for giving us children. One reason he gave children to you might be to help develop your ability to rebuke harmful behavior in others, which could also save your own child from destroying their life. ❖

PARENTING PRINCIPLE

Your tongue will tame or it will maim.

POINTS TO PONDER

- Do you tend to flatter people more or rebuke them more? What are the dangers of each?
- In what area do you need to be more assertive with your child?
- Who runs your home?

day186

BUILDING BRIDGES

Do not testify against your neighbor without cause—would you use your lips to mislead?
PROVERBS 24:28

As you raise your children, you will most likely learn a lot about your neighbors. Kids make friends. Friends come over and then you meet their parents. You will become friends with some new families simply because your kids hang out together. These new relationships may also create some issues. You won't share the same moral beliefs as some of these families. They might allow certain choice words in their home that you find offensive. They might watch movies you would never allow in your home. This will be challenging when you allow your child to spend time in their home.

Your children will learn about life by how you handle mishaps in these friendships. It's important to handle these issues in a Christ-like way. Don't fault your neighbor because they don't see things your way. You may have to set up certain boundaries because of the differences, but set the boundaries without throwing your opinion around or calling anyone names.

Learning how to be a good neighbor, despite having differences with others, is part of life. By doing so, you help your children know how to deal with "real world" issues. ❖

PARENTING PRINCIPLE

Instead of building animosity with your neighbors, build bridges.

POINTS TO PONDER

- What kind of neighbor are you?
- How do you typically handle issues with your neighbors?
- What can you teach your children about handling differences in friendships?

BALANCING WORK AND REST

A little sleep, a little slumber, a little folding of the hands to rest—and poverty will come on you like a thief.   PROVERBS 24:33–34

There is nothing wrong with rest. God rested on the seventh day of creation. We need rest, and it needs to be built into our family calendar. But in Proverbs 24:33–34, God is saying that we shouldn't fall in love with rest. If we are not productive in society and prefer to simply "waste time," we will become an unproductive leech and suck the resources from society.

We need to teach our children to find value in work. Social programs are necessary for the truly needy, but our children need to learn how to be a part of the workforce and not buy into the myth that getting something for nothing is easier. It isn't. In the end, they will find out that poverty isn't the way to life, and it's not part of what God desires for us! He created us to be capable of working and except for those who are not physically or mentally able, we need to work.

Be a parent who allows rest, but also instills a work ethic. It will be a blessing for your child! ✤

PARENTING PRINCIPLE

Rest is best when balanced with work.

POINTS TO PONDER

- Why do you feel a good work ethic is important for your children?
- Do you have a good balance of play, rest and work in your family?
- Who are good examples of this balance you can show your kids?

day188 july 7

GUARD THE GATES

Remove the dross from the silver, and a silversmith can produce a vessel. PROVERBS 25:4

Dross is a scum that forms on the surface of melted metal. In the case of Proverbs 25:4, the metal is silver. If a silversmith wants their vessel to be beautiful and pristine, they must remove the scum.

Teach your child how this principle applies to their life. If they allow "scum" in their life, the end product will not be as pure and refined as it should be. It will be drab and dull and have little luster. In other words, if you want a clean reputation, live a clean life. Simple to say, much more difficult to live. Start by teaching your child that they have three major gates through which things pass in and out of their life. The eye gate—what we see; the ear gate—what we hear; the mouth gate—what we speak. What they allow to pass through those gates will determine who they become.

If we monitor what goes through these three major gates to our life, we will have a better chance of producing a pristine vessel. Parents need to remember their children are watching their gate-control too! Your example matters. ❧

PARENTING PRINCIPLE

Guard the gates and help direct your fate.

POINTS TO PONDER

- How are you doing at controlling your own gates?
- How are you doing at monitoring your children's gates?
- How are you teaching your children to control their own gates?

192

SETTING THE TABLE

Like apples of gold in settings of silver is a ruling rightly given.   PROVERBS 25:11

At the time Proverbs was written, silver and gold were among the highest of riches. Though they are still valuable today, it's not likely they carry the same significance they did then. When the author puts this "apple of gold" in a silver setting, it is where it belongs, gold upon silver, displayed as it should be. Proverbs 25:11 is saying that when we rule rightly, our judgments and decisions are honored. And when we make right rulings with our children we have given them a most high blessing and reward.

To consistently rule rightly is nearly impossible. As a parent, you will sometimes miss the mark, but keep the bar high. Seek to honor God in all you do. Do not settle for mediocre parenting. Many have and it has brought severe consequences on our society. Your children will make their own decisions—just make sure they look back later in life and know you gave them a beautiful "place setting." It will be their call to take advantage of it or not—that's not on you. ✤

PARENTING PRINCIPLE

Leave your children a beautiful place setting that doesn't go on a table!

POINTS TO PONDER

- What are you doing to mature in your parenting rulings?
- How are you leaving your children a great legacy in their decision making?
- How will you maintain energy for this effort over the long haul?

day190

DRINK IT IN

Like a snow-cooled drink at harvest time is a trustworthy messenger to the one who sends him; he refreshes the spirit of his master.　　　　　PROVERBS 25:13

Let's put this verse in the context of parenting. When you receive news that your child has been a blessing to others or that they have been a good student in class—it's like a refreshing drink. It lightens your spirit and encourages you to press on in this parenting journey. We certainly need that, as parents don't usually receive a lot of accolades.

As parents, we may become so consumed by our own need for a "cool drink" that we forget our children need it as well, regardless of their age. When we bless our children with words of encouragement or we find a quality in them worthy of celebration—we become like a fresh drink to their spirit.

It's easy to think that we do enough for them already. But that can't be our attitude. We must stay in the mind-set that our words and deeds are seen as kind and uplifting to them. If you continue to foster this spirit, you can help bring them peace in the tough times and help build a good rapport between you. ❖

PARENTING PRINCIPLE

A fresh drink will quench your children's thirst and refresh their soul.

POINTS TO PONDER

- Who has been a refreshing drink for you?
- How could you be more refreshing to your family?
- How can you teach your children to be refreshing to others?

day191

FOLLOW THROUGH

Like clouds and wind without rain is one who boasts of gifts never given.

PROVERBS 25:14

When a person talks big about something they are going to do but then never follows through, it can be discouraging, especially if it happens in your family. When parents boast about what they might do or make promises they never fulfill, children experience a lot of disappointment. Proverbs 25:14 teaches us that it's like dealing with all the consequences of a storm and not getting the benefits of the rain.

If you promise somebody something, follow through and do it! If you make commitments to your children, don't let them down. If your children make commitments to others, make them finish what they started. For example, if you sign your child up for an activity but then halfway through they don't feel like doing it anymore, make them complete it. If they don't learn to be true to their word, you and others will lose respect for what they say they will do. If you always let them falter on their responsibilities, the only thing they will learn is how to falter. Teach them to be true to their word and that's what they will know. ✤

PARENTING PRINCIPLE

Big talkers are just like big mockers: they don't help anyone.

POINTS TO PONDER

- How often do you make big boasts without follow through?
- When have you seen this trait in your children?
- How will you curb it in your home?

# day192

PREVENTING MESSES

If you find honey, eat just enough — too much of it, and you will vomit. Proverbs 25:16

To find a treasure trove of honey in a comb is the equivalent of us coming home and finding our cupboards filled with a plethora of sweets. If you indulge yourself, it will make you sick now and even sicker later thinking about it. A delicate balance will help you enjoy some sweets now and look forward to another opportunity later.

A child doesn't know that balance. If you leave them alone in a room with a bag of candy, you will likely deal with a sick child later on. If you supervise them, they see you as a spoiler. What they see as the perfect opportunity, we see as a potential disaster.

Parents will need to monitor their children's consumption in many areas, not just with sweet treats. You must provide that delicate balance for your child until they develop sound judgment on their own. It's tough to think of ourselves as vomit stoppers, but it's our responsibility as parents to prevent some messes. Proverbs 25:16 suggests that we must accept that responsibility and do it with diligence. ❖

PARENTING PRINCIPLE

Teach your children the sweetness of doing everything in moderation.

POINTS TO PONDER

- What are you prone to overindulge in?
- How can you learn to be a delicate balance for your children?
- How could your family grow in this area of overindulgence?

GOOD NEIGHBORS

Seldom set foot in your neighbor's house—too much of you, and they will hate you.
PROVERBS 25:17

Have you ever had a neighborhood kid at your house who didn't know when it was time to leave? Worse yet, perhaps you have a neighborhood kid who has a parent who doesn't know when it's time for their kid to leave.

Here's all you need to know. Don't let that kid be your kid. Teach your children that while it's fun to play at the neighbor's house, they have to come home eventually. Too many parents see their children visiting at the neighbors as free child care.

Someone once said, "It takes a village to raise a child." You don't want to be known as the idiot of that village! Be sure you know where your children are and teach them not to "wear out their welcome." If they aren't yet familiar with that phrase, explain it to them. As parents, be sensitive to your neighbor's limitations. Build boundaries for your children and teach them the benefits of staying within those boundaries.

You want to be a family that the neighbors look forward to seeing and don't hide from. ✤

PARENTING PRINCIPLE

Good neighbors are called good because they know their boundaries.

POINTS TO PONDER

- How have you been a good neighbor?
- What could you do to assist your whole neighborhood with this issue?
- How can you teach your children to live within healthy boundaries in your neighborhood?

BE FAITHFUL

Like a broken tooth or a lame foot is reliance on the unfaithful in a time of trouble.

PROVERBS 25:19

If you have ever had an injury to your foot or a mouthful of pain, Proverbs 25:19 might make a lot more sense to you than to someone who has not. You can't rely on something that's not working. The same is true in family life. If you are an unfaithful parent, your child will never turn to you for the concerns or problems they face in life.

Unfaithfulness can take the form of inconsistent love and unreliable guidance. It's not just about making one mistake, but a more consistent pattern of unreliability. If you display moodiness or bring insecurity into the family, you can potentially be considered unfaithful.

Seek to change your behavior. You can do this on your own or by talking with a counselor and developing new patterns of behavior that will bring a steady diet of faithfulness to your family. Do not make excuses for yourself or blame something else — just own it and change it. As you do, you will win at home and become more satisfied with who you are in Christ. ❖

PARENTING PRINCIPLE

It's never too late to become faithful so you are not like a broken tooth or a lame foot to your children.

POINTS TO PONDER

- How are you a faithful parent?
- What could you do to improve some of your weak areas of faithfulness?
- Are your children becoming faithful themselves? How?

BURDEN BEARER

Like one who takes away a garment on a cold day, or like vinegar poured on a wound, is one who sings songs to a heavy heart. PROVERBS 25:20

You should comfort your child who has a broken heart and help them to heal. To that end, Proverbs 25:20 warns us against being insensitive to them as if their problems are not important and causing them even more pain. Don't punish them by unnecessarily taking away privileges during such a hard time or by pouring on criticism that can sting like vinegar on a wound. Don't take their broken heart too lightly.

When you sit by their bed and do nothing more than listen, you promote healing. Be sensitive to the fact that they are dealing with issues that are indeed heavy for them. The problems we deal with as parents may seem more significant, but to your children, their own problems seem huge.

Singing a song to a heavy heart might mean talking when talk is unnecessary, adding to your child's burden. Seek to be a burden bearer for your child by listening to them. Help them understand that life is filled with challenges and, when it's time, encourage them to move on. ✤

PARENTING PRINCIPLE

A heavy heart needs a light touch.

POINTS TO PONDER

- How do you lift your own heavy heart?
- What do you do to help relieve your child's heavy heart?
- What heavy heart issues do you need to be praying about right now?

# day196 july 15

BRING PEACE

If your enemy is hungry, give him food to eat; if he is thirsty, give him water to drink. In doing this, you will heap burning coals on his head, and the LORD will reward you.
PROVERBS 25:21–22

When our children are teased by a bully, the last thing we think of is how they can be nicer to that bully tomorrow. The idea of helping our enemy is counter-intuitive. Yet Proverbs 25:21–22 calls us to this type of thinking. Consider these ways to "heap coals" on an enemy.

Teach your children that taking revenge will typically only escalate the situation. The next and best step if possible is to remove themselves from situations involving this person. Encourage them not to do anything that gives their enemy a reason to come at them again.

The key is not worsening the situation. Too many parents do this by jumping in with both feet, both hands and a loud mouth, resulting in increased tension. Be a solution-orientated parent. Teach your children that kindness toward an enemy is what the Lord expects. Your child will learn to be much more Christ-like and balanced if you are, and in the end that enemy may become a friend. ❧

PARENTING PRINCIPLE

Bring peace and create solutions, not tension.

POINTS TO PONDER

- Who are potential or current enemies for your child?
- What would you tell your child about resolving conflict in healthy ways?
- How do you see them developing conflict resolution skills?

STOP THE SNAKES

Like a north wind that brings unexpected rain is a sly tongue—which provokes a horrified look.　　　　　　　　　　　　　　　　　　Proverbs 25:23

When someone in the family starts acting sly, they are a nemesis for everyone. They slither around and devise deceptive schemes that trip others up and cause turmoil. If you have a person in your family who is sly, call them out. When you do, their first instinct will be to slither away.

The best way to stop a snake is "dead in its tracks!" That's why we need to address sly, deceptive people with straight-up confrontation. They generally don't like it and won't look at you unless you make them. Catch their eye and don't let them look away. Describe to them how they are behaving and how it's affecting the family.

Right before a snake sheds its skin, it demonstrates distinct behavioral changes, such as increased nervousness or behavior that is defensive, unpredictable or aggressive due to the snake's vulnerable state. This could easily describe a sly-acting child. They are also in a vulnerable state, because they are acting outside of God's will.

Hopefully your correction will cause them to see the severity of their behavior—and stop any more horrified looks. ✤

PARENTING PRINCIPLE

Slyness is a snake in the grass for your family.

POINTS TO PONDER

- Who in your family has exhibited sly behavior?
- What are you doing to address those "sly" issues?
- How can you continue to protect your family from the "snake in the grass"?

 **day198**

CLEAN UP THE MUD

Like a muddied spring or a polluted well are the righteous who give way to the wicked.

PROVERBS 25:26

If you have ever watched a good family go bad, you have seen a sickening thing. I don't think any family ever wants or sets out to create "muddied water"—or giving way to the wicked—in their home, but some do fall victim to temptation or exhaustion.

Parents must be alert to their ever-changing home environment. Satan's attacks will most often be so subtle that the non-discerning parent can be easily fooled. The daily monitoring required to protect your home is tiring and therefore also easy to ignore. And if you feel you have already failed, you might just give up and let it go. Don't do that! Stand up for what you believe and know to be true. Even though these times will be stressful and seem too overwhelming, it will be worth it if you can get through the sludge.

Remember, parenting for Christ is not for the faint of heart. It will require lots of energy and often feel lonely. But you will receive your due rewards if you do not surrender to the ways of the wicked. ✤

PARENTING PRINCIPLE

If your well is pure your water will satisfy.

POINTS TO PONDER

- Are your children "muddying" the water?
- How can you protect your family from muddied water or, if necessary, clean it up?
- How can you combat the fatigue you will experience and not give up?

NOT TOO DEEP

[It is not] honorable to search out matters that are too deep. PROVERBS 25:27

At first glance, Proverbs 25:27 seems to say that shallow thinking is wise. But a closer look reveals a much more significant thought. The matters referred to are those things that, when sought out and uncovered, accomplish nothing.

The best way to illustrate this is to think about those times when you disagree on an issue with either your children or your spouse. Nobody is necessarily wrong but everybody is frustrated. When you spend all your time trying to get the other person to think your way, you are wasting everyone's time and causing division in the home.

Often one person will just want to be understood, which is good, but forcing another individual to think like them is destructive. In that scenario, they are delving too deep and it's not productive for anyone. In these matters it's more gracious to search deep enough to appreciate each other's point of view and then let it go! That is a depth everyone can share and doesn't dig at the issues that should be left alone. ✤

PARENTING PRINCIPLE

Dig deep enough to hit water but don't keep digging and ruin the well.

POINTS TO PONDER

- What do you want to discuss too often and too deep?
- How could you back off a bit in a particular situation?
- How can you help your family see and appreciate each other and your differences?

EXERCISE CONTROL

Like a city whose walls are broken through is a person who lacks self-control.

PROVERBS 25:28

Interestingly, many people who seem to lack self-control also seem to be able to control when they have it and when they don't have it. Often self-control is simply a matter of self-discipline.

Parenting without self-control is like fishing without a pole—it doesn't work very well. You will be grabbing at everything that swims by but you'll just end up all wet! If you struggle with self-control, just admit it. Then, don't try to justify your lack of self-control; just accept it as a character trait and move on to the next step. Lastly, realize that self-control begins with God-control. Start praying to God about changing this behavior and allowing him control of your life. Even though we claim to be followers of Christ, we like to do things our way, and it doesn't take long for our way to become the only way! Pray for God to direct your steps.

Becoming a parent with self-control will not be easy, but it will be necessary if you want peace in your home. As you change, God will use your example to help your children develop better self-control. ❖

PARENTING PRINCIPLE

Fish with a pole if you desire more control.

POINTS TO PONDER

- Where is self-control a struggle for you?
- What steps do you need to take to change this behavior?
- Where do you see your children lacking in self-control?

DON'T BE FOOLISH

Like snow in summer or rain in harvest, honor is not fitting for a fool.   PROVERBS 26:1

I'm sure you have never awakened in the morning during the middle of summer and opened your blinds to the sight of fresh-fallen snow. That would be foolish to even imagine. A comparison could be made with a parent who behaves in ways that are foolish and then expects honor from their children—think again!

Proverbs 26:1 also indicates that the same is true if your children make foolish decisions. Explain this verse to them and tell them that they will not be fit for honor if their decisions are foolish and do not respect God and you.

As children travel through the teen stages they will sometimes lose sight of how their attitude and tone are affecting others. Even when you point out their foolishness, they often won't see it. It's a good time to remind them that foolish decisions will never earn your trust. They may not like it, but this will be a place where you as a parent are not seeking to be liked. You are teaching the truth! ❖

PARENTING PRINCIPLE

Fools' names and foolish faces are always found in foolish places.

POINTS TO PONDER

- How might you be honoring those who are foolish?
- Where does our society do this?
- What can you do to help your children understand this truth and how it should affect their own behavior?

KEEP MOVING

Like a fluttering sparrow or a darting swallow, an undeserved curse does not come to rest.

PROVERBS 26:2

Have you ever had something said about you that you knew wasn't deserved but you couldn't stop people from saying or thinking it? You just couldn't get peace about it and no matter what you tried, it just didn't go away. It was like a bird fluttering and darting around, unable to rest.

The best way to deal with these comments is to ignore them. If you didn't start the fire, stop trying to put it out. Being able to "let it go" will be important for your family to move forward, and your children will learn from your example.

If an undeserved curse hasn't happened to your child yet, it will. By first grade they will probably have a couple of these experiences under their belt. If they have a sensitive personality, they will need you to guide them through these new challenges that are a normal part of life.

The good news is that birds that flutter and dart usually fly away. Over time and with good counsel most of us can move on too. ❧

PARENTING PRINCIPLE

If you didn't start the fire, stop trying to put it out!

POINTS TO PONDER

- What has happened to you in the past that you have had to let go?
- What are you dealing with now that you need to let go?
- How can you help your children learn to let go?

NOT A CALLING

Do not answer a fool according to his folly, or you yourself will be just like him.

PROVERBS 26:4

Some Christian teens feel it's their calling to go into the places where "foolish" teens go. They think it's a call of God because they will touch lives in a whole new way. Some can, but most can't! Too often the "rubbing of shoulders" with those who are foolish exposes the teen's immaturity and leads to some poor decisions.

Your children may justify the actions of some individuals that you call into question. Their tone will turn defensive, and your relationship may deteriorate. The problem is that you are seeing Proverbs 26:4 come to life. When your children constantly expose themselves to people who are making poor choices, then that behavior begins to look normal. They participate in things they used to deplore and it feels normal.

Talk now with your child about their commitment to purity and wise choices. You will not always be able to control their behavior, but you do have control of what you teach them. Those teachings will be remembered for a lifetime. ✤

PARENTING PRINCIPLE

If a fool full of folly comes calling, don't answer the door.

POINTS TO PONDER

- Where does your family risk making foolish decisions?
- Are you invested in your children's lives enough to know how they are doing with decision making?
- Can you think of some new ideas you can implement that will protect your family?

FOOLS RUSH IN

Like one who grabs a stray dog by the ears is someone who rushes into a quarrel not their own. PROVERBS 26:17

Most of us would never consider grabbing a stray dog by the ears—or at all. We are more likely to rush indoors if we encounter a dog we don't know.

This is good advice for most arguments we witness. Human nature would prompt us to get involved, but we run the risk of causing the disagreement to escalate because we are ignorant about what's going on.

Notice the key word in Proverbs 26:17 is *rushes*. It doesn't say we shouldn't get involved, but it counsels us to do so only after a bit of reflection and with wisdom. This is especially true when you are parenting more than one child. It's not unusual for one child to know how to get the other sibling in trouble. They will set you up to rush in and react without knowing the whole story. When you are tired from a long day of work, rushing in seems like the only option. But you could end up punishing the wrong child.

Take time now to establish a parenting protocol that you will practice during these moments. ✤

PARENTING PRINCIPLE

Fools rush in, parents should not.

POINTS TO PONDER

- How do you currently squelch your children's arguments?
- What is a possible parenting protocol you could follow to avoid rushing in?
- How could changes in your reactions benefit you and your home?

IT'S NOT FUNNY

*Like a maniac shooting flaming arrows of death is one who deceives their neighbor
and says, "I was only joking!"*   Proverbs 26:18–19

Jokesters can be hilarious, but they can also be harmful to a family. Consider the
person who justifies their wrong behavior by saying, "I was just joking!" This is
a person who doesn't take responsibility for what they do. It's also hard to teach
them anything if they claim they already know everything.

If you say "I was just joking" to your children and you use that tactic to keep
from having to deal with your own inappropriate behaviors—shame on you and
stop it! Parents who behave this way only confuse and frustrate their children. If
there is one child you have a harder time getting along with, they are probably the
one who is a lot like you. You may both be guilty of this behavior. If so, try holding
each other accountable to stop.

Though hiding behind inappropriate joking might at times seem trivial, it's
much more serious and concerning than it might appear. It's one of those issues
that can slip through the cracks and end up cracking the wall of the family's foundation. ❖

PARENTING PRINCIPLE

Hiding destructive behaviors behind joking is not funny.

POINTS TO PONDER

- When have you dismissed behavior by saying, "I'm just joking"?
- Does anyone in your family do that?
- How will you address joking if it's becoming inappropriate?

FIRE CONTROL

Without wood a fire goes out; without a gossip a quarrel dies down.   Proverbs 26:20

Gossip separates close friends and fuels a flame that spreads like wildfire. Gossip is sinful and can be responsible for the destruction of a family. Gossip is both a noun and a verb. It can be easy to fall into gossip and gossiping will sometimes be the catalyst for even more destructive behavior or consequences.

Dealing effectively with gossip is a sign of spiritual maturity. Parents who don't gossip and teach their children to refrain from it will create a beautiful home environment for growth! To try and eliminate gossip, insist that everyone follow these simple rules. Say only positive things about each other and about others outside the family. When you hear someone gossiping, ask the person who is speaking negatively of others to stop. Don't fuel someone's quarrel with gossip. As a Christian make sure you don't disguise a prayer request as gossip. Be sure you have permission to share it from the person who shared it with you.

If you speak negatively of others, that is what your children will learn to do. So first be a good example for them. ❖

PARENTING PRINCIPLE

Put out the fire by controlling your gossip desire.

POINTS TO PONDER

- How do you effectively stop gossiping when you hear it?
- How might you participate in gossip without even realizing it?
- How have you worked to prevent gossip in your home?

HARBORING DECEIT

Enemies disguise themselves with their lips, but in their hearts they harbor deceit.

PROVERBS 26:24

Watch out for people who sound like they care about you but are simply setting you or your family up for a fall. We can never really know a person's heart, but usually their actions will reflect more of their true character. Teach your children that the world is filled with people who say one thing but are actually thinking and doing something wrong that will affect you negatively. Many parents want to protect their children from knowing this, but if you expose them to it now when it's age-appropriate, they will be better prepared for the battles they'll surely face.

Harboring deceit is damaging and hurtful to all parties involved. If you have a child who is showing signs of harboring deceit, talk to them about it. They may be defensive and try to cover up what they are doing, but explain to them how their deceit will eventually be uncovered and leave a mark on everybody it touches.

Keep your home a place free and clear of enemies within and out of your home. ❖

PARENTING PRINCIPLE

Just because you don't see the enemy doesn't mean they aren't there.

POINTS TO PONDER

- What signs of harboring deceit have you noticed in others?
- What signs of deceit have you witnessed in your own family?
- How could you remove any deceit that is residing in your family—or in your own heart?

STOP DIGGING

Whoever digs a pit will fall into it. PROVERBS 26:27

Despite all the lessons from history, humanity still thinks they can pull a fast one.

Some people are convinced they can dig a pit of sin without falling into the pit. Our children are vulnerable to this kind of thinking. They will not see their digging as a pitfall; instead, they might call it "finding themselves." It's fascinating to see a group of kids standing together who dress alike, have similar hairstyles, have piercings in all the same places and yet crave to be unique. Uniqueness is not found by simply distinguishing ourselves from others physically. It is found in understanding and discovering what Jesus has in store for our particular life.

Help your children see and stay out of the pits of sin and stay up on the path that leads to wholeness in Christ. As parents, we need to be sure of our own distinctiveness in Christ and avoid digging our own pits or passing our pits on to our children. Build significance into your life, and let your children discover their own way to fully honor God by watching you live out your life honoring him — away from the pits of despair. ✤

PARENTING PRINCIPLE

Pit diggers become pit dwellers.

POINTS TO PONDER

- What pits have you dug and fallen into?
- How do you keep from digging more pits?
- What pits are your children at risk for digging?

BE TRUTHFUL

A lying tongue hates those it hurts.   Proverbs 26:28

If you have ever been lied to then you know how devastating it can be—especially if it's by someone in your own family. You feel hated, just as Proverbs 26:28 says. If you can get your child to see how lies hurt, it will help curtail their lying.

In general, liars hate to be lied to, but they don't mind lying to others. It is a bold statement to call what liars do "hate" speech. But that's what it is. It shows disdain and disrespect to the person who is being lied to. It's also a statement of disrespect about yourself if you lie.

Liars also will find it difficult later in life to totally trust others. This comes from an internal struggle with all they have seen and done to others. Help your children understand the dangers of lying, especially when they are young. Point out what others are going through as a result of lying. Some children will still choose to lie and then will learn from their own personal mistakes.

Lying is hateful and it hurts everyone involved. Be a parent full of truth and let that be a lasting memory for your child. ✣

PARENTING PRINCIPLE

Lying promotes hate while truth spreads love.

POINTS TO PONDER

- How have you been hurt by lies?
- How are you teaching your children that lies hurt and are a sign of hatred?
- What are you doing to promote truth telling?

LOOSEN THE NECK

Whoever remains stiff-necked after many rebukes will suddenly be destroyed — without remedy.   PROVERBS 29:1

Stiff-necked children are undisciplined children. Not because their parents haven't tried, but because they have refused to listen.

Stiff-necked people are difficult to be around. They are selfish, greedy and obnoxiously adamant about blaming everyone else for everything. They refuse to learn from or listen to anyone else. They are usually inflexible in their dealings with people.

According to this definition, are you or are any of your family members stiff-necks? If yes, how are you dealing with it? The latter question can be difficult to answer when you are in the midst of dealing with a child who is acting this way, but it needs to be addressed.

One of the best approaches to this situation is to pray for God to open their eyes to their weakness because that's exactly what it is, a spiritual weakness. It seems ironic that something so tough and stiff comes from something so weak. Next, make it clear to that child that by walking this path, their life is headed toward destruction. A third option is to consider professional counseling.

Do all you can as a parent to be tender and teachable so your children will do the same. ✤

PARENTING PRINCIPLE

A good daily neck-stretching will benefit everyone.

POINTS TO PONDER

- How might you be coming across stiff-necked?
- What type of stubbornness do your children deal with?
- What can you do to keep this out of your family?

WANDER FROM SQUANDER

A man who loves wisdom brings joy to his father, but a companion of prostitutes squanders his wealth. PROVERBS 29:3

A companion of prostitutes would experience natural consequences, but when it comes to our family the prostitutes Proverbs 29:3 is referring to are the scandalous things in our life that distract us and lead us to squander our wealth. The temptation of these desires is simply too great and powerful for many to overcome, and they end up in this very spot—squandered.

Look for the potential "prostitutes" that could destroy you or your children. There will be obvious ones, but pay close attention to those things that might seem inconsequential because they could be the most dangerous. Whatever lures your child away from the things of Christ could move them closer to squandering everything away.

On the other hand, Proverbs 29:3 instructs us to live with wisdom because that is much closer to the heart of God. A constant drip of wisdom into the veins of your family life will keep you in the center of God's focus. It will protect and guide your family through those temptation zones and keep you from the evils that could prostitute your family. It is a continuous and effectual walk with Christ that can help guard you from squandering. ❖

PARENTING PRINCIPLE

Keep away from the lures that only wisdom can cure.

POINTS TO PONDER

- What are the potential "prostitutes" of our family?
- How do we bring joy to our family?
- How can you protect your family from distractions?

NO STEALING

Whoever robs their father or mother and says, "It's not wrong," is partner to one who destroys.
PROVERBS 28:24

No parent could ever be prepared for their child to rob them. It seems a bit far-fetched to even think it could ever happen. Yet it does, and more often than we think.

Children rob their parents of peace and joy but then sometimes a child will actually steal money or other things from their parents.

That's why it will be essential to teach your children at a young age, how they are not honoring God's Word when they do these things. One of the best ways you can teach this is to make sure they don't see you stealing from your parents. If you are, change this behavior. After you set a good example, then you can call your children to new levels of godly commitment in their walk with Christ.

Too often, we don't want to admit our faults. We will defend and offend, but not submit. It is in the moment of submission that we fully understand the value of Proverbs 28:24. God is looking for a parent who will surrender their own personal gain for the benefit of their family. ❖

PARENTING PRINCIPLE

Honor your father and mother so your days will be peaceful and long upon the earth.

POINTS TO PONDER

- In what way may you have robbed your parents?
- How do you feel robbed by your children?
- What can you do to pass along a healthy parent-child relationship with your children?

NO NEED FOR GREED

The greedy stir up conflict, but those who trust in the LORD will prosper.

PROVERBS 28:25

We typically don't think of people who stir up conflict as greedy. We simply see them as trouble makers, unsettled people or the kind of people who argue for the sake of arguing. Upon closer examination, we can see a deeper, hidden agenda. People who cause conflict are all about having things their way, and ultimately that's greed.

When our children initiate conflict, we can usually trace it back to greediness. We attempt to resolve the conflict, but what we really need to do is get at the heart of the issue—greediness!

The opposite of greediness is to give thanks and trust in the Lord. As we help our children focus more on how they're blessed, and start to turn their eyes away from greed, we actually help them begin to prosper. It's how God's kingdom works.

We are blessed and honored by God focusing not on this world, but on the world to come. Our conflicts and deficiencies diminish as we think less worldly and more eternally. This will be a principle you will have to live by and teach every day. ❖

PARENTING PRINCIPLE

If we are filled with greed, we will be filled with need.

POINTS TO PONDER

- Where has your greediness caused a conflict?
- How do you handle your children's moments of greed?
- How are you teaching your children to trust in the Lord?

NOT SO FINE

Those who trust in themselves are fools, but those who walk in wisdom are kept safe.

PROVERBS 28:26

There will come a point in your parenting life when you will want to help your child deal with an issue, and they will tell you they've got it handled. In fact, their exact words will be, "I'm fine." That is a catch-phrase for what they really mean which is, "I'm not fine, and I don't know how to handle this."

This is the place where our children can fall into foolish decisions and actions. They can fall deeper into trouble because they trust in themselves, which is never wise. Wisdom seeks advice. Wisdom recognizes its own deficiencies and seeks counsel. Wisdom says, "I'm not fine and I know it." Your child will develop a false sense of security when they trust in themselves. Time and maturity will be the greatest teacher in getting your children to think beyond themselves.

A natural stage of developing independence is by trusting ourselves. The real challenge and test will be for you as parents to know how to let your children develop their independence by incorporating wisdom. It will be wisdom from God that genuinely keeps them safe. ♣

PARENTING PRINCIPLE

Don't look for wisdom within yourself but in the Lord.

POINTS TO PONDER

- When have you trusted in yourself solely and what were the consequences?
- How will you get your children to trust in God?
- When has your family been safe because of trusting in God?

DRIVE TO THRIVE

When the righteous thrive, the people rejoice; when the wicked rule, the people groan.

PROVERBS 29:2

It seems as though the wicked thrive in our society. They get a lot of attention and seem to advance in life in the spirit of celebration. But underneath, down where the truth exists, an entirely different story lives. A story often full of pain, sorrow and discontent, which can all lead to groaning. That's why it's important not to parent based on the trends of society, but to parent based on the Word of God.

God's Word teaches us to live righteously. He instructs us to raise our children to honor him and live with integrity. The result will be a home of rejoicing. We cannot live to see what others say about us, but we must live to please God and set an example for our children. We seem to spend a lot of time trying to create a good, false impression instead of impressing upon our children how to live well according to God's Word. That's what we're called to do.

It's important to understand "thrive" from God's perspective. Man's definition of thriving includes a plush lifestyle, where God defines "thriving" as deepening our life in him. ✤

PARENTING PRINCIPLE

Define your life by thriving in the Lord not the world.

POINTS TO PONDER

- How would you describe your home of origin—rejoicing or groaning?
- What would your children say about your parenting?
- What adjustments do you need to make to keep rejoicing in your home?

AVOID THE SNARES

Evildoers are snared by their own sin, but the righteous shout for joy and are glad.

PROVERBS 29:6

Parents will go to great lengths to protect their children from snares. They will spend whatever money it takes to get them involved in activities that will help keep them from falling into a bad situation. The reality is that kids can still fall into evil lifestyles. They might not see it coming and they certainly won't agree with your observations, but God's Word is true. They will be snared.

When you have a child caught in the snare of sin, it can be all consuming. It will drain your energy as you pray and seek to help remove them from the snare. The only true way to get them loose is to eliminate sin. As much as sin ensnares, obedience to God releases.

Your children will find full freedom in their understanding of the love of Christ. They will be influenced greatly by your Christ-like lifestyle. When you are living in the day to day, it's difficult to see the big picture. Instead, live knowing that teaching your children how to avoid the snares of sin will help them attain a joyful life in Christ. ❖

PARENTING PRINCIPLE

To be freed from a snare is a burst of fresh air.

POINTS TO PONDER

- What are the snares that have tripped you up as a parent?
- How do you help your children see potential snares?
- What snares do you need to overcome as a family?

MAKE PEACE

Mockers stir up a city, but the wise turn away anger.　　　　　PROVERBS 29:8

To show restraint from anger is a noble and much desired trait. If you can do that as a parent, it will greatly benefit you as you deal with relationship issues with your children. Although it's not always easy, turning away from anger is a choice. Unfortunately, in an effort to prove we're right, most of us simply stir up anger.

Think about how often you've rolled your eyes or made a mocking gesture while your child talked to you. When you do that, your body language sends a clear message that you don't agree with their statement. You might have even ridiculed them by repeating a phrase back to them imitating their voice. This type of response will *never*, and that's the right word, facilitate a normal, healthy conversation. It is wiser to show them respect by listening to them, even when you don't like what they're saying. A reasoned, steady response will always trump a hardy and foolish one.

Stop stirring up the pot and be a parent who facilitates peace and earns the reputation of someone who turns away from anger. ❖

PARENTING PRINCIPLE

Remove the family from danger and turn away from anger.

POINTS TO PONDER

- What would your family say about your ability to turn away from anger?
- How can you improve in this area?
- Who has been a good role model for you in this area?

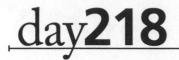

day**218**

DISCIPLINING FOR PEACE

Discipline your children, and they will give you peace; they will bring you the delights you desire. PROVERBS 29:17

I don't imagine many parents equate discipline with peace. Often a child doesn't understand discipline nor do they see it as a benefit. That's why parents are responsible to establish a disciplinary system. These are guidelines that help keep your children safe as they learn to live within boundaries.

When we hear the word boundary, we tend to think limitation. It's a word that can have negative connotations, even though in this case, it's very positive. While discipline will help your children in the long run, during those moments when you enforce those established guidelines, peace may be elusive.

Peace will come, though, as a result of all the time, effort, and energy you spent developing and maintaining structure for your children. Your children may not always be excited about the boundaries that exist for them, but eventually they will come to appreciate them. Your goal as a parent is not to become best friends with your children, but to be their best advocate and protector. Ironically, later on, they will call you their friend as they begin to understand the wisdom of your decisions and those boundaries you developed for their benefit. ❧

PARENTING PRINCIPLE

If you want peace, put peace in place.

POINTS TO PONDER

- What are some of the discipline techniques you use that work?
- What are some techniques that have failed?
- What are some new techniques to consider?

LEAD ON

Where there is no revelation, people cast off restraint; but blessed is the one who heeds wisdom's instruction.   PROVERBS 29:18

It's healthy from an emotional, physical and mental standpoint when we know we have a purpose and direction in life. It is critical to the health and well-being of your family. As a parent, invest some time seeing the big picture that God has prepared for you and your family, and then share that vision with them. Don't get so bogged down in the details that the joy of life is sucked away, but help your family see there is a purpose for their existence.

For example, show them the significance of why you live in the neighborhood you do. Talk about your involvement in peoples' lives and the importance of sacrificing for the purpose of helping others. This can develop into a way of life, instead of something that is regimented or forced. Through this process your children will begin to feel a good sense of self-worth because they are being used for a higher calling. As they mature and develop, this calling will become more significant and could lead them into their future career.

Your efforts to develop your family's purpose will ultimately help your child develop their life purpose and cause them to be forever grateful. ❖

PARENTING PRINCIPLE

If you don't lead, your children can't follow.

POINTS TO PONDER

- What is the revelation your family is following?
- How can you develop your family in this area?
- Why is this so important?

MORE ACTIONS, FEWER WORDS

Servants cannot be corrected by mere words; though they understand, they will not respond.   PROVERBS 29:19

In a family, we can replace the word *servant* with *children* to understand the meaning of Proverbs 29:19. Servant refers to anyone under your authority. Our children will generally need more than words to correct their behavior. Parenting a two year old child will quickly reveal the nature of disobedience that comes to all humanity. Words, mere words, are usually not enough.

If you have ever witnessed a parent repeat empty threats, you understand the importance of taking action to correct behaviors. For example, take away a child's favorite privileges. Confine your child to their room until they are ready to adopt a humble and loving spirit. You must break their will when it is bent on disobedience. Most children will respond to this parenting technique and learn the lesson you are trying to teach. Some will not.

Remember, all of this is for their good and not just because you're the parent. You are trying to help them in the long-run. Stay in control of your emotions while administering these disciplines.

If necessary, talk to a pastor or counselor for additional ideas if your attempts to gain control do not work. Do not tolerate defiance. ❖

PARENTING PRINCIPLE

Let your actions speak louder than your words.

POINTS TO PONDER

- What are the techniques you use beyond words to correct your children?
- What techniques typically work?
- What new ideas for correction would benefit your family?

TAKE FIVE

Do you see someone who speaks in haste? There is more hope for a fool than for them.
PROVERBS 29:20

Before we can deal effectively with our children, we should examine our own lives as parents.

Do we speak in haste? Are there certain phrases that just fly off our tongues that we later regret? Do we regularly have to seek forgiveness because our rant wasn't necessary?

A parent who is prone to ranting is setting themselves up for a difficult future with their child. Remember, children become adults and will someday respond to you as adults. You don't want their response to be one of bitterness and frustration because of your inability to control your tongue.

A quick remedy that might help you in your moments of haste is to stop and "take five." Excuse yourself from the situation and take five minutes to calm down and think before you respond to challenging circumstances. That small amount of time can make a big difference in the outcome.

If you display control over what you say, your children will be more likely to as well. Hopefully they will see how disciplined you were and seek to respond the same way with their own children. Your control is shaping their lives and also the lives of your grandchildren. ✤

PARENTING PRINCIPLE

Haste makes waste!

POINTS TO PONDER

- What steps do you take to control what you say?
- Where do you struggle with control?
- Where do you see your children struggling with control?

ANGER MANAGEMENT

An angry person stirs up conflict, and a hot-tempered person commits many sins.

PROVERBS 29:22

Do you have an angry person in your family or extended family? A person that everybody dreads being around at holiday time? The one who makes even the simplest of conversations risky? They can create drama in an instant and they blame everyone else for what's happening.

I hope and pray that person isn't you. But remember it could be. If we don't deal with our inner struggles in a Biblical and godly way, the potential is there for building up tension and exploding with anger.

Your children may be prone to developing issues with anger. In the early stages, they may display behavior that involves secluding themselves from others. It may also lead to uncontrollable tantrums and aggressive behavior. Watch for clues that indicate they may be struggling with anger. Seek professional help if necessary.

Some of this behavior is normal, but it still needs to be addressed. You want to prevent your child from always creating conflict and developing sinful behavior. You want to avoid them being the one no one wants to be around. ❖

PARENTING PRINCIPLE

Deal with it now so you don't deal with it later.

POINTS TO PONDER

- Who is that person who causes conflict in your family or extended family? How are you helping them?
- How are you managing anger in your children?
- How can you be proactive in dealing with conflict?

HIDE PRIDE

Pride brings a person low, but the lowly in spirit gain honor.   PROVERBS 29:23

It seems negative to be lowly in spirit, but in this case it's positive. This "lowly in spirit" refers to an understanding that life is not all about you. It's more about your desires and your thoughts being centered on the bigger picture of how to use your life to bring glory and honor to Christ. There's no room for that to occur if you are filled up with pride.

Pride makes you self-seeking, self-glorifying and selfish! It's a fine line to teach your children to be proud of who they are without letting them become proud of who they are. Confusing? Probably. Here's the way to understand what this means.

When our pride comes from seeing that our accomplishments are because of Christ in us, then we exhibit a healthy pride. That is appropriate and should be celebrated. But if our pride comes from believing we've done everything in our own strength, and that we are the object of worship, we have fallen into sinful pride.

Teach your children that their accomplishments are awesome but that they must balance that with the fact that God is the giver of all gifts. Remind them daily! ✤

PARENTING PRINCIPLE

You must lose pride to gain respect.

POINTS TO PONDER

- How can you help your children have high self-esteem without pride?
- How do you help them identify their strengths and weaknesses?
- How do you keep that balance in your life?

FIGHT FEAR

Fear of man will prove to be a snare, but whoever trusts in the LORD is kept safe.

Proverbs 29:25

At some point we all fear man. There will be days when your children will fear man. It's a part of life. Teaching our children to trust in the Lord on those days will lead them to safety.

In reality, life will someday put our children between a rock and a hard place. In Proverbs 29:25, it's called a snare. Whatever you call it, it's part of life. Instead of protecting your children from it, prepare them for what may come.

We've all heard of people who have been put in very fearful situations, and have survived because of their trust in God. Make sure your children know those stories. Also tell them of some of the Biblical examples where martyrs of the faith have given their lives while trusting in God.

When you raise your children as Christians, you need to be prepared for the consequences should they follow the example of Jesus. It could lead them into some incredibly difficult places, where they will need to understand how to live without fear of man but in the trust of God. ❖

PARENTING PRINCIPLE

If you raise your children Christian, then raise their trust in Christ and lessen their fear of man.

POINTS TO PONDER

- What is the "fear of man" that you carry?
- What "fear of man" do you see your children facing?
- How are you teaching your children to trust in God and not fear man?

day225

SERVING JUSTICE

Many seek an audience with a ruler, but it is from the LORD that one gets justice.

PROVERBS 29:26

A teenager will often try to get everyone to argue for their side so that they can flaunt their high position. In these cases, many teens believe if they get the mob's approval, they will prove they are right, and yet their tactic is all wrong!

The Lord is the final exacter of justice. Even when it doesn't look like we're winning, if we continually honor him with our decisions, then justice will be served. The problem we have is that we want to define justice. We have a hard time submitting and accepting that we can't make all the rules and always get the result we want.

Your children are no exception. They are experts at trying to get you to decide in their favor by telling you only part of a story or sharing only the details that make them look good. As their parent, pray for wisdom to discern and knowledge to understand how Christ would handle these circumstances in your home. In doing so, you look to the one who determines the final justice and you will be wiser for seeking him. ✤

PARENTING PRINCIPLE

If the buck stops here, then *here* should be God.

POINTS TO PONDER

- How do your children try to work things in their favor?
- What do you do to see through their schemes?
- How do you teach them to avoid this behavior?

# day**226**

CHARM AND BEAUTY

Charm is deceptive, and beauty is fleeting; but a woman who fears the LORD is to be praised.
PROVERBS 31:30

Our culture sends messages to young girls that say, "Charm is most important and beauty is all that matters." Ironically, both messages are rotten to the core. All charm and beauty will pass away, but a person's good character can last forever.

Helping our daughters and sons understand the concept of recognizing inner beauty and character will be instrumental to their healthy development. Teaching it is helpful, but it won't guarantee their survival through this passage to adulthood. A child's personality and temperament will be a huge factor in determining how they cope with cultural messages.

Introduce your children to people you know who are a great example of this godly inner beauty. At some point you may need these individuals to speak into your child's life. Do not see this as a weakness or an inability on your part to meet all of your child's needs. Instead, think of it as an opportunity for them to grow beyond the realm of your family. It is a step in preparing them for the real world and through their growth in Christ. ✤

PARENTING PRINCIPLE

Do not be fooled by the foolishness of mankind.

POINTS TO PONDER

- Who are the positive role models involved in the life of your children?
- How can you help your children develop "inner beauty"?
- How can you prevent some of the negative influences of our culture from getting through to your children?

THE B-I-B-L-E

All scripture is God-breathed and is useful for teaching, rebuking, correcting and training in righteousness.   2 TIMOTHY 3:16

The Word of God is a solid foundation for any home. It helps you understand why you parent the way you do and it's critical for eternal purposes.

Parents often base their family rules and guidelines on traditions and themes that are not biblically based. This leaves their children with nothing to fall back on other than those traditions. That's why our foundation must be built on Scripture. Our teaching, rebuking correcting, and training must be backed by Scripture. We use God's Word to support and explain why we do what we do. Otherwise, the rules would constantly change based on cultural desires. The next generation would not learn to pass on faith and the result could be a faithless society. It's not hard to imagine what could happen if that occurred because we see some of the results all around us today.

Continue to know and teach God's Word to your children. Help them get God's principles into their lives so they can withstand the tests and trials they will face. The best hand-held note that we could ever give a child is the Word of God. ✤

PARENTING PRINCIPLE

The B-I-B-L-E—yes that's the book for me and my children!

POINTS TO PONDER

- How are you integrating Scripture into your family life?
- What positive outcomes have you seen as a result?
- How has Scripture been a help to you in parenting?

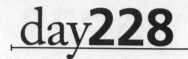 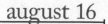

day228 august 16

WHAT THEY WANT TO HEAR

For the time will come when people will not put up with sound doctrine. Instead, to suit their own desires, they will gather around them a great number of teachers to say what their itching ears want to hear. 2 TIMOTHY 4:3

Your child will favor people who let them do what they want. The natural bent of a child is not toward obedience. They will be defiant and deceptive, which will alarm you. Don't worry, as your child is normal.

Parents can easily fall into a pattern of always giving in to their children's desires because they want the best for them. Scripture clearly teaches that this will result in an unhealthy spiritual condition known as selfishness! If unchecked, your children will always surround themselves with people who only say what they want to hear. This is a dangerous place. It is inbred and dysfunctional.

Always surround yourself with people who will speak Biblical truth into your life, especially when you don't want to hear it! It is wise to do so as it protects what Scripture teaches you to do and is beneficial in guiding your parenting steps. It ensures that you have God's Word as the basis for your family life. ❖

PARENTING PRINCIPLE

If you stick your fingers in your ears, make sure you are shutting out the right voices.

POINTS TO PONDER

- Do you allow people to speak truth into your life?
- How are your children at receiving advice?
- How could your family improve in this area?

HEADS UP

But you, keep your head in all situations . . .   2 TIMOTHY 4:5

What a challenge! If the verse said at least some or most situations, that would seem reachable, but to keep our head in all situations, that seems impossible!

Most of us don't have to think very long to remember a time recently when we did not have complete control in dealing with a situation involving our child. Instead of defending your actions in that moment, consider what you could have done better. If you have a hard time seeing your weaknesses, then invite a third-party to give you their observations and offer you some guidance.

Our control in parenting needs to be above reproach. We will never do it perfectly, but we should always strive to improve. The growth that we experience as we work on "keeping our head" will be obvious to our children. It will also inspire them to consider following your example.

Keeping our head will sometimes mean changing our tone and words or improving our body language. It will definitely mean eliminating all temper tantrums. If you would be embarrassed to let someone see how you act when you are dealing with your child, then you need to change. ❖

PARENTING PRINCIPLE

If you act like a child, don't be surprised when your kids do.

POINTS TO PONDER

- How do you "keep your head" when dealing with issues?
- What would your children say about your control?
- Who could you talk to that would help you control your impulsiveness?

SELF-CONTROL

Similarly, encourage the young men to be self-controlled.   Titus 2:6

The teacher in Titus 2:6 is helping the people living in the culture of that time to understand what makes a healthy environment for families. The thought is simple and applies to us today as well. When we help our sons (and daughters) develop self-control, our families and society as a whole benefit greatly.

Consider that we live in a time where we celebrate uncontrolled behavior. The crazier and wilder the actions, the more attention we give them. Just think about how well those movies perform that base their plot on obnoxious conduct. The attention given is often what seems to condone the behavior and what people consider their right.

Your child might not like the discipline you teach them that leads to self-control, but when they become adults they will understand it better. Even when your children's defense is that "everybody else is doing it," be adamant about teaching control because eventually they will see that everybody is not doing the right thing.

Notice that Titus 2:6 says to encourage them to be self-controlled. It will ultimately be their decision as they become adults. Hopefully your good guidance as well as your example will lead to self-controlled children who become self-controlled adults. ❖

PARENTING PRINCIPLE

Display self-control and your children will likely follow!

POINTS TO PONDER

- How do you maintain your self-control?
- How is your child developing this on their own?
- Where is your child struggling in this area?

LIVE DIFFERENTLY

In everything set them an example by doing what is good. In your teaching show integrity, seriousness, and soundness of speech that cannot be condemned, so that those who oppose you may be ashamed because they have nothing bad to say about us.

TITUS 2:7–8

Titus 2:7–8 speaks to the importance of setting a good example of behavior in your family. You should never sacrifice your child on the altar of "a good family name." Instead you should ensure that your children understand that as you live, others in your neighborhood will either want what you have or they will use you as the example not to follow.

To promote a sound example, this will involve living with a high degree of integrity that even if spoken against, no one believes, because they have observed how you lived. Sadly, too often the opposite is true. Often we aren't as good as our reputation because we are better at hiding flaws.

That's why it's important to seek to set an example of living, that even when your family is facing difficult times, is hard to dispute. In the end, your family will leave an impact on those you live around. It might be the reason God has planted you in that neighborhood—someone there needs your love! ✤

PARENTING PRINCIPLE

Don't play a game with the family name.

POINTS TO PONDER

- What are you known for as a family?
- What influence do you have in the neighborhood?
- How could you be a better influence?

A HEAVENLY VIEW

For the grace of God has appeared that offers salvation to all people.　　Titus 2:11

It's interesting that Titus 2:11 appears in Scripture soon after a verse that talks about how slaves should respect their masters. Titus 2:9 is a verse that needs cultural context to make sense. It should not be seen as condoning slavery but rather dealing with the reality that slavery existed and how guidance was given to help the circumstances slaves found themselves in.

Titus 2:11 teaches us that salvation is for both master and slave. Our children need to see that the love of Christ exists for all people. When we see all people as God's children, we get a heavenly view of this world. Help your children see and embrace this view. To do so will mean your children will see no color, no creed and no social class better than another. You will help them see this world the same as Jesus does!

There may come a point when your child battles with God because of the differences between their blessed life and those less fortunate. You will need to be aware of these inner growth moments of your child and then teach them that God loves and offers his salvation to all. ✤

PARENTING PRINCIPLE

God's grace is free to everyone you see.

POINTS TO PONDER

- How do you handle deep issues?
- How are you at helping your children understand the "deeper" issues of life?
- How does your faith help your teaching?

WATCH OUT

Warn a divisive person once, and then warn them a second time. After that, have nothing to do with them. You may be sure that such people are warped and sinful; they are self-condemned.   TITUS 3:10–11

Divisive people are poison to a family. They hinder and destroy every good thing. They invent new ways to cause harm to a home. The traits of a divisive person include stirring up conflict, not knowing when to stay quiet and using a smile like a sword. Their behavior is no good.

Your children need to learn to recognize divisive people and stay far from them. If you have a family member or child who seems to fall into these behaviors, address it and correct them. Don't let it go unchecked.

Titus 3:11 implies they are warped. In other words they don't think clearly. Their mind does not seek godly things but instead chooses to pursue evil patterns. Parents need to be aware of these people who could be potential influences on your child's life. Protect them from it. This can only happen if you are involved in the life of your child and stay involved until they learn to recognize these distractions on their own. ❖

PARENTING PRINCIPLE

The evil ways of a divisive mind will hinder yours if you are so inclined.

POINTS TO PONDER

- What traits of decisiveness have you witnessed in others?
- What traits have you seen in your own family?
- How can you protect your family in this area?

KEEP PERSPECTIVE

But avoid foolish controversies and genealogies and arguments and quarrels about the law, because these are unprofitable and useless. Titus 3:9

There are usually two types of people in every family. Those who like to hash everything out and those who like to let things pass. Although there are times when discussion and a deeper understanding will be profitable, there will be other times when the "let it go" philosophy will be best.

How often has something trivial in your family grown into something huge? Your children have witnessed this and have learned from that example. Use discernment to determine when an issue is really big enough to take center stage. Otherwise, know when it's profitable to say you're sorry and learn to let it go. If you ask older people what they wish they would have done more of in their life, they will often say "let things go."

Everyone should learn this early on in their family life because of how it will benefit their home. Teach your children to forgive each other and to not bring those issues back up later after they've been resolved. Be willing to grow if this is your weakness as a parent. You might be frustrating your children to no end with your constant bombardment of an area you always focus on. ❖

PARENTING PRINCIPLE

Know when to say when!

POINTS TO PONDER

- What is the useless area you "beat like a drum"?
- How can you change this?
- How are your children at letting things go?

THE CASE FOR ETERNITY

Your throne, O God, will last for ever and ever.   HEBREWS 1:8

It's important to help your children understand the eternity of God. Teach them the reason for your trust in God, which is because he will be there forever and ever.

Show them practical ways to see eternity. You can take them to a beach and ask them to count the grains of sand. When they realize how long that would take, you can tell them to imagine counting them all, then starting over and counting them again. If they never stopped—that would be eternity. You want to get a picture in their mind of a seemingly endless number. Then have them compare that thought to the existence of God. He will always be there.

Be prepared for a few questions. It's okay to admit you don't have the answer for everything, because then you can introduce them to the principle of faith. We may not understand all there is to know about eternity, but we trust in the God who will be there throughout all eternity. The bottom line for all of us is that it is our faith in God that will ultimately sustain us all. ❖

PARENTING PRINCIPLE

God is God—always has been, always will be.

POINTS TO PONDER

- What do you understand about the eternity of God?
- How can you continue to help your children understand these concepts?
- What can you do to help your children yield early to God's sovereignty?

TRUST IN THE PROOF

He also says, "In the beginning, Lord, you laid the foundations of the earth, and the heavens are the work of your hands."   Hebrews 1:10

Science could prove the existence of God considering all the proof available, but there are too many who will do whatever they can to ensure this never happens.

Take time as a parent to do your own research into the scientific proof that supports Biblical teachings and instill this into your children. In a public setting, if your child simply says "God made the earth" they could be ridiculed. That's why they need to back up their beliefs. Without that basis, they may start to doubt the Biblical training you have given them.

Many children will grapple with this at deep and difficult levels. You will have to patiently wait or carefully guide them through this challenging time. The bottom line is they will eventually develop their own belief system but at least you want to know that you have given them a proper foundation of truth from which to build on.

Be sure to teach them how God laid the foundation of the earth and provided the scientific support to prove it's true! ❖

PARENTING PRINCIPLE

The eyes see what the mind must help us understand.

POINTS TO PONDER

- How can you help your children understand God's creation?
- What good scientific proof have you given your children to help them?
- What steps can you take to offset some of the secular teachings your children are exposed to?

LISTEN AND SOFTEN

Today, if you hear his voice, do not harden your hearts. HEBREWS 3:7–8

A soft heart is a parent's dream. When our children display a teachable spirit, we can celebrate as parents. If their heart begins to harden, our home can become a very difficult place to be.

When your child develops a hard heart, first try and find out the reason. Usually you'll find it's something they are hiding or getting involved with that's causing this shut down. If they won't talk to you, then seek the advice of a pastor or professional counselor. Dealing with hard hearts is not unusual. It's part of family life. You simply don't want to see it grow into a deeper issue and then cause more problems in the house.

One of the keys to getting our children to soften their hearts is by displaying a soft heart ourselves. Even if at some point if they do develop a little hardness in their heart, it will hopefully soften again if they see that in you.

Notice Hebrews 3:7–8 says "If you hear his voice." This means we must be listening to Christ for direction in our lives. Teach your children to seek Christ as they face issues, and he will keep them soft and teachable. ✤

PARENTING PRINCIPLE

When God speaks, listening is learning.

POINTS TO PONDER

- How have you made your heart soft and teachable?
- What causes your heart to harden?
- How are you helping your children develop soft hearts?

SAVING SOULS

See to it, brothers and sisters, that none of you has a sinful, unbelieving heart that turns away from the living God.   HEBREWS 3:12

Of course Hebrews 3:12 is referring to the Christian kingdom of brothers and sisters, but it also applies to a family.

What if everyone in our family all worked to help each other stay close and accountable to God? What if our children wanted to make sure they did everything possible to see that their siblings sought after God? We can! At the least it should be our goal.

To accomplish this means there should be a lot of love and forgiveness flowing back and forth and everyone should be allowed to mature at their own pace through each stage of life. This won't be easy because it's normal for siblings to be impatient with each other. So as you parent, exude patience while your children develop and mature through each juncture of life.

In the end, your patience, love, forgiveness and grace will hopefully help them see why we need to be that way toward each other. Again, it will never be perfect, but do what you can to help them be mature adults that care about each other's eternal souls. ❖

PARENTING PRINCIPLE

Keep your eyes on the prize — the eternal destiny of all in your family.

POINTS TO PONDER

- How do you encourage your family to be understanding?
- How could your family improve in this area?
- What can you do to help your children develop a love for each other's souls?

START ENCOURAGING TODAY

But encourage one another daily, as long as it is called "Today," so that none of you may be hardened by sin's deceitfulness.   HEBREWS 3:13

As a parent, it's hard to believe that the innocent child at your feet could become a defiant, hard-hearted person. But it can happen. After all the effort and energy you put into raising them, they can one day become a stranger. Many parents can testify to this very situation.

One of the ways that we can seek to offset this change is to encourage them daily. That's right. Spend a little time every day finding something good to say about each other in the family. Too often we end up only sharing our frustrations. That negative trend can develop into a common theme of the home.

Before you go to sleep each night, talk to your children about something you see in their lives that inspires you. Focus on it and tell them why it delights you. Let them see the joy in your face. Make this a regular occurrence. Your children will then look forward to seeing you coming. This could be a new trend you can begin in your home today. If that happens, you can be assured your home will be a great place to live. ✤

PARENTING PRINCIPLE

Encouragement today can help prevent hardening tomorrow.

POINTS TO PONDER

- How do you get encouraged?
- How have you developed encouragement in your home?
- What could you do to bring more encouragement to your family?

A STRONG SHIELD

Every word of God is flawless; he is a shield to those who take refuge in him.

PROVERBS 30:5

Your children will need a place of refuge. Even with all your efforts, you will not be able to provide what God provides. He is the ultimate defender. Ironically, he also knows when we need to be tested and exposed. You will watch with helpless eyes at times when your children, through all stages of life, face situations that you cannot control.

These are the times when God will take your children to new depths with him. He will be their shield. As life progresses, you may experience the pain of a serious health problem or a devastating loss with a child or grandchild, but even then God's greater purpose will prevail. His shield may not look like we would want it to, but that's God's decision. Sometimes we are too busy comparing or keeping up with the Jones's instead of keeping our priorities straight. Our eyes should be on the bigger prize of a family that puts their trust in God.

Learn how to trust your children to God. You need to understand his flawless word and believe that his shield is sufficient for molding your children into who he wants them to be. ❖

PARENTING PRINCIPLE

The deeper we go the more we know.

POINTS TO PONDER

- How have you seen God's shield in your life?
- How have you seen his shield with your children?
- How can you grow deeper in trusting God with your children?

SAY WHAT?

Do not add to his words, or he will rebuke you and prove you a liar.   PROVERBS 30:6

When you are talking to your children and validating your point using Scripture, don't misuse it. Too often in our haste to prove a point, we will make God's Word fit what we have to say instead of fitting what we have to say in what God has already said. Your children will see right through it. The sad part is they will begin to disrespect God's Word because they have seen you disrespect it. In the end, you will not fool your children but you will look like a fool.

Instead of speaking when you are seeking to teach your children about a topic, simply write a Scripture down that fits what you want to say and lay it on their pillow for them to see. God's Word will penetrate far deeper into their soul than you will ever hope to with your mouth. They may never mention that they saw it, but remember his Word doesn't return void.

As Christian parents we have the support of the Bible and we need to be more aware of its guidance for everyday life. ✤

PARENTING PRINCIPLE

If you *lean on* the Word of God your children will be able to fall back on it.

POINTS TO PONDER

- When have you used his Word incorrectly?
- Are you using God's Word for guidance with your children?
- How could you benefit from more study of it?

NO LIE

Keep falsehood and lies far from me. PROVERBS 30:8

If you want a daily prayer that is great for your family and children it's this, "Lord, keep lies far from us." If lies ever find a foothold in your home, they can be very difficult to eradicate.

Lying leads to lying. Children can easily fall into lying. In fact, there most likely will be a stage where your child does lie. It's built into our DNA. Be aware of it and don't overreact to their behavior.

However, you will need to be swift in dealing with the lies and pray the results of your actions will rid it from your family. In addition, you need to pray for the Lord to keep lies away from your family, but if any seep in that he will show you how to deal with the situation and resolve it.

Also in order to keep false truths to a minimum, you need to embrace being a truthful parent. Keep lies out of your personal life. Keep lies out of your business dealings. Keep lies out of your relationships. In doing so, you help keep the family and home falsehood free. ✤

PARENTING PRINCIPLE

Lying leads to lying.

POINTS TO PONDER

- When have lies been an issue in your family?
- What can you do to protect your family in this area?
- How will you help your children deal with lies?

day243

OUR DAILY BREAD

Give me neither poverty nor riches, but give me only my daily bread. PROVERBS 30:8

When we have too little, we fall into jealousy and theft. When we have too much we fall into complacency and self-reliance.

What we can learn from Proverbs 30:8 is not to give our children everything, as it does an incredible disservice to them. They will have no need to rely on God, because everything they think they need is provided. If you don't learn this early on, you will find out soon enough when those "things" don't satisfy your child and they go searching for the next "thing."

On the other hand, to make it difficult for your children to have anything will take the life out of them. As parents, we need to balance this for our children. This equalization is often influenced by our own family of origin. If we seek God for understanding of this delicate balance of needs and wants, we will most likely find the sweet spot for our family.

Jesus prayed that the Father would give us "our daily bread." Pray for your family that you would get only what you need each day. ❖

PARENTING PRINCIPLE

Give us this day our daily bread and help us not to let it go to our head.

POINTS TO PONDER

- How has God provided your "daily bread?"
- What is your understanding of the balance between poverty and riches?
- How are you teaching your children to give thanks for their daily bread?

day244

BALANCING TENSION

The righteous detest the dishonest; the wicked detest the upright.   PROVERBS 29:27

Your children need to understand the tension that exists because of good and evil in the world. They need to understand how this tension comes right down to the living room in their house.

When children commit dishonest deeds, conflict will arise because the rest of the family is trying to promote good. It may be as minor as your child stealing a cookie from the cookie jar, but it will cause conflict between you and them. When your teenager plagiarizes on a paper, there will be consequences that will lead to opposition! Helping your children understand you don't condone dishonesty will benefit you as a parent because they will know to expect correction when they lie. If their dishonesty becomes a regular issue, you may see them start to withdraw from you, or an older teen may decide to leave to avoid your correction. As difficult as that may be, you need to continue to discipline them.

Remember, we parent for the long-term health and wealth of our children. Don't give in to momentary lapses of dishonesty to avoid conflict. Your conflict will only increase ahead if you decrease your parenting responsibilities. ❖

PARENTING PRINCIPLE

When you don't know the facts, don't be fooled by fiction.

POINTS TO PONDER

- Overall, how have you promoted a home of honesty?
- How do you build principles of honesty into your children?
- What are the benefits of honesty you can discuss with your child?

day245

GOD KNOWS

There are those who curse their fathers and do not bless their mothers. PROVERBS 30:11

Some parents will know the sorrow and deep meaning of this verse. Maybe you fall into that group. No parent ever wants to feel this sorrow from any of their children. If they do, they have many questions. Why us God? What did we do wrong? How have we sinned against you? Why are you punishing us? Why can't we just have peace like this or that family? All fair questions and ones that God understands.

God's first children were Adam and Eve. He set them up to win. A perfect garden in a perfect place, and they chose to disobey. Their actions cursed the land God had given them. I'm guessing you have never blamed God for their choices. Instead, you thought they were foolish and guilty for making bad choices. Let that bring comfort to you. If today your child is choosing to live a life inconsistent with God's teaching, remember that's their decision.

You don't get to determine how your children will live their life. You seek to influence it, but they are responsible to answer to God. Find release and peace in the Lord today. He alone knows the heart of our children. ❖

PARENTING PRINCIPLE

God is perfect, but Adam and Eve were not.

POINTS TO PONDER

- How do you handle your disappointment when your kids fail?
- How do you move forward with your life?
- What lesson have you learned from this devotional?

day246

september 3

ROLLING EYES

Those whose eyes are ever so haughty, whose glances are so disdainful. PROVERBS 30:13

Disdainful is an appropriate word for describing the disrespectful looks you will get from your children. You may tell them you won't tolerate it, but they may ignore you. There may even be a day when a smirk or two will be thrown in with their rolling eyes.

If you know it's coming, you can prepare for it. The best preparation is to make sure you don't return the look. Doing so will only negate the corrective action you need to take.

Recall how *you* rolled your eyes at *your* parents so you can relate to how your child is feeling. As you do so, you will be more understanding of how your child is learning to navigate through this step toward adulthood.

The point we need to extract from Proverbs 30:13 is that these behaviors do happen. We can wish and hope it won't, but it does, regardless of how sweet they seem as toddlers. Be aware of where your child is in their development. When they hit the eye-rolling stage, simply accept it as another phase you have to work through. Be diligent about it. Don't let it go unchecked or their defiance might increase. ❖

PARENTING PRINCIPLE

Haughty eyes are expected but not respected.

POINTS TO PONDER

- What looks or glances do you have that affect your family?
- How do you handle these looks with your children?
- How can you prepare for these issues down the road?

THE ANTS GO MARCHING

Ants are creatures of little strength, yet they store up their food in the summer.

PROVERBS 30:25

All God's creatures can teach us lessons. If you have ever observed an ant farm or watched an ant carry a piece of food to its destination, you will be amazed by its strength. They work all summer to store up food that sustains all the ants in the colony during the winter.

If an ant can do that, how much more should we, as people, know how to provide and store up what is needed in our lives? Use these lessons from the ants, to teach your children how to observe and learn from other creatures. This will help them to develop the ability to learn on their own from what they see.

Consider making this a family project and encourage your children to watch other animals and write down their observations. They can observe the family pet or they can go outside and watch the birds and squirrels. All creatures have lessons to share. Have everyone share their findings with each other. This could be a great way to build time with your family and have fun while you learn how to provide. ✤

PARENTING PRINCIPLE

All creatures great and small have a lesson for us all.

POINTS TO PONDER

- What lessons have you observed in the things around you?
- What observations do your children make from their environment?
- How can you make this family fun?

THE GODLY PATH

This is the way of an adulterous woman: She eats and wipes her mouth and says, "I've done nothing wrong." PROVERBS 30:20

The phrase "I've done nothing wrong" will be one you deal with as a parent. Initially you will want to respond with a smirk to curb your child's foolishness, but it may be wiser to step back and help them see why their phrase is immature.

Notice how Proverbs 30:20 says, "This *is* the way!" In other words, an unchecked, selfish person who is out for themselves, will always excuse their behavior and justify their actions.

That is the exact spot your child will find themselves in if they veer off the godly path you have sought to guide them along. When they justify their inappropriate actions, you need to wisely remind them how others have unsuccessfully traveled this path too. Use Proverbs 30:20 as an analogy to show them how people who do bad things don't wait and take responsibility for their actions. It's always somebody else's fault.

Use your own life experiences and times of foolishness to help steer your child back onto the road less traveled. ❖

PARENTING PRINCIPLE

Just because a path is well worn that doesn't make it a wise choice to follow.

POINTS TO PONDER

- What actions do you tend to justify that are not helpful for your family?
- How do you handle it when your children don't own up to their responsibility?
- What are you doing to help them see the error of their ways?

SPEAK FOR OTHERS

Speak up for those who cannot speak for themselves, for the rights of all who are destitute.

PROVERBS 31:8

Who in our society cannot speak for themselves? Certainly the poor can be included but also those sold into slavery as well as the unborn children in their mother's womb who need to be heard. To discern who these groups are and to help our children and ourselves understand how to apply this verse is a great way to grow deeper with God.

From the beginning, God has cared about those who cannot care for themselves. Jesus took this to a whole new level, and certainly many ministries have been founded to carry out this mission.

The question for us is what can we do to make a difference in these destitute lives. Do we invite them over for dinner? Do we let our children, at an appropriate age, learn about their plight or do we try to keep them from seeing this side of the world?

If we raise our children to be Christians, then we should raise them with an awareness of the desperate needs of our society. Let them learn and grow in such ways that they can be the hands and feet of Jesus. ✤

PARENTING PRINCIPLE

Don't turn a deaf ear to those who already can't speak.

POINTS TO PONDER

- Who are the destitute among us?
- What are you doing as a family to help the destitute?
- How could you get more involved in touching those lives?

WALK A MILE

Speak up and judge fairly; defend the rights of the poor and needy.　　Proverbs 31:9

It's easy to look at some among us who are poor and be judgmental of how they live. That is until you try to imagine growing up in their environment. Proverbs 31:9 challenges us to think of the plight of those you are talking about before you actually speak.

All of us are guilty of speaking negatively about those who are less fortunate than we are. And guess what—our children are watching! Our example will either cause them to join in the ridicule or rebel and do something to help the poor.

You've heard the saying "Don't judge a person until you have walked a mile in their shoes." Maybe a mile isn't enough. We need to spend time understanding the culture of those who are in great need before we can know how to help them. Judge fairly when you see a beggar on the street. Some may be there by choice, but others are not. Seek to make your family's life a reflection of this verse as you speak up and defend the rights of the poor and the needy. ❖

PARENTING PRINCIPLE

Don't judge a person until you have lived, to some degree, their life.

POINTS TO PONDER

- How do you ensure as a family that you judge fairly?
- How have you sought to teach your children about the poor and needy?
- How could you be a better parent in this area?

OBJECTS OF LOVE

A wife of noble character who can find? She is worth far more than rubies.

PROVERBS 31:10

Teaching our sons what to look for in a wife is an important step in the life of a parent. Most of what society throws at us in regard to women is lust and sex. It's easy to see why women could be viewed as objects of sexuality and not as people.

When we understand that our goal as men is to see women (and men, for that matter) as spiritual beings, our whole view changes. We value daughters and wives because we see them as God's daughters first. They are to be valued for who they are on the inside. Appearance is important, but ultimately our sons need to see that as we love a woman like Christ loved the church, we show unconditional love. This is not based on appearances or intellect, but on something much deeper—the person inside.

Help the men in your family begin to see how television and movies can distort our view of women. Tell them how you see the women in your family from God's perspective. Train up children who will be like Christ in his love for his family. ❖

PARENTING PRINCIPLE

Help your son become a man and not stay a boy! Help your daughters remember their own value!

POINTS TO PONDER

- Husbands, how has your view of your wife changed?
- What have you done to set a good example in this area?
- How do you protect your child from the sexist view of society?

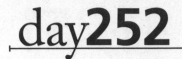# day**252**

RELY ON THE WORD

For the word of God is alive and active. Sharper than any double-edged sword, it penetrates even to dividing soul and spirit, joints and marrow; it judges the thoughts and attitudes of the heart. HEBREWS 4:12

The Word of God is a central tool in the hand of a parent. There will be family moments when you will need to rely on the Word of God alone for guidance and direction. When nothing around you makes any sense, God's Word always will.

Teach your children early and often about God's Word. Take a verse that is easy to understand and recite it at bedtime until your children are able to memorize it and say it alone. You might put the verse to music or a rhythmic pattern for easier recollection. As your children grow older, hopefully these verses will become a regular part of their language. At some future date that simple verse will be what penetrates their heart and soul and brings them peace and comfort through difficult circumstances.

We often underestimate Scripture's power. It penetrates us to the very core. When you can't get to your children, God's Word can! Continue to rely on him for strength as you and your children grow in his Word. ❖

PARENTING PRINCIPLE

Knowing God's Word is knowing God himself.

POINTS TO PONDER

- How do you use God's Word to grow?
- What are you doing to instill Scripture in your children?
- What did you learn today from God's Word?

SURRENDER!

Nothing in all creation is hidden from God's sight. Everything is uncovered and laid bare before the eyes of him to whom we must give account. Hebrews 4:13

A day is coming when we will give an account for how we parented. We will be responsible to God for what he has entrusted to us. On that day, we will want to hear, "Well done good and faithful parent." We earn that by the way we live today. God sees all we do. Any hidden or unexposed secrets or lies keep us from reaching our fullest potential.

Openly confess to Christ today all that he already sees and knows. Come clean and pure before him. Be willing to let him have control of all you do. You will be a better person and parent as a result. And you will discover this is a daily need. Living in an imperfect world, parenting imperfect children and simply being human requires us to acknowledge God's omnipotence. He sees all we do. He knows our every thought.

Let's spend less time trying to get away with stuff and more time in complete surrender. After all, this is what we as parents want from our children. Let's give to God what we desire from our children. ❖

PARENTING PRINCIPLE

We can run but we cannot hide—it's futile to try.

POINTS TO PONDER

- How are you seeking to be more open to Christ?
- How are you a good example for your children in this area?
- What growth do you see in your children in this area?

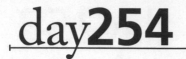

HOLD ON

Therefore, since we have a great high priest who has ascended into heaven, Jesus the Son of God, let us hold firmly to the faith we profess.   HEBREWS 4:14

Someday your children's faith will become their own. You need to prepare for that day and be aware that it is usually a process and not instantaneous. Your teaching that Jesus Christ died and rose again to ascend into heaven will be a foundation for that belief. In fact, it will be what you hope they eventually base their faith on. You cannot be their faith holder. Faith is an individual belief. This will be true for each of your children.

The best thing we can do is continue to give to the high priest in prayer and seek his divine providence over our children. Satan has plenty of pitfalls, so we must do all we can to seek God's blessing and protection for our children and then yield them to him.

The yielding part will be one of the most challenging things you will ever face if your child is not chasing after God. Be willing to yield even if your child is not. And hold onto your faith. ✤

PARENTING PRINCIPLE

Grab onto the pole of faith and pray your children's growing hands have the same desire.

POINTS TO PONDER

- What are you doing to hold onto your faith?
- What threatens your grip?
- How are your children growing in their personal faith at their particular age?

THRONE OF GRACE

Let us then approach God's throne of grace with confidence, so that we may receive mercy and find grace to help us in our time of need. HEBREWS 4:16

Notice Hebrews 4:16 doesn't say, "If we ever have a time of need." It's assumed that there will be those times.

When they come, approach God's throne boldly. Come before him knowing he is God and he loves you and wants to help you with your children. When we pray, we receive God's grace and mercy. His grace brings peace and his mercy brings hope. God will ultimately be the one who can touch your children. Therefore, you can approach confidently because of his consistent faithfulness to be there for us.

That might be your very circumstance today. If so, be encouraged that God sees your trial. He knows what you and your child need. Pray for him to meet those needs and know that he may see a perspective about the situation that you can't see. Look to him for peace and strength today and know he has cared about parents for eons. As you trust your burden to him, feel the mercy and grace that is available to you. ❖

PARENTING PRINCIPLE

When you approach the throne, it sets a tone!

POINTS TO PONDER

- What do you need to bring to God today?
- How are you at boldly approaching God and understanding that he cares for you?
- How can you pray for your children to continue to yield their lives to God?

day256

LOOKING BACK

Now faith is confidence in what we hope for and assurance about what we do not see.

HEBREWS 11:1

There were several men and women in the Bible who were known for their faith. Abraham, Ruth and Job are a few examples. We need to remember they dealt with issues just like us. Their days of parenting were filled with challenges and trials of all kinds. They made it through because of their faith and their hope and belief in what could not be seen.

This is all part of the wonders of the world of parenting. Remember, you will not see your child's full potential in the middle of a temper-tantrum. When they snub their nose at you, it will be difficult to imagine their potential for Christ. In those moments, faith will have to hold you to the duty that is parenting.

When we look back at the saints of the Bible, it's in retrospect that we see clearly. We may never visibly see the plan God has for our children, but by faith we trust that when we look back from the eternal view, it will have all been worthwhile. As Hebrews 11:1 teaches, we need to do all this with confidence. That is a reflection of a life dedicated to honoring Christ. ❖

PARENTING PRINCIPLE

Learning to believe in what is unseen is called faith.

POINTS TO PONDER

- How have you developed your faith?
- When do you or your children struggle with faith?
- How are you helping your children develop theirs?

DISCIPLINE IS GOOD

Because the Lord disciplines the one he loves, and he chastens everyone he accepts as his son.
HEBREWS 12:6

Discipline is a topic we need to hear more about. It's almost a lost word in our society because people have become afraid to discipline for fear of violating someone's rights. When worrying about protecting those rights becomes more important than protecting our children's future, that's a concern.

The Lord disciplines those he loves and therefore we must also discipline the ones we love. In doing so we show our children we care, even though they may not see it that way. As a parent, you must embrace and accept this responsibility. It is yours. Don't put it off on the teachers, the neighbors or your parents. They are certainly part of the support team that surrounds your children, but discipline should always start in the home.

Enforce it by establishing structure in your home and setting boundaries for your children. When those boundaries are crossed, have a specific plan of action that includes disciplining your children and requiring them to suffer consequences. Help them understand that those consequences are a direct result of their behavior and not your behavior. This teaches them to develop a sense of responsibility that will yield the results you desire as a parent. ❖

PARENTING PRINCIPLE

Discipline won't happen unless you are disciplined.

POINTS TO PONDER

- How does the Lord discipline you?
- How does discipline benefit people?
- What is your disciplinary style?

SEEK PEACE

Make every effort to live in peace with everyone and to be holy; without holiness no one will see the LORD. HEBREWS 12:14

In a family, there will be times when having peace will be a challenge. Siblings will not always be patient or understanding of each other. They will not be mature enough to see what you can see as a parent. You will get tired of dealing with these situations. In the middle of it all, Christ will call you to continue making an effort. That means going the extra mile, and then going that extra mile again, even when you're exhausted.

If you can get the whole family to abide by this, you will be much closer to having a house of peace. It's unlikely your family members will always be willing to go beyond the ordinary, but it should be the goal.

Remember, achieving peace in a home will be similar to parenting—it's a journey. It's something you need to work at all the time and as a parent you must be the example.

Creating a home of peace is the same as creating a little piece of heaven on earth. Do all you can to get it! ❖

PARENTING PRINCIPLE

Experiencing peace in your home is like experiencing a little piece of heaven.

POINTS TO PONDER

- What are you doing to go the extra mile?
- How do your children practice this principle?
- What can you do to increase the peace in your home?

EFFECTIVE DISCIPLINE

No discipline seems pleasant at the time, but painful. Later on, however, it produces a harvest of righteousness and peace for those who have been trained by it.

HEBREWS 12:11

We could write all these devotionals on discipline and it probably still wouldn't be enough. Discipline is a critical foundation for sound parenting.

It's important to note that effective discipline will involve discomfort for everyone involved. If it doesn't, it probably won't work. Now this is not to be used as any justification for action that would be abusive. Instead, we are reminded to continually think of methods that can be employed to effectively get the attention of your children. Sometimes what works as discipline on one child may not be effective with another.

One of the best ways to make sure your discipline is effective is to know what your child enjoys and how removing that pleasure might be very hard for them and thus teach them a lesson. You can be aware of the things they enjoy by simply observing their behavior. When discipline is needed you merely take away one of their preferences and you will get their attention. Don't give into their kicking and screaming and you will soon experience the benefits of discipline. The effective discipline of a righteous parent brings results. ❖

PARENTING PRINCIPLE

Kicking and screaming is all about scheming.

POINTS TO PONDER

- What are the unpleasant discipline actions you are incorporating with your children?
- How are these methods effective?
- What circumstances prevent you from incorporating these methods at times?

TOUCHED BY AN ANGEL

Do not forget to show hospitality to strangers, for by so doing some people have shown hospitality to angels without knowing it.　　　　HEBREWS 13:2

It would be an incredible feeling to discover that you had been kind to an angel, but it's even better just knowing your kindness touched another person. When you reach out to others, you don't always know the long-lasting impact you are making. It's important to teach your children to show love to all people and that the possibility of touching an angel exists.

If you are a "go to" family in your neighborhood and your home is a place where people feel welcome, your children will benefit from that environment. If they see kindness regularly displayed in their home life, there's a good chance they will desire a life that impacts the world with their servant spirit.

Teach your children to show hospitality to strangers. As adults, they may pursue a ministry that could place them in risky situations, but how sweet it will be to know they're serving God in that way. They don't have to be in a ministry to show kindness. Be thankful if they are doing it in their neighborhood, their workplace or across the globe. ❖

PARENTING PRINCIPLE

Be an angel to a stranger and reap heavenly rewards.

POINTS TO PONDER

- How does your family show hospitality to others?
- What are you doing to impact strangers?
- How do we help our children discern between the dangers and the needs of a stranger?

THE LOVE OF MONEY

Keep your lives free from the love of money and be content with what you have, because God has said, "Never will I leave you; never will I forsake you."   HEBREWS 13:5

Kids learn to love money. It gets them what they want at the store. It sinks in after a while that the more money you have, the more stuff you can get. It's an innocent attraction at first, but as we have all discovered, it doesn't take long before it becomes an obsession. Your children think the neighbor kids have more toys than they do and jealousy forms. Instead of defaulting to contentment, it makes them want more.

Though there are no perfect answers to this problem, one way to help your children develop a thankful spirit is to serve through a mission trip locally or in a different part of the world. See how people live who don't have as much as they do. Like us, most of our children have wants but not really needs. Don't be guilty of overwhelming them with luxury or you will only build a love for money in them. Teach them that money is a means and a necessity in life, but it's not to be worshiped. ❖

PARENTING PRINCIPLE

Do not bank on monetary contentment.

POINTS TO PONDER

- When have you fallen in love with money?
- How do you keep money it its proper perspective?
- How will you help your children maintain a healthy balance with money and contentment?

day262

PURE JOY

Consider it pure joy, my brothers and sisters, whenever you face trials of many kinds, because you know that the testing of your faith produces perseverance.   JAMES 1:2–3

Are you going through a trial in your family life? Do you consider it a blessing? Probably not!

But James 1:2–3 says these trials teach us perseverance, and that when we have stood the test we become more mature! Many families give up in the middle of the test. They never experience the blessing of the maturity that comes from hanging in there.

God has a perfect plan for you and your family. The issue is that we define the word *perfect* differently than he does. He sees the big picture and knows the areas in which we lack perseverance. He allows the testing to bring maturity to us and glory to his name. Pure joy seems a little extreme, but it reflects an ability to appreciate things from God's perspective.

If you're in the middle of a trial and each day is a battle, you're missing an opportunity to let your children see how to deal with conflict positively and represent the kingdom of God. Embrace this new normal you may be facing today and grow. ❖

PARENTING PRINCIPLE

Don't be fooled. Pure joy often looks like the devil's ploy.

POINTS TO PONDER

- What trial are you facing that could benefit from a new perspective?
- How could you improve your situation with a shift in attitude?
- What are you showing your children through this current trial?

THE GIVER

If any of you lacks wisdom, you should ask God, who gives generously to all without finding fault, and it will be given to you.   JAMES 1:5

How comforting to know that God does not base his giving of wisdom on our perfection. He assures us that if we need wisdom, he will be faithful to give it to us. In fact, he emphasizes it will be provided with great generosity.

This helps us make a shift from not knowing what to do with an issue our child is experiencing to knowing that God wants us to bring him our issues. He created us so he knows exactly the piece of advice we need. As we seek him in prayer, we will find peace and a sense of direction. There may be times when you seek God and don't feel anything, but don't give up. God will be faithful.

Just as you want to meet the needs of your children, God wants to meet your needs and exceed your expectations! Focus in on an area you need wisdom and pursue it like you would air if you were drowning. Your relentless seeking and asking will result in his relentless guidance and direction. ✤

PARENTING PRINCIPLE

Where there is a will there is a way.

POINTS TO PONDER

- What is an area you lack wisdom because you have failed to ask God?
- Are you quick to want an answer or quick to give up asking?
- How have you taught your children to seek God for wisdom?

JUST BE THERE

My dear brothers and sisters, take note of this: Everyone should be quick to listen, slow to speak and slow to become angry.   JAMES 1:19

Step one to a good relationship with your child is to be quick to listen. When your child reaches the age where they can tell you things about their life or issues they are dealing with—listen. Please understand that you might not ever need to respond. The tendency for every parent is to feel like you need to supply all their answers, but often times it is most helpful to simply listen and learn.

If step two is needed, it is wise to be slow to speak. Measure your response. If it's defensive or attacking, reconsider what you plan to say. When your child listens to you, make it worth their while. If you develop this type of relationship, they will probably pursue you often with issues.

Third, don't allow your conversation to take an angry tone. The moment this happens, you have lost any chance of making a point or making a difference. Sadly it happens too often.

Determine today that you will begin to improve your ability to converse with your child by practicing these three steps—steps that are Biblical and thus have the very foundation of truth. ❖

PARENTING PRINCIPLE

Wise parents open their ears more than their mouths.

POINTS TO PONDER

- How would you rate yourself as a listener?
- How can you prevent your conversations from turning angry?
- How can you improve communication with your children overall?

ACT ON IT

Do not merely listen to the word, and so deceive yourselves. Do what it says.

JAMES 1:22

The Word of God speaks in a way that can penetrate your soul and spirit. If we read it, however, without following up with action, we can deceive ourselves.

We need to put into practice what we read. As parents we often condemn our children for their actions when what we are doing in our lives would fall into the same category—disobedience! We must be careful not to become so regimented in our teaching of God's Word that we turn our children off to what God might say because we continually shove our thoughts down their throats. By this method, our children will end up living a life of condemnation where they hide all their weak spots. This can lead to a very disobedient lifestyle.

Instead, ask your children what a verse means to them and let them begin to develop a love for God's Word and a desire to be obedient to it. Talk to them about being responsible for what they know and accountable for what they do. Share stories of your own learning experiences as you grow in this area of doing what Scripture teaches. ✤

PARENTING PRINCIPLE

Listen and then act on it!

POINTS TO PONDER

- What have you learned from listening to God's words?
- How often do you act on what you've heard?
- How have you helped your children develop their skills for listening to God's Word?

day266

ONE SMALL SPARK

Likewise, the tongue is a small part of the body, but it makes great boasts. Consider what a great forest is set on fire by a small spark. JAMES 3:5

It weighs only a few ounces, but it can destroy a family. The tongue is the most dangerous part of your body when it comes to your family. Words will either build people up or tear them down. You will be respected or rejected based on how you speak, whether it's through emails, texts or other modes of communication.

These newer ways of conversing allow for even more explosive phrases to emerge because they require no face-to-face contact. It's as simple as pushing a send button. Soon the forest is burning because of that one seemingly small spark. But when you consider the deceptiveness of Satan, it all becomes clearer. He chooses to use a small body part, because he knows the big destruction it can reap on families.

Have you succumbed to his deception by way of your harsh words? Have you been the victim of someone else's verbal assault? Learn from your past experiences and from James 3:5 that God expects us to control our tongues. Teach your children the benefit of living without starting fires. ❖

PARENTING PRINCIPLE

Where there is smoke, there is a loose tongue.

POINTS TO PONDER

- What have you learned about your tongue?
- How do you get good control of it?
- By what example are you teaching your children in this area?

DREAMS COME TRUE

But the wisdom that comes from heaven is first of all pure; then peace-loving, considerate, submissive, full of mercy and good fruit, impartial and sincere.　　JAMES 3:17

Who wouldn't enjoy a home that exhibits the traits mentioned in James 3:17? The wisdom of God will bring a pureness to our house. No longer would we be about ourselves, but about everyone in the family.

This type of home would be a parent's dream. A home where peace reigns and everyone loves the peace. Your children are considerate of each other and submissive to your authority. Their thoughts are impartial and their actions sincere and everyone is full of mercy.

This dream can become a reality if you seek God's wisdom from heaven with all your heart. It needs to become as repetitive as breathing. Breathe in the wisdom of God, breathe out these beneficial traits.

Be sure to discern pure godly wisdom from the Bible and not the wisdom that comes from the world. When you start to see the results listed above, celebrate like crazy! Be faithful to seek God on all occasions in many ways as you grow in him with your family. ❖

PARENTING PRINCIPLE

A sweet home comes from a sweet loan from God's hand of love.

POINTS TO PONDER

- Where do you typically go for wisdom?
- Do you see any of the traits listed in this verse in your family?
- What can you do to continue to develop these traits in your family?

CREATE PEACE

Peacemakers who sow in peace reap a harvest of righteousness.   JAMES 3:18

When you hear the garage door opening because your spouse or one of your children is coming home, what's your first thought? Is it joy because you are looking forward to seeing them or is it dread because they're home? If it's the latter, then the peace is gone. When your family hears you entering the home what do you imagine their first thoughts are?

You should give high consideration to that first thought you have when someone walks in your house. It reflects the atmosphere that surrounds your home. As parents, we need to make sure we bring peace to our family. Of course, you must discipline and correct, but do it all in an effort to bring peace.

Take time today to analyze your own actions as a parent. If you are creating unnecessary conflict in your home, eliminate it. Before we teach our children how they can contribute to maintaining peace in the home, we must be doing all we can.

A peaceful home will bring about better health, more productivity, less stress and overall joy to the family. No home will have perfect peace, but we can be consistent in our efforts to try. ❖

PARENTING PRINCIPLE

When you open the door, make sure peace enters before you.

POINTS TO PONDER

- How peaceful is your home?
- What benefits can a peaceful home bring you?
- How can you improve the peace in your home?

SUBMIT

Submit yourselves, then, to God. Resist the devil, and he will flee from you.   JAMES 4:7

Teach your children how to resist Satan. Help them understand that you can't run toward him and be freed from the traps of sin. For example, if you go places where people are engaging in unhealthy activities, you will probably fall into them too. It's hard for teens to understand this because they feel invincible at their age.

Your children need to run from those places. The very act of running from Satan is submitting to God. It's what he asks us to do. As we submit, God's favor and blessing will come upon us. It's a choice. We can chase Satan and be defeated and discouraged or we can submit to God and have peace and strength even in the tough times.

Make sure your children understand that submission to God doesn't mean life will always be easy. Life isn't fair. There will be times when you submit to God but you won't feel like you're winning the battle. Remember, it's not about winning and losing, it's about obedience to God.

Our goal is to flee the devil. You will find you and your family in a much better place if you are all submitting to God. ❖

PARENTING PRINCIPLE

If we resist, God will assist.

POINTS TO PONDER

- How do you resist the devil? How are you teaching your children to resist the devil?
- How could you improve as a family in this area?
- What helps you submit yourselves to God?

MISTY MOMENTS

Why, you do not even know what will happen tomorrow. What is your life? You are a mist that appears for a little while and then vanishes.   JAMES 4:14

The concept of life and the brevity of life is a delicate issue to discuss with children. When it's age appropriate, we should help them understand how as humans we only have a brief time on this earth.

They may understand this if they've already had a loved one pass away. Maybe it was a beloved pet, a grandparent or possibly a sibling. Regardless, be prepared to help your children understand that life is precious and passes quickly. They probably won't want to dwell on it a long time, but at least plant the seed.

One way to help your children understand this is to demonstrate what James 4:14 suggests. Using a squirt bottle, spray some water in the air and show them how it immediately vanishes. Explain to them that to humans life seems much longer, but to an infinite God life is mist. They may not understand it completely, but it will become clearer as they age. Your illustration will be more memorable in preparing them for further development in understanding life. ✤

PARENTING PRINCIPLE

A misty moment can cause misty moments.

POINTS TO PONDER

- How do you deal with the concept of life as a mist?
- What have you done to help your children understand the brevity of life?
- What other illustrations could you use to help them understand?

SPEAK POSITIVELY

Don't grumble against one another.   JAMES 5:9

Have you ever been around a grumbler? It can be pretty frustrating. Day in and day out, they just complain about everything and anything. Even when you try to say something positive and encouraging to them, they only stop for a moment, and then go at it again—grumbling!

Some children will tend to lean this way for a variety of reasons. It's normal for some grumbling to occur in the family, but persistent complaining from a child is unacceptable. When you notice someone developing a pattering of complaining, try to pinpoint the root of the problem.

Are you as parents setting the grumbling tone? Is there a friend or schoolmate influencing your child? Try to correct their behavior by explaining the importance of speaking positively to others. Tell them what it's like for other people to be around a grumbler, using an example they can relate to. For those children who don't willingly comply or even try to correct their behavior, you might consider further discipline.

If they don't respond to any punishment, think about using a professional counselor who can deal with the behavior at a much deeper level. There may be underlying developmental issues to consider. Be patient as this type of behavior doesn't change overnight. ❖

PARENTING PRINCIPLE

Don't let a grumbler cause you to be a tumbler.

POINTS TO PONDER

- What do you grumble about?
- What do your children tend to complain about?
- What can you do to correct grumbling when you see it?

HOLY, HOLY, HOLY

Just as he who called you is holy, so be holy in all you do.   1 Peter 1:15

Holiness is not a common word we hear, but it's something we should practice every day. God set Jesus as our standard. His flawless, perfect life is our supreme example. To consider what Christ did for us is beyond human understanding. Constantly forgiving, ever faithful and always loving.

We have all failed at times in our quest for holiness. There is no perfect parent or person, but we should continually strive to reach new levels of holiness as we pursue God's will for our life. When we fall short, we need to admit our defeat and grow from the experience, but not give up the pursuit to live like and for Jesus Christ.

We need to teach our children to seek holiness too! Help them understand what holiness looks like. If you can use people they know as role models of holiness, it will help them to better understand how to be holy in all they do. Talk about who were role models for you.

You might also make a list of behaviors associated with holiness to give your child tangible ways to achieve these qualities in their life. ✤

PARENTING PRINCIPLE

Holiness should not be just a church word, but a life pursuit.

POINTS TO PONDER

- How are you growing in holiness?
- How have you taught your children to pursue holiness?
- What are some holiness traits you can pursue in your home?

THE TASTE OF CHRIST

Like newborn babies, crave pure spiritual milk, so that by it you may grow up in your salvation, now that you have tasted that the Lord is good.　　　I Peter 2:2–3

Watching your baby experience some of their first food tastes is fun. They make faces that cause you to burst out laughing. Those first expressions soon give way to sucking some foods in and spitting some foods out. And through it all your little baby begins to grow and mature.

The same is true for your children spiritually. When they begin to learn about God, you want those first experiences to create an inner desire for them to know more. Your goal as parents should be to make Christ contagious and not condemning. We all want our children to desire to love Christ and not only just out of duty.

Our own example of a genuine and heart-felt love for Christ will be the most obvious and easy way to teach this principle. However, if being involved in church, reading the Bible and praying appears as a chore and not something you love, it will not inspire your children.

Do all you can to help your children develop a love for the taste of Christ. ❖

PARENTING PRINCIPLE

Show Christ as your inspiration, not your desperation.

POINTS TO PONDER

- How do you show you love your relationship with Christ?
- How do you make Christ contagious for your children?
- What are you doing to grow yourself and help your children grow in their taste for Christ?

YOU ARE SPECIAL

But you are a chosen people, a royal priesthood, a holy nation, God's special possession, that you may declare the praises of him who called you out of darkness into his wonderful light.

1 PETER 2:9

With six plus billion people on earth, it's easy to think we might not be very special as individuals. But because of Christ's love for us, we are exceptional. He makes us unique and important in light of eternity.

Teaching your children their importance in Christ will have a lasting purpose. When their best skills are all they rely on, it won't be enough. There will always be someone who can run faster, jump higher or get better grades. While it's important to teach children to strive for their best performance, their reason for significance must rest in Christ alone. When their human successes fall away, their value will be sure and secure in Christ.

Let this principle guide you as you parent. Then after you've passed away, your legacy will live on. Remember, God called you out of darkness into a great light. This light will guide your way, guard your heart and keep the dark roads visible.

Rely on God for all things, including your self-worth. ❖

PARENTING PRINCIPLE

We are special to Christ for no special reason except that he created us.

POINTS TO PONDER

- When don't you feel special to Christ?
- How do you help your children know they are special to Christ?
- How has God's light kept you on track as a parent?

ALWAYS CHOOSE GOOD

Live such good lives among the pagans that, though they accuse you of doing wrong, they may see your good deeds and glorify God on the day he visits us.   1 PETER 2:12

Your children will struggle when they do right but then are accused of doing wrong. You will understand because it has probably happened to you. The natural response to this circumstance is to attack back and be defensive. Instead, continue doing good and eventually your deeds will bring glory to God. Notice the glory is not for us, but for God.

Consider the life of Christ as an example. Any bystander who watched him being slapped and ridiculed would have thought he was weak not to respond. In the end Christ won and still wins. Today his name remains above all names.

It's not easy to commit to respond like this in every situation. It's painful and difficult because you appear to be weak and losing. But learn through Christ's example that winning is not of this world. In fact, don't strive to be winners on this side, but work to be winners in the life to come.

Be faithful to set this example for your children, and your eternal rewards will be great! ✤

PARENTING PRINCIPLE

Live to please God, not people!

POINTS TO PONDER

- How do you handle false accusations?
- How can you help your children deal with these?
- What example of false accusations from your life can you share with your children?

FREEDOM RINGS

Live as free people, but do not use your freedom as a cover-up for evil.   1 PETER 2:16

Freedom is something soldiers in our society fought for so we could live in peace. Unfortunately many individuals confuse freedom as a cover up for evil. They do things that are questionable and justify their behavior by saying it's within their individual rights.

Teach your children that freedom is first and foremost from God. He has blessed us with Christ who forgave us all our sins and granted us freedom from the bondage sin keeps us in. God even gives us free will, the right to choose whether Jesus Christ is our Savior. We also have the freedom to live and work where we want as well as do what we like.

Freedom is good, except if we use it in a way that destroys our life. It is a delicate balance, but help your children understand the difference between freedom and rights. Be sure of your own understanding of freedom and then lead by example as you instruct your children.

Other people's beliefs about freedom will have influence over your children. It's important to be sure your faithful instruction on freedom is what they adopt as they mature. ✤

PARENTING PRINCIPLE

Just because it's my right doesn't make it right!

POINTS TO PONDER

- How do you live free?
- What do your children understand about the difference between rights and freedom?
- How can you better help your family grow in this area?

RAISING CHRIST FOLLOWERS

For it is commendable if someone bears up under the pain of unjust suffering because they are conscious of God.   1 PETER 2:19

There are incredible challenges in raising your children to be followers of Christ. If you see him and his life as the ultimate example of perfect purity, then be prepared to suffer if you or your children expect to follow him. Following Christ's example sounds perfect until you get to that place of suffering.

When you consider that hundreds of Christ followers suffer daily simply because of their faith, you become aware of the potential for this to happen to your child. If they decide to serve in a place that brings you fear, you must decide to support them even if you don't like it. Releasing your children to follow God as he leads them is part of parenting. You don't get to decide his will. You get to pray, provide and plead for their protection. Just don't be a hindrance for what he has planned for them.

You will be amazed what your blessing and support will mean to your children. They probably have more inner fear than you, so don't exacerbate those, but come along side and seek to bring peace as they honor God. ✤

PARENTING PRINCIPLE

When it's time, let them go!

POINTS TO PONDER

- What do you do to let your child find their own direction in life?
- How are you preparing to be a parent of adult children?
- What did you learn from your parents in this area?

THE SHEPHERD SEES

For "you were like sheep going astray," but now you have returned to the Shepherd and Overseer of your souls.   1 PETER 2:25

At some point in your parenting journey you might have a child who "strays." Of course, you pray that a quick and single correction brings everything back to order. But if not, you must believe God has a purpose in it!

This verse calls the Lord the shepherd and overseer of our souls. When a child strays, it is usually a soul issue. While your guidance and restrictions help define the outer actions of your child, only the Lord can change the soul.

Because of this, we need to understand the importance of committing ourselves to pray for our child's soul. If we yield that to God, parenting will be much more pleasant. Even during the difficult times, God remains our shepherd. There may be days when we feel lost as parents, but the Shepherd will always know where to find us.

The ultimate prayer is for our lost child to find their way back. Our children are his sheep and he sees the attacks Satan lays before them. In the end we want to see that God is faithful to our family. ✣

PARENTING PRINCIPLE

We are the sheep of his pasture!

POINTS TO PONDER

- How did God reach you in your "straying" moments?
- What will you do to keep yourself under his care?
- Do you have any wayward "strays" in your family or extended family that need prayer today?

A TEAM APPROACH

Finally, all of you, be like-minded, be sympathetic, love one another, be compassionate and humble.   1 PETER 3:8

It's great when family members are like-minded! When we think and work together as a team, so much can be accomplished for Christ and each other in that family atmosphere. Add to that a sympathetic servant spirit, and the rewards are even better. When family members can relate to and understand each other, there is a greater chance for compassion and humility to prevail in the home.

Every parent would want to adopt this verse for their family, but the reality is that we won't always be able to create this type of environment. But we need to seek it individually first and then pray for God to grant all of our family members this spirit. And it all starts with this spirit of humility.

Calling our family to these standards and goals is helpful in creating positive home environments. Certainly this is a verse we can use for such guidance. It might be Scripture you can put on the wall or certainly read at dinner time. Get these thoughts into the minds of your children and do what you can to build a solid home. ❖

PARENTING PRINCIPLE

When we all work as one the home is a lot more fun!

POINTS TO PONDER

- What do you do to build a like-minded home?
- How do you handle things when the family doesn't act like-minded?
- How can you build humility in your family?

LOVE LIFE

Whoever would love life and see good days must keep their tongue from evil and their lips from deceitful speech.   1 PETER 3:10

The Bible seems a bit redundant. In many verses, we see almost a rhythmic reminder to watch our tongue and guard ourselves from deceitfulness. Maybe it's because God knows humanity. He knows that without constant reminders, we easily fall into the enemy's traps.

It's probably why parents often sound like a broken record. Your children get ready to leave the house, and you rattle off the same reminders you did the day before because you aren't sure they're listening or heeding your advice. Parenting would be more enjoyable if we could say something once and be done because our children immediately obeyed.

These recurring speeches come from wanting our children to love life and see good days. We know that can happen if we teach them to live totally submitted to the authority of Christ and to develop a good relationship with their family.

You don't get to make their choices for them, but you can influence them by choosing to be faithful and committed to helping them keep their tongue from evil and their lips from deceitful speech. ❖

PARENTING PRINCIPLE

Saying and hearing something important over and over makes it easier to remember.

POINTS TO PONDER

- How well do you love life?
- When do you see this love for life in your children?
- What can you do to continue to protect your lips from evil?

EYES AND EARS

For the eyes of the Lord are on the righteous and his ears are attentive to their prayer.

1 PETER 3:12

There is a good reason to be a righteous parent and seek to honor God in all we do. We want him to hear our prayers and for our prayers to be answered.

His ears are tuned to us as we live in obedience to him. There will be times you'll wonder if he's listening, but by faith you can know that he is. He sees all that we are doing, and is more involved than we can understand. Think of a time when you didn't think he was involved in something, but now in retrospect you can see clearly he was involved.

Remember that for whatever you are dealing with today. Those countless nights of prayer are not unseen or unheard. That wayward child isn't lost from God's eyes. There may be a much bigger picture God is painting that you can't see. That's not always easy to accept, but it gives us hope that one day we will see how his plan is always best. Be faithful in prayer and he will be faithful in his response. ✤

PARENTING PRINCIPLE

God sees your hurts and hears your feeblest of mumbles.

POINTS TO PONDER

- What do you need to give in prayer to God today?
- How have you seen his work in the past?
- What issues and burdens are you trusting him with because of your faith?

DEEP LOVE

Above all, love each other deeply, because love covers a multitude of sins.   1 Peter 4:8

Your deep love of your children will help you survive parenting. During this journey, you may be accused, abused, reused and misused. You will be at low points you would never have imagined and high points that you can't believe. That baby you hold could become a bundle of pain. It's just part of the deal. Your undying love will be what helps you get through it. It's what Christ did for you and now you get to do it for your children.

One of the reasons we need to stay faithful to love is because one day our children will experience something similar from their children by putting them through great and challenging days. Your children won't forget your example of faithfulness as a parent who paved the way. If you are prone to be a quitter, resist the urge to give up and remember that God's love will sustain you.

If you had a parent who never gave up on you, you understand the importance of this love. If you had a parent who gave up on you, then you understand this concept even more. Press on and keep love at the forefront of all you do! ✤

PARENTING PRINCIPLE

Deep love should be cherished not abandoned.

POINTS TO PONDER

- What kind of love did your parents show you?
- How has that affected your love for your children?
- How could you show more love?

LIVING THE DIFFERENCE

However, if you suffer as a Christian, do not be ashamed, but praise God that you bear that name.   I PETER 4:16

Our children need to know that being a Christ follower might not always be easy. They could be ridiculed or even suffer physically because of their belief in Christ. What should make us unique as Christians is that when that happens, we respond in love and are not ashamed. We know that Christ set an example of loving those who didn't love him.

These lessons begin in the home. Teaching your children to love each other even when they don't feel like it is a way to honor Christ. When other kids treat your children unfairly, it will take great strength not to respond with hatred.

As Christians, our reactions should be the opposite of those who show hate. When we model behavior based on love, we are showing our children that we fully understand what it means to completely surrender to Christ. It's what Christ expects from those who follow him. That's why he tells us the way is narrow and filled with difficulty, but the rewards are eternal. You will need to remind yourself and your children of that often. ♣

PARENTING PRINCIPLE

Parenting from Christ's perspective will call you to sacrificial living.

POINTS TO PONDER

- When have you suffered for Christ?
- How have you honored his name in the midst of suffering?
- How are you preparing your children to understand suffering?

GREAT EXPECTATIONS

Be shepherds of God's flock that is under your care, watching over them — not because you must, but because you are willing. 1 PETER 5:2

Our children are certainly part of the flock under God's care as well as our care. Most days we do what we can for our kids because we are willing, but that doesn't mean there won't be times when we do it because we must.

It will be challenging, but you will survive those times when you are dead tired and your child needs one more thing. Remember, it's not your duty to give them everything they ask for, but to discern what is best for them. This is especially true in the formative years. You have to teach your children about boundaries in order to help them respect you and others as they enter adulthood.

God's expectation for us as parents is to be available to our children. It doesn't mean being at their beck and call, but we need to carve out time for them or leave gaps in our schedule in case they need to talk. Being there for them doesn't mean simply handing out money and stuff; it means being available for wise counsel and guidance and doing so with a willing spirit! ✤

PARENTING PRINCIPLE

Our children are in God's flock before our flock!

POINTS TO PONDER

- What makes you a "willing" parent?
- What is a "must" part of parenting for you?
- How do your children know you are available for them?

CAST OFF

Cast all your anxiety on him because he cares for you. 1 PETER 5:7

It's no secret that parenting brings on anxiety. At first, it's the anxiety of having a new little bundle of joy to care for daily. Then it's the first fever. The first time they choke. The first time they fall. All of it brings anxiousness.

Unfortunately it doesn't stop there because then they start to walk and the worry shifts to what they will get into. Will they run out in the street? Will you lose them in the grocery store? During the teen years, the consequences of their decisions could be more serious and this only increases your anxiety levels.

While it's normal to experience this, Christ invites us through it all to cast our anxiety on him. We don't have to deal with it alone! However, once we cast our anxiety on him, we need to make sure we don't take it back.

Seek to become a parent who prays and hands over your anxiety to God. Every parent will experience anxious moments in their journey, but they can rest easy knowing God is there to help them. They just need to let him! ❖

PARENTING PRINCIPLE

After you cast your cares, don't reel them back in.

POINTS TO PONDER

- What do you tend to get anxious about as a parent?
- How are you learning to cast your cares on God?
- What is a care you need to submit to him right now?

day286

FINDING HOPE

I pray that the eyes of your heart may be enlightened in order that you may know the hope to which he has called you.   EPHESIANS 1:18

Parents, dedicate yourself to praying that your children's heart and soul will be aware of God's hope. That they will know it for themselves. That their experiences with places and people of faith will ultimately call them to God and not turn them off to faith.

When they understand this from their own soul, they will experience hope. Without hope, this is a pretty tough world. Because of technology, our children will be exposed to more negative news than we ever were. If you do much blogging or read threads on websites, you can see how critical people can be. It's easy to hide behind a computer screen and write hurtful comments.

That's why their soul needs to be secure in the hope that only Christ can bring and why we need to pray this for them. We cannot protect them forever. They must learn how to defend themselves with the sword of the spirit. Also pray that they will be a positive influence on others who don't know this hope. Pray Ephesians 1:18 over your children so they will be enlightened. ❖

PARENTING PRINCIPLE

When Jesus gets their soul, he'll take full control!

POINTS TO PONDER

- What do you pray daily for your children?
- How can you be more specific in your prayer life?
- Where do you see your children discovering their hope in Christ?

LIVING WITH GRACE

But because of his great love for us, God, who is rich in mercy, made us alive with Christ even when we were dead in transgressions—it is by grace you have been saved.

EPHESIANS 2:4–5

Seeing your children experience grace is a wonderful thing. They don't know how much they need it, but as a parent you know because you realize your own need for grace.

Let's first remember that it is by grace we are saved. It's nothing we do, nothing we can pray for, and nothing we can accomplish on our own. Simply put, it's a gift from God and one that we need to pass on to our children. They will need it just as we do.

There will be times when you feel a lack of grace. During those moments, take time to read over these verses and let the truth of God's Word soak in. In this place of reading and seeking, you will find renewed strength because it is part of his living Word speaking into your life. Let it become a regular habit, and you will be much better equipped to teach your children how to obtain the grace they will need.

It is by grace we are saved and it is by grace we are able to be godly parents. ✤

PARENTING PRINCIPLE

God's grace is how you get your grace!

POINTS TO PONDER

- What causes you to struggle with grace?
- What do you know now about grace?
- How will you teach your children about grace?

day288

THE POISON OF ENVY

For where you have envy and selfish ambition, there you find disorder and every evil practice.   JAMES 3:16

Envy rears its ugly head in every family. Parents show favoritism. Siblings feel resentment. Families quarrel over possessions. It happens! During this process, family members start acting selfishly to prove a point or to get people on one side or the other. Unfortunately it all leads to disorder and the opportunity for evil to penetrate into the very core of your family life.

Sadly, most people, including your children, do not receive correction regarding envy in a positive way. In fact, they tend to become more defensive and divisive. You still need to address the issue, but understand that until the Lord deals with them, you may be tackling this topic more than once. For that reason, be careful not to develop bitterness toward them as that will lead to more disorderly conduct.

Teaching your children, when they are very young, how to love and respect their siblings will be important. Curbing envy early on will help avoid these behaviors following your children into adulthood when it's more difficult to tame.

As a parent, seek to keep your own life free and clear of envy because that will be remembered by your children. ❖

PARENTING PRINCIPLE

Envy and greed are poison indeed.

POINTS TO PONDER

- Is your home one that fosters envy?
- How can you keep envy out of your family?
- What situations cause your children to be envious?

FIGHTING BATTLES

What causes fights and quarrels among you? Don't they come from your desires that battle within you?   JAMES 4:1

At the heart of most family quarrels is a person who is probably not at peace in their heart. That's why it's important to help your children see their selfish inner struggles so they can understand how it ties into quarreling.

It's much easier to point out the flaws in another person rather than admit and recognize our own faults. That's why James 4:1 is bold in helping us see that if there is an issue then everyone involved needs to examine their own hearts.

In family life, you will frequently see displaced anger. You or your child might have a conflict at work or school, but you take your frustration out on other family members. We do this naturally because we figure our family will always forgive us. This thinking is wrong. If practiced too often, a wall can be built that takes years to knock down.

Family members need to have boundaries with each other. Of course, never allow physical violence, but mental and emotional abuse can be just as devastating. Parents need to keep this in check and always address the responsible party and require change. ✣

PARENTING PRINCIPLE

Eliminate battles in your home by identifying the battles family members harbor inside.

POINTS TO PONDER

- What causes quarrels in your family?
- How are you addressing these quarrels?
- How are you helping your children see how their little struggles can cause big quarrels?

day290

DISCOVERING GOD'S GIFTS

We are God's handiwork, created in Christ Jesus to do good works, which God prepared in advance for us to do.   EPHESIANS 2:10

Helping your child understand their calling from God is a great assignment for a parent. You will see hidden talents and then direct your children to pursue the skills needed to develop their gifts. In the midst of their instructive guidance, be careful not to name their life calling, because that must come from God. It is a process that could take time. A parent's job is to help their children move through it and allow them to discover it on their own. If it's not clear, they will learn how to adjust their focus just like we did.

Notice it is God who has prepared this work in advance for your children to do. It was laid out before they were born. There are times it will feel like God doesn't know the road they're traveling but then you will realize he actually paved the way.

Teach this to your kids. Help them see God's handiwork in their lives even if it's not always a perfect picture. All things work to bring him glory! ✤

PARENTING PRINCIPLE

The best way you can help your children discover their God-given gifts is to guide them, not override them.

POINTS TO PONDER

- What unique talents have you already seen in your children?
- How can you help your children develop this talent?
- What should your child be doing to help in this process?

BEYOND IMAGINATION

Now to him who is able to do immeasurably more than all we ask or imagine, according to his power that is at work within us. EPHESIANS 3:20

Imagine getting more than you asked for. What if you got a call from a local gas station and they said you would receive a free tank of gas if you came to their station. When you arrive to fill up your tank, they surprise you and say that you will actually be receiving a year's supply of gasoline. That's more than you had imagined.

That's God's love for us. He wants to do more for us and our children than we can even imagine. Ephesians 3:20 indicates that it comes from his power that lives within us. We usually think of this in terms of "stuff" but it's more about spiritual meaning. It's an abundance of his plan of spiritual formation and guidance. It deepens us and takes our children away from the selfish desires of this world into the realm of new dimensions of life with Christ.

All the more reason that as parents we must continue to grow in Christ and experience new depths of his love. ✤

PARENTING PRINCIPLE

If you can measure God's love for you, then you haven't found the depth he desires for you.

POINTS TO PONDER

- How do you see God's immeasurable love in your life?
- What have you discovered about yourself in light of God's immeasurability?
- How will you surrender your children to God's power?

HEED THE CALL

I urge you to live a life worthy of the calling you have received. Ephesians 4:1

Paul wrote Ephesians 4:1 from a jail cell. One of the most prolific and influential writers in the history of mankind considered it a privilege to pen these words in the place God called him to be — prison.

What an example for us as parents to recognize our place in God's kingdom. It may not be the status you imagined. It may have some frustrations you could live without. It may not be what you planned, but God chose it for you. Do you see it as a worthy place? Do you fight it or accept it?

Paul says we are urged and must give an all-out effort to please God through our life calling. As parents we can please God by raising our children to honor him. We must seek his continued blessing and support as we celebrate or struggle through our calling. Our children are watching how we accept this life of worth set before us. If we do well, they learn well. If we give up, it's likely they will follow.

Be content in your place today and heed the call. ✤

PARENTING PRINCIPLE

A change in attitude can change everything.

POINTS TO PONDER

- How do you see your life calling as worthy?
- How have you been a good example for your children in living out your calling?
- Where do you struggle, if at all, in accepting your life calling?

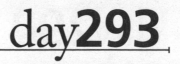

BEAT THE DRUM

Be completely humble and gentle; be patient, bearing with one another in love.

 EPHESIANS 4:2

Beating the drum of humility, gentleness, patience and forgiveness will be part of your parenting journey. You will be humbled daily by things you experience. Just when you think you have figured one thing out, another thing will arrive and you will find out how humble life can make you. So will your children.

Your children will need gentleness as you humble them with correction and discipline. Patience will be needed at every turn. You will need patience to teach them patience. Be faithful in endurance as well. You will need to be a step ahead of them for your family to stay together and continue on a path toward Christ. Let God guide you and let Ephesians 4:2 encourage you as a reminder that God walks with you in everything and he understands why you need these qualities.

To remember that a family needs humility, gentleness and patience will require your focus. It won't happen by accident. You need to teach it relentlessly.

These attributes will not be natural in your children. It will come from your teaching and example. ✤

PARENTING PRINCIPLE

Families don't acquire these attributes automatically, parents must keep their hands on the controls.

POINTS TO PONDER

- How do you grow in these areas as a family?
- When are you tempted to put it on "autopilot"?
- What can you do to sustain this effort for the long run?

 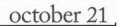

day294 october 21

BODY PARTS

From him the whole body, joined and held together by every supporting ligament, grows and builds itself up in love, as each part does its work. EPHESIANS 4:16

Our family is a body made up of different parts. As bodies grow and each person fulfills its function, the family will be complete.

Parents are at the core of what holds the family together. The children become living, breathing appendages that help parents reach new levels of growth in their life. As those children grow and eventually break off to become their own family, hopefully the message of Christ is spread to the next generation. That's how the gospel is advanced when families grow and reproduce themselves into the next generation.

Naturally there is no guarantee that your children will have the same belief you hold. It's your responsibility to teach and train up your children and then pray they listen. You can hope they absorb your wisdom as they grow and eventually form their own appendages—your grandchildren.

Our goal as parents is to develop a properly functioning family body and help each part understand its importance and purpose. Knowing this analogy helps to clarify everyone's role. God uses the visual of the body to help us understand how the family should function. ❖

PARENTING PRINCIPLE

Feed and care for your family the same as you do for your body.

POINTS TO PONDER

- What does your family body look like?
- How do you know if your family is functioning properly?
- In what ways could you improve the function?

CLEAN UP THE TALK

Do not let any unwholesome talk come out of your mouths, but only what is helpful for building others up according to their needs, that it may benefit those who listen.

EPHESIANS 4:29

A family is a place where unhealthy talk can thrive. It's easy to get used to it, and then it starts to take root and become part of our everyday life.

It's a good practice to never allow negative talk about others in your homes. You might discuss a situation that's bad and talk about the people involved, but don't let it become a gossip or criticizing session. As written in Ephesians 4:29, Christ desires talk in our home that will build others up. This includes how you talk about your own family members.

When you forbid unwholesome talk from family conversations, you are building up your children in a couple of ways. One way is that they will learn how to discuss issues and people without doing so in a negative way. Also, you create a positive home environment that your children know is a safe place.

As you strive for wholesome talk in your home, God will be honored and your family will benefit. Let your home be one that sees the good in life. ✤

PARENTING PRINCIPLE

Unwholesome talk leads to an unwholesome walk.

POINTS TO PONDER

- How would you describe the talk in your home?
- Where does your family need help in this area?
- How can you continue to improve as a family?

LIVE WISELY

Be very careful, then, how you live—not as unwise but as wise, making the most of every opportunity, because the days are evil. EPHESIANS 5:15–16

As parents we need to be wise and keep our eyes open, for the days are evil. Satan wants us to fall asleep and ignore all the stuff around us that could harm our home. Instead, we should be alert and make the most of every opportunity.

Be prepared that you will not always be wise and therefore you will fail in certain areas of parenting. Every parent looks back in retrospect and sees where they could have done better. It's one of the curses of parenting. It's better to focus on the positive. Even in looking at our faults there are opportunities to learn and pass onto our children what we now see clearly.

It's been said that smart people learn from their own mistakes, while wise people learn from the mistakes of others. You will experience both during your days of parenting. You will be pleased at how you seized an opportunity, and you will be disappointed that you let another pass by. It's all part of growing in wisdom. ❖

PARENTING PRINCIPLE

Seek to live as wise parents and become surer and secure in Christ.

POINTS TO PONDER

- What is something you learned the hard way?
- What is something you learned from other parents' mistakes that helped you to be a better parent?
- How can you keep growing and learning?

LEARN TO OBEY

Children, obey your parents in the Lord, for this is right.　　　EPHESIANS 6:1

The idea regarding obedience was not born out of a parent's need to demand respect or feel good about themselves. It's an idea that came from God, and we want our children to do it because it honors him.

Make sure your children know Ephesians 6:1. Explain how God has commanded them to obey him just as they are to obey you. The process of learning how to obey their parents will help your children learn to submit to the authority of God.

These commands seem so simple, yet we have all discovered how hard they are to carry out. One reason is because we live in a world of good and evil. The evil forces continually work hard to distract us in ways we don't always see to keep us and our children from full obedience to God.

It will take our parenting focus and our children's compliance to fulfill this verse. Make it a priority. Be sure to parent from Biblical certainty and not personal traditions. We are to call our children to obedience as we live a life honoring and pleasing to God. ♣

PARENTING PRINCIPLE

Teach your children to obey for there is no better way.

POINTS TO PONDER

- How are you parenting "in the Lord"?
- What can you do as a parent to help your children understand this is a Biblical principle?
- Where do your children struggle in showing obedience?

HONOR FIRST

"Honor your father and mother"—which is the first commandment with a promise—"so that it may go well with you and that you may enjoy long life on the earth."

EPHESIANS 6:2–3

Honor your father and mother! This is a lost art in our society. Unfortunately, when children become adults they confuse honor with allowing their parents to continue to control them.

To do everything your parents say after you have established your own home doesn't represent honoring. Honoring is remembering who they are, what they have done for you, respecting them and taking care of them as they age. Too often parents manipulate their children by quoting Ephesians 6:2–3. That's dishonoring!

Honoring involves helping your parents understand that your home will be established by you, hopefully incorporating many of the principles passed on by them. Honoring them includes making sure they're not left to fend on their own. You can help them with provisions if they are struggling, and listen to them and gain wisdom from their unique perspective.

We can teach our children by establishing this type of honoring relationship with our parents. As you honor your parents, you will be known as a great son or daughter. The direct promise from God is that you will enjoy an extended lifespan. ❖

PARENTING PRINCIPLE

As you honor your parents, you will be honored.

POINTS TO PONDER

- How well do you understand what honor means?
- How do you honor your parents?
- How will you ensure your children are prepared to establish their own home?

A DIFFERENT STANDARD

Fathers, do not exasperate your children; instead, bring them up in the training and instruction of the Lord. EPHESIANS 6:4

I don't believe any father has ever gone through their life and not exasperated their children at some point. It will happen. When a child shows that exasperation, the natural response is for a father to show equal exasperation right back. Instead, God calls us to a different standard. Our response should be to instruct our children and help them grow in the Lord.

A huge advantage we have available to us as Christian parents is the Word of God. It not only guides us, but it provides us reasons for doing what we do. Let's be certain that we train our children using God's Word and not man-made directives that will only exasperate our children.

A parent's job is to continually teach their children and not give up because we don't think we can handle it. With God, we can handle anything that comes our way! Using his daily wisdom and guidance we will hopefully help and not hinder our children.

This will call you to new levels in Christ and you may feel inadequate. But you can and you will handle it. Some parent out there has dealt with much more than you ever will, and they made it—so will you! ✣

PARENTING PRINCIPLE

Use the Bible more as you teach your children and you will exasperate them less.

POINTS TO PONDER

- What tends to exasperate you with your children?
- How do you exasperate your children?
- How could you learn to frustrate your children less?

day300

THE REAL BATTLE

For our struggle is not against flesh and blood, but against the rulers, against the authorities, against the powers of this dark world and against the spiritual forces of evil in the heavenly realms.   EPHESIANS 6:12

It's hard to believe your struggles aren't against flesh and blood when your two year old is screaming and you can't get them to stop. When your teenager is belligerent and you're getting nowhere. That's not your real battle.

Although these are obvious flesh and blood issues we tackle, the point of Ephesians 6:12 is that it's the inner fight against the evil of darkness that's causing all these struggles. Don't diminish this. Don't pretend it doesn't exist. But don't overdramatize it either.

More importantly, find a balance in recognizing where evil comes from and how it's affecting your family. Pray for God's protection over your family. Remember, the power of Christ is far greater than the power of Satan. That battle has already been won. Christ defeated the grave and evil has lost.

Claim that promise over your family and seek to honor God in all you do as a parent. God will provide, bless, protect and defend you as you seek him. ❖

PARENTING PRINCIPLE

Know that Satan is your real enemy, not your children.

POINTS TO PONDER

- How much time do you spend fighting flesh and blood?
- How could you get a better understanding of who the real enemy is in your house?
- How are you seeking God to grow in victories?

ALWAYS PRAY

And pray in the Spirit on all occasions with all kinds of prayers and requests. With this in mind, be alert and always keep on praying for all the Lord's people.   Ephesians 6:18

As you read Ephesians 6:18, you can see it's all about attentiveness. It's important that you are continually aware of what is going on in your family and to pray about everything.

What a privilege that we have to pray to God on behalf of our children and family knowing that he hears and answers our prayers. That should encourage us even more to offer prayer to God. Be grateful for the freedom God gives us to pray with assurance and that no prayer is ever wrong. However we pray, whenever we pray or why we pray doesn't matter to God—he loves it all!

When possible, pray specifically for the needs of your family. You can pray for your children's health and strength, their future calling, their friendships, their future mate as well as for their protection and provision. Pray too, for your parenting skills.

You can't go wrong with prayer. Simply pray and seek God's face. Do it when you are driving. Do it when you are showering. Do it when you are resting. You get the point—pray! ✤

PARENTING PRINCIPLE

Never stop praying for your family!

POINTS TO PONDER

- What are some of your regular prayer practices?
- How can you focus better on prayer?
- What have you taught your children about prayer?

day302 october 29

A LEGACY

Whatever happens, conduct yourselves in a manner worthy of the gospel of Christ.

PHILIPPIANS 1:27

Teaching your children to handle every situation in a manner that honors Christ is quite noble. Most times we haven't done it that way ourselves. And therein lies the best instruction we can give.

We will fail and they will fail. We will act selfishly sometimes and they will too, but if we also work hard to live a life that is honoring to Christ, then our children will also seek to emulate that behavior. It will help our children understand how their lives have a greater purpose than just fulfilling their own needs.

As a benchmark for how we are to live, we are called to compare to Christ. He is worthy of our worship and imitation because in everything he faced, whether persecution or triumph, he conducted himself in a heavenly way. Our goal should be to live heavenly in our homes.

Every Christian believes they're going to heaven. Let's seek then to make our home a picture of heaven by the way we conduct ourselves. You may not see all the benefits of your work in your lifetime, but you will have left a legacy of Christ in your family. ❖

PARENTING PRINCIPLE

Whatever you face you can face with certainty in Christ!

POINTS TO PONDER

- What have you done to model Christ in every situation?
- How are you growing in this conduct?
- How are your children growing in this?

TEACH HUMILITY

Do nothing out of selfish ambition or vain conceit. Rather, in humility value others above yourselves, not looking to your own interests but each of you to the interests of the others.
PHILIPPIANS 2:3–4

If you've ever met a person who thinks mostly of themselves and considers themselves more highly than others, then you have experienced someone who is vain. Do you remember what you thought about that person? Were your children exposed to that vain attitude?

Most likely that experience was not pleasant. That's why it's important that we raise our children from another perspective, one that involves seeing others more important than ourselves. It's a lifelong lesson that you will have to be diligent about teaching through constantly looking to the interests of others. It will be challenging with children at different stages of growth. While one child may understand and seek to be a servant, another might see it as an opportunity to take advantage of a sibling. You will need to adapt your lessons based on each child's unique personality to help them develop selflessness and lack of conceit.

When we think we have become somebody, we have—nobody! Helping your children grow and mature in self-assurance without self-conceit is a task parents cannot take lightly. ✤

PARENTING PRINCIPLE

Vain is pain with no gain.

POINTS TO PONDER

- What is the difference between confidence and conceit?
- When have you dealt with vanity in your life?
- How will you build confidence in your children but not conceit?

day304

october 31

REPLACE GRUMBLING

Do everything without grumbling or arguing, so that you may become blameless and pure, children of God without fault in a warped and crooked generation.

PHILIPPIANS 2:14–15

Children love to complain, grumble and argue. If you have parented for any length of time, you have seen it. It can drive you crazy.

Part of our role is to help them see that it is detrimental to their life. They probably won't see it until they are older, but don't let it deter you from correcting it. If we seek to parent that way without grumbling and complaining, while correcting these behaviors in our children, we will be ridiculously like Jesus. However, it's much more likely that our grumbling will need correcting along the way.

If we can remain committed and faithful to the task of teaching this to our children, we will set an example of what God calls a warped and crooked society. When we understand our purpose is much higher than what we sometimes see, it will motivate us to reach that next level. God's blessing and grace will be upon you as you seek to honor him with your own blameless and pure motives and desires. ❖

PARENTING PRINCIPLE

When we replace grumbling and complaining with purity and blamelessness we have accomplished a great task!

POINTS TO PONDER

- What is the thing that causes you to argue?
- How are you seeking to grow in this area?
- Where do you lack consistency in correcting your children's grumbling and arguing?

day305

TWINKLE, TWINKLE

Then you will shine among them like stars in the sky as you hold firmly to the word of life.
PHILIPPIANS 2:15 – 16

Most parents dream that their children will shine like stars. Chapter two of Philippians is all about the reflection of Christ's example in humility and servanthood. The end result is a "shining" moment when Christ became the savior of the world because of his willingness to die to self.

If we want our children to shine like stars, it won't happen because they make the final cut in American Idol. It won't be because they're the best player on the soccer team or the brightest student in school.

It will come from helping them live a deep life in Christ and helping them see the difference between God's idea of stardom and our society's definition of it.

It's easy to get caught up in man-made stardom because of the world we live in. But when you see yourself falling into that trap, own it, and then get back to the business of raising your children for the sole purpose of honoring Christ. In other words, help them shine like stars! ✣

PARENTING PRINCIPLE

When you shine like a star in God's kingdom, the light is more radiant.

POINTS TO PONDER

- How can you train your children to be stars for Christ?
- What examples can you use to show them the difference between God's stars and man's?
- How are you fooled by earthly stardom?

LOSS IS GAIN

What is more, I consider everything a loss because of the surpassing worth of knowing Christ Jesus my Lord, for whose sake I have lost all things.   PHILIPPIANS 3:8

Paul, the author of Philippians, obviously reached a place and depth in Christ that few of us will ever attain. However, from that depth, his teaching has shown us something about what it means to be completely and utterly surrendered to God. Paul says that in that place you will consider everything you have endured, ever known or ever accomplished and none of it will compare to what you will discover in the most intimate relationship with Jesus Christ.

Through this journey of parenting, you will lose time, money, sleep and a piece of your heart, but in the end most parents will say it's all been worth it.

Though most of us won't even come close to fully understanding Paul's depth and knowledge of Christ, we should be inspired to try. We should seek God in everything and work to deepen our spiritual maturity. This is an area where Paul went long and deep. Most of us prefer the short and out patterns, but if we want to know God intimately, we must go long and deep. ✤

PARENTING PRINCIPLE

What looks like loss is most likely gain!

POINTS TO PONDER

- What have you lost for the sake of Christ?
- How have you learned from your losses?
- How can you help your children grasp this verse?

THE PRIZE

Forgetting what is behind and straining toward what is ahead, I press on toward the goal to win the prize for which God has called me heavenward in Christ Jesus.

PHILIPPIANS 3:13 – 14

A key ingredient to a healthy family is this — forgetting what is behind. Let go of some of the stressful situations that have occurred in your family and strain toward what is ahead. It won't also be easy, but it's usually best. Be committed to the future and do not let the past define your family. Naturally, there are consequences for past decisions, but don't let these consequences keep you from letting God use whatever your family has faced as a light for him in the days ahead.

Remember we are pressing on toward the prize of heaven. Your children will love that image because they love prizes. If you can help them see how they win in the end, it will be a great motivating force to drive them.

The old adage that everyone wants to go to heaven but nobody wants to die is especially true for children. Just like you, as they age, they will appreciate having the challenge of seeing heaven as a wonderful place. It will continually look better and better! ✤

PARENTING PRINCIPLE

Heaven is not behind us — it's ahead!

POINTS TO PONDER

- How have you learned to forget the past and move on?
- How do you press on toward the prize?
- How can you help your children understand that heaven is a prize?

DON'T FRET

Do not be anxious about anything, but in every situation, by prayer and petition, with thanksgiving, present your requests to God.   PHILIPPIANS 4:6

You will have anxious parenting moments. It seems absurd to tell parents not to be anxious because it seems impossible, but that's what God is telling us to do.

It is good to practice responding to situations immediately with prayer instead of anxiety. When your child is running a 105° temperature, pray, don't panic. When your child continues to do poorly in a class, pray and seek help, don't lose sleep. When you can't find your teen—pray!

If prayer becomes your default in anxious moments, you will benefit. If you trust God with all you do as a parent and rely on him in a crisis, it will help you to continue to grow. Philippians 4:6 also suggests that we keep a spirit of thanksgiving instead of anxiety. Be mindful that you have God to turn to and be thankful. What if we were all we had? How helpless and painful life would be—as well as hopeless!

However, by prayer and petition, we have hope as we cast our anxiety on Christ. He will help lift our burdens and carry us when we can't sustain ourselves! ✣

PARENTING PRINCIPLE

If you are anxious you're probably not praying!

POINTS TO PONDER

- What is your default—anxiety or prayer?
- What can you give thanks to God for even in the anxious moments?
- How are you growing in trusting God more?

IN HIS STRENGTH

I can do all this through him who gives me strength. PHILIPPIANS 4:13

There is a gentleman named Eric who can balance just about anything on his chin. It is an incredible thing to see. He starts with a golf club and places it on the tip of his chin and balances it while he walks around. Then he moves up in degrees of difficulty by balancing a chair on his chin. Next he hoists a sofa, which weighs more than you can imagine, on his chin and then lastly he balances a full canoe in the same spot.

Eric's stunts are a great demonstration of doing all things through Christ. The little things seem possible, but when we get to the gigantic stuff that "all things" begins to feel a bit absurd. However, just as you might be skeptical whether Eric can balance a canoe on his chin, you also might not believe we really can do all things through Christ. Parenting will bring some "I can't do it" moments. Christ reminds us often that he is capable of everything. Maybe not the way we see it, but when we see life through his perspective, all things become possible because of him, not us. Celebrate victory through Christ! ✤

PARENTING PRINCIPLE

When he says all things, he means all things in his strength.

POINTS TO PONDER

- Where do you find your strength?
- When do you have weak faith trusting Christ to give you strength?
- What do you need strength for today?

A HEAVENLY PERSPECTIVE

God will meet all your needs according to the riches of his glory in Christ Jesus.

PHILIPPIANS 4:19

Philippians 4:19 should be comforting for parents as it conveys that you can handle anything that comes at you because God is there to meet all your needs. It doesn't say there won't be trials, but that he will help you manage whatever challenges you encounter.

He will do so according to his riches in glory. In other words, you will have a heavenly perspective on earthly issues if you trust in Christ. He understands everything you're involved in. He actually sees it at a deeper level because he created everyone who is involved. He knows the personality quirks. He knows the way you cope. He has the staying power, through his grace and mercy, to keep you going.

Don't let difficulties put a damper on parenting. It's a great and awesome privilege that compares to none. Most times, it will bring you incredible joy, and when it doesn't, always know you have a mighty God to rely on. He watches over all you do as a parent of his children. ❖

PARENTING PRINCIPLE

God will meet all of your needs, even those you don't realize you have.

POINTS TO PONDER

- What need could Christ help you with today?
- How do you lay these needs before Him?
- How are you teaching your children to go to God?

HE HOLDS THINGS TOGETHER

He is before all things, and in him all things hold together. COLOSSIANS 1:17

What ultimately holds a family together? The obvious things like time together, love, patience and kindness come to mind, but the real super glue that helps a family stick together is by loving and believing in Jesus Christ.

Look around. There are families falling apart everywhere. There are neighborhoods disbanding because of divorce and the residual effects from it. That in turn is causing communities and countries to suffer.

And the one thing that would help in holding people together is Jesus Christ. It sounds simplistic, but he is where we can find hope and healing. If your family can maintain their integrity to the cause of Christ, then your family has great potential to make a difference for Christ. If other families are inspired by your example, then family by family we can turn the tide — start a revolution if you will for Christ!

He is before all things, in all things and after all things. As parents we can find great comfort in Colossians 1:17 because it gives us the confidence to teach our children what we believe about Christ. We can remain faithful because the one we look to is faithful! ❖

PARENTING PRINCIPLE

He holds you when you can't hold things together!

POINTS TO PONDER

- How does Christ hold you together?
- How is he helping you hold your children together?
- Where do you need to recognize his holding strength?

day312

HIT THE TARGET

Continue to live your lives in him, rooted and built up in him, strengthened in the faith as you were taught, and overflowing with thankfulness.   Colossians 2:6–7

As parents, we can leave a lasting legacy for our children if we live as Paul suggests in Colossians 2:6–7. Our goal, however, should be to reach far beyond the day-to-day issues that arise with our children and look at the big picture so we can see our lives from an eternal view.

Our target should be to introduce our children to the Bible and pray they will be built up by his Word. We must show our children faith, not simply through our words, but in our actions. Lastly, we need to model gratefulness by speaking thanksgiving over everything in our life, no matter how small.

Most of us would love to see this happen while our children are growing up in our home, and it can to some extent, but we know it takes years to learn the lessons of Christ. It is a patient parent who understands this and daily toils to fulfill the mission God has called them to. ✤

PARENTING PRINCIPLE

Once the target is set, you know where you're trying to get.

POINTS TO PONDER

- What have you done to keep your eye on the goal of this verse?
- How have you seen your family grow in Christ?
- How do you keep a spirit of thankfulness in your home?

TASTE AND SEE

See to it that no one takes you captive through hollow and deceptive philosophy, which depends on human tradition and the elemental spiritual forces of this world rather than on Christ.
COLOSSIANS 2:8

As parents, we must first guard ourselves against the deceptive forces of this world and then we must guard our children. This protection doesn't mean never allowing them to see the evil of the world, because that can backfire. Instead, we must seek Christ for wisdom on how to let them be in the world, but not of the world.

Some children will be more prone to want to taste and see that the Lord is good while others are eager to taste and see if the world is good. Their choice will become more obvious as they enter the teen years.

If they hunger for the world, make sure you stay involved and guide them because of the captivity of hollow and deceptive philosophies. You will need to pray fervently for you and your children, and then stay faithful and trust that the Biblical foundation you laid will ultimately touch their heart and soul. ❧

PARENTING PRINCIPLE

Feed your children Biblical principles and they will hopefully hunger for the Lord.

POINTS TO PONDER

- When has your family been deceived by any hollow philosophies?
- What are you doing to keep Christ at the forefront?
- How can you pray for protection from these philosophies?

HE HAS OVERCOME

And having disarmed the powers and authorities, he made a public spectacle of them, triumphing over them by the cross. Colossians 2:15

Great news! Christ has won the battle over all the issues that we might have as a family. Whatever it is that hurts your relationship with your children, Christ has already overcome. That is where we put our hope! He did so by triumphing over death through the cross. In him we have and hold victory.

Victory will not always look like we won. We need to help our children come to grips with understanding what this means. They will need the power of the cross to overcome some of the difficult situations they will encounter. We will want them to understand that only Jesus has the ability to disarm the power and authorities of this world.

Teach your children how to grow in the Lord daily and spend time with Christ on their own so they can uncover his power for themselves. The ultimate goal is that our children will discover the discernment and wisdom that we have gained over the years. Pray they will see it in us and then find it themselves. ❖

PARENTING PRINCIPLE

We are not the final authority—he is!

POINTS TO PONDER

- How has Christ triumphed over circumstances in your life?
- How are you helping your children discover his power?
- What is one step you can take to help your children grow in Christ?

GET CONTROL

Learn to control your own body in a way that is holy and honorable.

1 Thessalonians 4:4

We need to teach our children to honor their bodies by showing them how to make good, healthy behavioral choices. Educate them on how to eat well and exercise regularly and how to live in moderation. We can teach discipline by modeling discipline. If addictions or behaviors rule our lives, we won't be able to fully submit to Christ as ruler.

This will become important when our children want to indulge in bad behaviors and then justify the need for it. Certainly hormonal changes and clinical issues can affect our children and their bodies, but even then we need to seek help and give them the resources and tools that help them remain in control.

Many of the issues our children face will be selfish acts of their own choosing. They must be held responsible for those behaviors in order to learn about control. They won't change immediately, but hopefully over time. Give your children the opportunity to grow! It may produce pain at times, but from the pain you will see gain as they learn to maintain control. ❖

PARENTING PRINCIPLE

If you don't control your body, your body will control you.

POINTS TO PONDER

- How do you exercise good control over your body?
- What is an area of struggle for you with your body?
- What examples of good choices are you showing your children?

QUIET AMBITION

And to make it your ambition to lead a quiet life: You should mind your own business and work with your hands, just as we told you.   1 THESSALONIANS 4:11

God created us with the desire to provide for ourselves and not depend completely on others to meet our basic human needs. Certainly there are times we may need help, but the goal is to learn how to care for ourselves through the strength of Christ. That's not always easy because it seems to be in opposition to what our society practices.

Knowing this, we must seek to teach these skills to our children by giving them responsibilities and helping them cultivate ambition that will contribute to society and glorify God. As they begin to influence others in their life, these principles can take hold and help them make a difference in this life. They should be mindful of the world around them, but mind their own business and quietly do the work for which they have been called.

Based on how we do family life, they will either understand the concept and make a difference in the world or fail to see it and add to the increasing problems around us. ❖

PARENTING PRINCIPLE

Busy people are generally happy people, but busybodies don't get much work done.

POINTS TO PONDER

- What are your family ambitions?
- What are your personal ambitions?
- How can you help your children develop ambition?

day317

IT'S NOT OVER

For you know very well that the day of the Lord will come like a thief in the night.

1 THESSALONIANS 5:2

Nobody spends a lot of time discussing the promise that Jesus Christ will return one day.

Scripture reminds us that this day should not surprise us. That's why we need to be prepared. Sadly, many Christians view that preparation as storing up and shelving things away instead of eagerly anticipating with joy what Christ has in store for us all.

It's important that our children know that this time is coming. It should not be taught to induce fear but to help them realize God's plan for the earth. Don't be surprised if this day initially seems like a disappointment to them. They are young and will want to focus on all the life they have yet to live. So make sure your children understand it in an age-appropriate way.

Your children can be joyous about today and their days ahead but they can also eagerly look forward to the day Christ returns. His return is beyond anything they will ever experience in their greatest moment of joy on earth! ✤

PARENTING PRINCIPLE

Joy comes from knowing it's not over at the end of time.

POINTS TO PONDER

- How have you prepared yourself for Christ's return?
- How do you help your children prepare in a healthy way?
- What examples can you use to describe how much better heaven will be?

A GOOD RESPONSE

Make sure that nobody pays back wrong for wrong, but always strive to do what is good for each other and for everyone else.   1 THESSALONIANS 5:15

Paybacks and family life seem to be intertwined. When we are wronged, we wrong back, which often leads to prolonged family problems.

If you want to start a new trend in your family, then it must start with you as parents. If you have been mistreated by a family member, you need to show your children how you can forgive and not seek to avenge that behavior. It's natural to want to, but with Christ you don't need to. You may be the first in your family to do it Christ's way, and it will be well worth it.

Try taking a step to show love where you have previously shown hate. It might be the reconciling factor for the generations yet to be born. Use wisdom in your choices and make sure you operate within safe boundaries.

Our goal as parents is to make sure we don't pass on to our children examples of wrong doing but examples of doing things right with Christ. If we teach them one way but do the opposite, we teach them hypocrisy! Nobody wants to follow a hypocrite. ❖

PARENTING PRINCIPLE

Hypocrites are not family fit!

POINTS TO PONDER

- When have you been guilty of wrong for wrong?
- What can you do to change this?
- How would this change benefit your children?

NOBODY'S PERFECT

May your whole spirit, soul, and body be kept blameless at the coming of our Lord Jesus.

1 THESSALONIANS 5:23

What a prayer for our children—especially in a world that will fill them with flaws and discouragement that may cause them to fall.

Through it all we need to pray that they will be kept blameless. When our time on earth comes to an end, the question won't be regarding our perfection because we already know the answer. The real question is, were we blameless? In other words, have we been forgiven for the things we have done to others and have we forgiven those who have done things to us?

There will be situations when our children are at fault. Use those opportunities to teach them how to be blameless even when they are to blame. We don't get to choose if our children lead a blameless life, but we can pray that they will and that the Lord will give them guidance.

We can live the example of blameless for them and then watch them pursue it on their own. That's when parenting moves from hands on to hands off with special emphasis placed on the off. ❖

PARENTING PRINCIPLE

Blameless is another word for beautiful!

POINTS TO PONDER

- Where have you not been blameless that you need to seek forgiveness?
- What can you do to protect your body, soul and spirit?
- How can you continue to grow and help your children in this area?

PASS IT ON

So then, brothers and sisters, stand firm and hold fast to the teachings we passed on to you.
2 Thessalonians 2:15

Think of all the teachings that your parents and grandparents passed onto you. Have you captured many of these teachings in your heart and have they become a big part of who you are? Are they based on God's Word or are they merely life experiences?

Your children are now formulating their own belief system and the teachings you share could be something they hold onto for a lifetime. Are you teaching eternal principles? Are they based on God's Word? It's worth evaluating regularly and then making changes if needed to ensure you are faithful in sharing Biblical truths.

In 2 Thessalonians 2:15, Paul is reminding the Thessalonians of their forefathers and their forthcoming. It is good to keep our place in perspective at times. We will live this period of our heritage. Our forefathers have passed truths onto us and now we get to pass them on to our children and forthcoming grandchildren.

Be diligent at the task. Keep all your priorities in order and stand firm yourself. You will be referred to with pride in the years to come! ❖

PARENTING PRINCIPLE

Stand firm and hold fast and your principles will last.

POINTS TO PONDER

- What teachings do you appreciate from your heritage?
- What Biblical principles are you passing along?
- How do you see your children beginning to understand these principles?

THE REAL WORLD

And pray that we may be delivered from wicked and evil people, for not everyone has faith.   2 THESSALONIANS 3:2

When children are little they think everyone is like their parents. It's called innocence.

Over time, children will see the reality of this world outside of their home and will quickly surmise that not everyone is like their parents and not everyone has faith. It's why we want to protect them from the world. Of course that's not only impossible, it's unwise.

Parents who have isolated their children soon regret it because when those children discover the outside world, it often overwhelms them and they quickly lose their innocence. The reality is that the more you can help your children understand the wickedness around them, the wiser they will be.

Teach your children that not everyone believes in Christ and that wickedness and evil people do exist. Help them understand that it won't always be easy when good and evil collide, but their faith in action can make a positive difference in those situations. Make sure they believe their faith will carry them through all situations. ✤

PARENTING PRINCIPLE

The less you protect your children from the world, the more insight they'll gain about the world.

POINTS TO PONDER

- What are safe ways you can introduce your children to the real world?
- How have you helped your children recognize good and evil?
- How do you help your children understand that faith is a personal choice?

CHANGE IN DIRECTION

May the Lord direct your hearts into God's love and Christ's perseverance.

2 THESSALONIANS 3:5

While our children are young, we are responsible to direct their hearts. We usually pray for Christ to give us wisdom with this direction. But as our children become adults, we must step back and release that direction to them. Then our prayer becomes for the Lord to direct their hearts.

Just like when we were young and ready to embark on the world, we couldn't see all that life had in store for us. We dealt with many unexpected challenges. Our children can't see everything ahead either, and they will no doubt face various trials. They will need the perseverance of Christ to get them through. Hopefully, they will call on God's strength just like we taught them when they were little.

As we watch them navigate life, our commitment to prayer will be our greatest gift to them. While we can physically help them at times and speak encouragement into their lives, the most supreme effort we can make is to continue to pray! Meditate on 2 Thessalonians 3:5 in seeking God's care over your adult children. ✤

PARENTING PRINCIPLE

When you let your children go, let them go bathed in prayer.

POINTS TO PONDER

- How are you preparing to let your children go?
- How can you share the benefits of prayer with them?
- What other Scripture can you find to pray over your children?

THE POWER OF HIS NAME

Here is a trustworthy saying that deserves full acceptance: Christ Jesus came into the world to save sinners—of whom I am the worst.　　　　　　1 TIMOTHY 1:15

If Paul was able to call himself the worst sinner, then we need to look at our deficiencies outside of Christ. Paul's point here was to simply acknowledge the importance of knowing Christ and making him a priority in his life.

Our children need to understand that their value won't be completely realized until they fully know their place in the kingdom of God. As a Christian, our life is eternal. Therefore we don't live to focus on what is accomplished in this life. Parents must be careful to maintain a balance between celebrating their children's accomplishments in life without letting those accomplishments define their life.

We must help our children understand that we deserve nothing we have and nothing we achieve comes close to what Christ did for us in saving our lives. No matter what our accomplishments, our family lineage, or our name, we are the worst when compared to Christ's supremacy. This is not about condemnation but about recognizing the power of his name. ❖

PARENTING PRINCIPLE

Recognizing our worst compared to Christ will bring out our best.

POINTS TO PONDER

- How do you view your unworthiness in Christ?
- Why are you grateful for his salvation?
- How will you explain to your children about recognizing their worth without Christ?

day**324**

THE ONLY WAY

There is one God and one mediator between God and mankind, the man Christ Jesus.
                                                              1 TIMOTHY 2:5

God's Word makes it clear that there is one way to heaven. First Timothy 2:5 is crystal clear and an important Biblical truth to teach to our children.

In a society that continues to seek new ways to heaven, the simple truth is that Jesus is the only way. He is the one who paid the price for our sins. We must believe this truth or not. There is no middle ground.

Our beliefs will continually be challenged by an onslaught of theories and faiths that disagree that Jesus is the only way. Your children will wrestle with this concept at some point too in their development. That's why it's important to have 1 Timothy 2:5 grounded in their life. You might be called narrow-minded or judged for your belief, but hold steadfast. If your children have doubts, be open to listen to their point of view, but keep using God's Word to back up your beliefs.

God will reward you as you faithfully continue to proclaim the name of Jesus Christ as the one and only mediator. ✤

PARENTING PRINCIPLE

Don't back down, just back up your beliefs with the Word of God.

POINTS TO PONDER

- Why do you believe Jesus is the one and only mediator?
- Why is this hard for "the world" to believe?
- How are you teaching this concept to your children?

EXERCISE FAITH

For physical training is of some value, but godliness has value for all things, holding promise for both the present life and the life to come.   I TIMOTHY 4:8

It's important to teach our children how to take care of their bodies. This not only includes healthy eating, but helping them understand the importance of exercise in relation to stronger bodies. All of this is of some value. At least that's what the Word of God calls it—of some value.

We all know people who become obsessed with exercise, but there is only one area we should obsess about and that's growing in godliness. That's healthy! The reason is because it helps us in this life and the life to come. It has eternal significance. Our nature is to invest and indulge in the things that are temporal because that's what everyone else is doing, which makes it seem normal.

God calls us to recognize a not-so-normal standard for us and our children. We need to see our children as eternal beings and then we will be all the more inclined to keep this world and the world to come in proper balance. ✤

PARENTING PRINCIPLE

Make sure that your workout plan includes exercising your faith.

POINTS TO PONDER

- Do you or your family have any unhealthy obsessions?
- How are you balancing this present life versus the eternal?
- How do you help your family grow spiritually?

SET THE EXAMPLE

Don't let anyone look down on you because you are young, but set an example for the believers in speech, in conduct, in love, in faith, and in purity.   1 TIMOTHY 4:12

Let your children know that they don't have to wait until they are older to be an example to others. Don't discount their abilities or wisdom just because they are young.

Consider the areas of speech and conduct. They can be taught to resist the urge to speak in the same language as the culture around them. When they do, they will stand out and shine like a star for Christ. They can act in a way that is different from their peers so that even adults will take notice of and be inspired. Many times our children are capable of more than we realize.

First Timothy 4:12 also calls for youth to set an example in the areas of love, faith and purity. If our children can grasp this truth when they are young, they will make an even greater impact for Christ. God will do amazing things through their life, and our own families will be enhanced by their godliness. ❖

PARENTING PRINCIPLE

The examples set by young people can make an even greater impact because of their age.

POINTS TO PONDER

- Why is this a hard concept for adults to grasp?
- How can you explain this concept to your children?
- In what areas of your children's lives can you start implementing this concept?

FAMILY MATTERS

But if a widow has children or grandchildren, these should learn first of all to put their religion into practice by caring for their own family and so repaying their parents and grandparents, for this is pleasing to God.   I TIMOTHY 5:4

We learn from 1 Timothy 5:4 that God expects us to care for our parents and grandparents because they have cared for us. This way of family life is often mocked by our society, but we need to recognize it has value. It's not surprising that God's plan for the family is very functional. Nobody does it perfectly, but God is pleased when we seek to honor him and his Word because therein lies great wisdom.

When you teach your children the meaning of this Scripture, help them to understand that you aren't sharing it for the sake of sharing, but because you believe what you are passing on has eternal implications. What was written 2,000 years ago is still relevant for today, and it will be 2,000 years from now.

God is good all the time. His patterns for living are designed to encourage your family. Seek his ways and your family will be blessed. ✤

PARENTING PRINCIPLE

Show care and respect for your parents and it is likely your children will care for you.

POINTS TO PONDER

- How have you cared for your parents?
- What are you teaching your children by your example?
- What more might you be able to do for your parents?

day**328**

SEEK CONTENTMENT

But godliness with contentment is great gain. For we brought nothing into the world, and we can take nothing out of it.   1 TIMOTHY 6:6–7

There's a reason God wants us to be content with what we have. A day is coming when we will leave taking nothing with us, just as we came with nothing!

When our children see us living with this mindset, they will gain a greater respect for us and for the eternal. If you have learned to be content, be patient as your children grow in their contentment. It does not come naturally. Remember, you are more mature. While you are releasing the things you have attained, they are in the gathering stages.

If you get frustrated by their lack of contentment then you are forgetting what it's like to be their age. You may also realize that the older you get as a parent, the more frustrated you can become with your children's selfishness. You will need to learn to extend that patience to the last child as you did with the first.

It will require extra focus to stay content especially when those around you aren't there yet! ✤

PARENTING PRINCIPLE

I can take my children only as far as I have gone!

POINTS TO PONDER

- What examples of contentment and godliness are you setting?
- What signs of contentment have you seen in your children?
- How could you help them more in their journey?

THE VALUE OF MONEY

For the love of money is a root of all kinds of evil.   1 TIMOTHY 6:10

A little boy was heard talking to his dad about money and how it can cause someone trouble. The dad said, "Son, money is the root of all evil." The six year old boy replied, "Yes, dad, and man needs roots." Humorous, yet true. We have to balance the fact that we need money without letting money cause us to stumble and crash.

In order to teach your children how to manage money properly you will need to understand their personality and watch how they handle their money. One child will let it burn a hole in their pocket while another child will pinch it too tightly. Both ways can be detrimental and lead to some unhealthy behaviors.

Talk with your children early on about some basic budgeting principles. It will help them greatly when they get their first paycheck. A simple idea to encourage their frugality is to put a dollar in their savings account for every penny they find and save. Those little things teach the value of a dollar and will guide them into financial freedom in the future! ✤

PARENTING PRINCIPLE

Teach your children that money isn't evil, but the way we use it can be.

POINTS TO PONDER

- What trouble has money ever caused you or your family?
- Who has modeled good money management skills for you?
- What age-appropriate budgeting techniques can you teach your children?

COUNT THE BLESSINGS

Command those who are rich in this present world not to be arrogant nor to put their hope in wealth, which is so uncertain, but to put their hope in God, who richly provides us with everything for our enjoyment.   1 Timothy 6:17

God wants us to enjoy life. This will come from putting our hope in him and not wealth, which is fleeting. Certainly there are times when the burden of parenting and the overwhelming nature of life prevent us from the enjoyment that should be common in our family.

That's why you need to take time today to reflect on all the blessings God has given you. Many of us are in a place of little or no need. We have people around us who love us. We have a good place to live and food on the table. Our children may not be perfect, but we have a good relationship with them. We can get together and celebrate with our family.

Your children will be more joyful if they see you enjoying life. If you set a positive tone in your home, it will flow throughout. Change your focus if you need to and live to enjoy the things God has already given you. ✤

PARENTING PRINCIPLE

If you enjoy today, it won't slip away.

POINTS TO PONDER

- How do you enjoy your life?
- How can you find joy when you are facing tough circumstances?
- In what ways do you enjoy your children?

GOD POWER

The Spirit God gave us does not make us timid, but gives us power, love and self-discipline.
2 TIMOTHY 1:7

Some children are more timid than others. This is not a negative trait. In fact, as a parent there will be times that you will appreciate that spirit. It can make the home more peaceful.

Children who are more timid and sensitive need to know that their faith and witness for Christ can still be bold and powerful because of the love and discipline found through Christ. He has saved us and called us to his holiness—not because of our personality, but because of what he can do through our personality.

In our boisterous society, a child with a timid personality can often feel like they don't measure up. People may even assure them that someday they'll come out of their shell, as though their personality isn't good enough. That can be discouraging.

Help these children know that they are enough in God's eyes because he created them that way. They don't have to be a type-A personality to make a difference for Christ. It's a wise parent who helps each child to appreciate their own unique personality! ✤

PARENTING PRINCIPLE

It's not who you are, it's whose you are!

POINTS TO PONDER

- What various personalities live in your home?
- How do you appreciate personalities unlike your own?
- How can you help your timid child see how they can be bold and powerful for Christ?

SOUND TEACHING

What you heard from me, keep as the pattern of sound teaching, with faith and love in Christ Jesus. 2 TIMOTHY 1:13

Paul wrote this verse in a letter to Timothy, but what a beautiful Scripture for parents to reflect on in regard to their children.

Our goal as parents should be to live and teach the things of God that are sound. Things that will stand the test of time. Occasionally, however, we may fail to teach anything and end up saying things out of frustration with life or with our children.

Unfortunately, it's those words our children seem to remember the longest and will sometimes hold against us when they get older. You might be clinging to something hurtful right now that your parents said many years ago. It might be adversely affecting your parenting.

In order for you to develop a good pattern of sound teaching, you may need to begin by taking steps to forgive your parents. Then seek forgiveness from your children for any offenses you made against them.

Our sound teaching will be a strong influence for our children as it aligns with our faith and love in Jesus Christ! ❖

PARENTING PRINCIPLE

Sound teaching is pleasant to hear and nothing to fear.

POINTS TO PONDER

- How were you affected by your parents' teaching?
- What patterns of teaching have you established with your children?
- Where can you improve in your teaching patterns?

GOD'S ARMY

Join with me in suffering, like a good soldier of Christ Jesus. 2 TIMOTHY 2:3

To ask our children to join us in a life of suffering can seem morbid. However, when we put it into proper perspective, with all the saints who have gone before us, it can become very clear.

As Christian parents, we need to understand that our lives and those of our children could be adversely affected by our walk in faith. Think about the martyrs of faith and recognize the price they paid to impact the world for Christ. Consider that most of the Bible stories you read to your children have a character who suffered for Christ.

These stories aren't over and done. The Christian life is on a continuum, and our children are part of that continuum. We must be extremely open about our willingness to suffer if necessary for our faith. We might be called to endure ridicule, mental hardship or adverse health issues that lead to suffering.

In our suffering, we are called to be good soldiers of Christ's humility and grace. It's not pleasant to think of these worst-case scenarios for our family, but we must prepare ourselves and our children for suffering. ❖

PARENTING PRINCIPLE

Suffering is never easy but it will bring glory to God.

POINTS TO PONDER

- How have you suffered?
- How have you handled your suffering?
- What are you doing to help your children view suffering as an opportunity to honor Christ?

A MATTER OF RULES

Similarly, anyone who competes as an athlete does not receive the victor's crown except by competing according to the rules. 2 TIMOTHY 2:5

Even though we know it's right, sometimes we don't like to play by the rules. Consider if basketball players didn't play by the rules. What if they could carry the ball, run out of bounds and shove other players down but never be called for a foul. The integrity of the game would be lost. People would stop playing, and the game would be done.

The same is true in our family life with our children. We can't let them do whatever they want. Our home would quickly be overrun by out-of-control children and the family's integrity would suffer. Of course children will sometimes challenge the rules and do their own thing, but they will soon learn that the rules are for their benefit. People generally operate best within boundaries.

Be faithful in continuing to establish rules and guidelines in your home. They will help you when the game gets out of control. If you allow a child to do whatever they want, it can potentially upset the balance of the family.

Children will actually find freedom when they abide by the rules. ✤

PARENTING PRINCIPLE

A good balance of rules is a great parenting tool!

POINTS TO PONDER

- What are your family rules?
- How are your children at understanding and respecting the rules?
- How are you helping them with this?

VALUE WORDS

Keep reminding God's people of these things. Warn them before God against quarreling about words; it is of no value, and only ruins those who listen.   2 TIMOTHY 2:14

Have you ever been in an argument with someone in your family and you knew it was pointless to continue talking but you couldn't quite shut your mouth? Do you remember how you then started arguing about what words each other had said and how that became another argument? Do you know what that is called? Pointless! And it happens in family life!

In order to stop this, set goals in your family of knowing when to stop talking. Try to put an end to pointless arguments and quarreling. If it's your tendency to talk too much, recognize this weakness and seek help. Let someone hold you accountable to change this behavior.

If you have a child who tends to quarrel easily, try removing them from the person they're quarreling with and invoke a cool-down period. Usually after a break, a child can be reasonable again and continue their conversation peacefully. Eliminating wasted words will bring more peace to your home. ✤

PARENTING PRINCIPLE

If you are wasting words, you are wasting opportunities for peace.

POINTS TO PONDER

- Who in your family is prone to quarrel?
- How do you know when to stop talking in an argument?
- What steps could you take toward improvement in stopping quarreling?

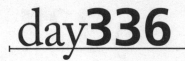# day**336**

SPREAD THE WORD

God's word is not chained.   2 TIMOTHY 2:9

For decades, people have tried everything to suppress God's Word. It has been burned, confiscated, spit on, torn up, shredded, buried and anything else you can imagine. Your children need to be aware of the efforts others will take to eliminate Scripture and subdue it.

Fortunately, nothing has succeeded because the Bible remains one of the best-selling books of all time. It is as alive today as it was when it was first written. No matter what has been or will be tried, God's Word will remain because it lives in our hearts and souls. This is why we need to teach it to our children so they can embed it in their minds. Once it's committed in their minds, it travels to their hearts and souls where it comes alive. It has no chains and no limits!

What a great comfort for us as parents to know that when we pass from this earth, the Lord remains to continually guide our children through God's Word and by the wisdom of the Holy Spirit.

Thank him every day for this great and perpetual unending gift. ✤

PARENTING PRINCIPLE

Be a part of the human chain that links God's Word to the next generation!

POINTS TO PONDER

- What have you seen people try to do to stop God's Word?
- How have you made God's Word come alive to your children?
- In what ways have you shared God's Word with others?

CHATTER THAT MATTERS

Avoid godless chatter, because those who indulge in it will become more and more ungodly.
2 TIMOTHY 2:16

There are television shows based on godless chatter. Just turn to any channel and the evidence is there. It's the norm in our society. Our homes can quickly become just like what we watch and see. In fact, when we don't participate in godless behavior, we actually look like the odd person out.

Don't let that stop you from maintaining your beliefs. Work hard to keep the conversations in your home pleasing to God. Do not let inappropriate discussions in and let it become a squawk house! Hold firm in this area and you will see the benefit as your children become adults. They will come to appreciate the difference they see and feel in your home. It will be a safe home for conversations that don't criticize others.

Our job is to raise godly children so we need to do all we can to eliminate the factors that could destroy that effort. Starting today, set a tone of positive dialogue in your home and let it begin with you. ✣

PARENTING PRINCIPLE

Speak chatter that matters to God and those around you.

POINTS TO PONDER

- What is your weakness in the area of godless chatter?
- How do you correct this behavior in you and your children?
- What can you do to keep your home free from godless chatter?

GROWING PAINS

Flee the evil desires of youth and pursue righteousness, faith, love and peace, along with those who call on the Lord out of a pure heart.   2 TIMOTHY 2:22

As a parent, have you ever considered that evil desires are a normal draw for a child? If not, 2 Timothy 2:22 reminds us that it is. God created us to mature from childhood to adulthood knowing we will develop an independent streak where we will fight for our freedom. It's during this time that we face the evil desires of youth. Our children will likely have the same experience.

Be assured that it is normal for our children to battle through this stage. That's why we must teach them to seek righteousness, faith, love and peace — all things they need but won't seem to want during this transition to adulthood.

God gave 2 Timothy 2:22 to parents as a reminder to stay faithful and never give up prompting your children about what they should pursue. Do it in love, never forgetting your own struggles through that same transition years before. Use your experience to assist and guide them.

Pray for the Lord to bless your children in this time of growth! ♣

PARENTING PRINCIPLE

Your assistance through this transition is more important than their resistance!

POINTS TO PONDER

- How did you transition from teen to adult?
- Where are your children struggling with this transition?
- How could you provide more assistance?

SHARE VERSES

Keep this Book of the Law always on your lips; meditate on it day and night, so that you may be careful to do everything written in it. Then you will be prosperous and successful.

JOSHUA 1:8

If there is anything we can count on in this world, it is that Scripture is all God-breathed. We need to use Scripture when guiding and disciplining our children.

It's a great idea to share Biblical verses with your children all the time. Write a verse on a post-it note and stick it where they'll see it. Text a verse to your children on occasion and remind them of Biblical truth. Select a verse to memorize as a family. Just like us, if your children have these truths in their minds it could make a difference in the middle of a temptation or in a moment when they are sharing their faith. The point is, Scripture is useful in just about everything we do.

It's why the early fathers taught their children by putting Scripture on their foreheads and binding it on their arms. They used little bands to actually clip these godly thoughts to their bodies. Let's learn from history and take God's Word at face value—it matters and it can make a difference in our children's life! ❖

PARENTING PRINCIPLE

If it's God-breathed, it will help you achieve!

POINTS TO PONDER

- How do you memorize Scripture?
- How has Scripture been of value to you?
- How are your children getting Scripture into their life?

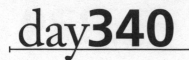

day**340**

STAY THE COURSE

I have fought the good fight, I have finished the race, I have kept the faith.

2 TIMOTHY 4:7

What a testimony to our children if we can live up to 2 Timothy 4:7 and feel confident reciting these words in our final moments.

Make it your goal in life to fight the fight worth fighting. This includes learning to lay aside the distractions that can quickly arise in your family and in life and do all you can for the kingdom of God.

Be sure you finish the race, especially in the area of parenting. Many parents tend to drop out once their kids leave home. But the fight isn't over until our days on earth are done. Some of our most influential moments will occur when our children our adults. It gets tiring, but we need to remain strong for our children to the very end.

Our primary goal should be to know we have kept the faith. To die believing in the very thing we lived for. If we remain faithful, we will enter the presence of God! ✤

PARENTING PRINCIPLE

What a day it will be when it's Jesus we see!

POINTS TO PONDER

- How are you living this verse?
- In what area of parenting do you feel like you might be falling behind in the race?
- What kind of legacy do you want to leave for your children?

PURITY FIRST

To the pure, all things are pure, but to those who are corrupted and do not believe, nothing is pure. In fact, both their minds and consciences are corrupted. TITUS 1:15

We want to be parents with pure minds. If we keep our minds pure, we will be able to have pure thoughts and pure guidance as we instruct our children. If we corrupt our minds we will have a warped and corrupted mind as we work with our children, which will have a detrimental effect on them.

Imagine holding up a dirty glass of water in front of your eyes. Everything you view while you are looking through that glass will be tainted. You can use this illustration to help your children understand why they need to avoid things that are dishonest and help them identify potential areas of immorality they could fall into at their age.

As parents, we are continually faced with temptations that could lead us into corruption. Identify what might be tainted in you today and be faithful to seek God to cleanse and purify your heart and mind! As you do, you will experience a new freedom in parenting those God has given to you! ❖

PARENTING PRINCIPLE

Christ is the cure for keeping things pure.

POINTS TO PONDER

- What in your life has the potential to taint you?
- What are you concerned about that may corrupt your children?
- How are you seeking to stay pure and help your children be pure?

BE A WITNESS

In your teaching show integrity, seriousness and soundness of speech that cannot be condemned, so that those who oppose you may be ashamed because they have nothing bad to say about us. TITUS 2:7–8

When you live with a high degree of integrity you are a witness to everyone. As parents, when we live above reproach because of our integrity in Christ, our children are blessed. We do not do it for them only, but they will receive the benefits of our faithfulness.

Sometimes our children will be the opposition talked about in Titus 2:7–8. They won't always appreciate our ways, but they won't be able to say anything bad about how we are living. In fact, as they grow up they will hopefully be grateful for those character traits. That's why we need to focus on the long-term.

If we live for the short-term applause and our children's gratefulness, we might be disappointed. But over time, our commitment to integrity, seriousness and soundness of speech will be rewarded.

Stay true to your beliefs. Be faithful today and again tomorrow. As the tomorrows pass, you will have done the very thing you desired to do—leave a heritage that's godly! ✤

PARENTING PRINCIPLE

The sound teachings of today will be appreciated in the future tomorrows.

POINTS TO PONDER

- How would you classify your teachings in relation to this verse?
- How do you react to your children's opposition?
- When have your children shown gratefulness for your teachings?

IN HIS AUTHORITY

Remind the people to be subject to rulers and authorities, to be obedient, to be ready to do whatever is good.   TITUS 3:1

What is consistent throughout Scripture and in the way Jesus lived is that he taught people to respect the rule and authority of the land. In his day, there were many things that happened that were against the word of the Lord but people were still called to abide by the law. Although we can certainly work to change a law that is in opposition to our beliefs, we also have to accept that God is allowing that law for a reason.

Jesus was able to teach this because of his authority and his ability to see the bigger picture. Often we get caught up in the moment and fail to really look beyond our own circumstances.

Teach your children how to respect the law of the land even when they don't agree with it. God's Word teaches that no law and no man or woman comes into power without his authority. When we follow the laws, we are doing so out of obedience and respect for God, not necessarily out of agreement. ✤

PARENTING PRINCIPLE

We must follow the laws of man but not necessarily the ways of man.

POINTS TO PONDER

- What laws do you have trouble accepting?
- What can you do to reconcile some of the laws you don't agree with?
- How are you teaching your children to respect these laws?

HANDLE WITH CARE

If your brother or sister sins, go and point out their fault, just between the two of you. If they listen to you, you have won them over. But if they will not listen, take one or two others along, so that "every matter may be established by the testimony of two or three witnesses." If they still refuse to listen, tell it to the church; and if they refuse to listen even to the church, treat them as you would a pagan or a tax collector. MATTHEW 18:15–17

The advice in this verse is very helpful in family situations when you have a family member or extended family member who is regularly hostile and it's beginning to affect the peace in your home.

Simply follow the teachings of this verse. In order to avoid a situation where it's your word against their word, you may find it wise to have a third party involved. Give the decisive person two warnings. If that doesn't produce the desired results and if a third, independent party agrees that you are right, you should remove yourself from further involvement with that individual, at least temporarily.

You can be a great role model for your children of how to handle difficult people that you love. Be thankful Scripture gives us clear instruction for these situations. Be open to the teaching and guidance of Christ in your life through these learning experiences. ❖

PARENTING PRINCIPLE

Don't run from trouble, but don't invite it either!

POINTS TO PONDER

- What challenging people have you had to deal with in your family?
- How did you handle it?
- What did you learn from it that you could teach your children?

TEACH HIS WORD

Only be careful, and watch yourselves closely so that you do not forget the things your eyes have seen or let them fade from your heart as long as you live. Teach them to your children and to their children after them. DEUTERONOMY 4:9

The Old Testament is filled with direction and guidance for parents. Long ago, God established that it is a parent's responsibility to pass along his teachings to the next generation. This is the best way for our children to learn. When we falter in that responsibility, we put our children at risk and leave them exposed to the godless teachings out there.

Our children will become much more tempted to respond to those other teachings if we haven't grounded them in God's Word. Those Bible stories that seem so simple at the time are a way of connecting them to the almighty God of the universe. They need to discover the one true God for themselves, but we must do all we can to make sure they're at a place where he is reachable.

When we remember that God's influence is timeless, we renew our strength and are called to parent with wisdom another day. ❖

PARENTING PRINCIPLE

Insulate your children with God's Word, and those godless teachings may not be heard.

POINTS TO PONDER

- Where have you faltered in teaching God's Word?
- What other teachings have your children been exposed to?
- What has been your response to those teachings?

day346

A DAILY CALL

These commandments that I give you today are to be on your hearts. Impress them on your children. Talk about them when you sit at home and when you walk along the road, when you lie down and when you get up. Tie them as symbols on your hands and bind them on your foreheads. DEUTERONOMY 6:6–9

God's Word calls us to teach our children his principles no matter what we are doing. Deuteronomy 6:6–9 says to impress his love on our children when we are sitting, walking, lying down or talking. We are to tie them, bind them and continuously instill them. What a calling!

God is serious too because he calls us to do it all the time. We are to evaluate our daily lives and make sure that whatever we are doing, we are always looking for the opportunity to make a mark for Christ's sake.

In our homes, we might have words on our walls that represent what our family stands for. These small things will be what our children remember about us. Talking about and living for God daily will influence them in the same way—they will remember. Pass that on to your children and be part of God's big plan to call your family to make a difference for Christ! ✤

PARENTING PRINCIPLE

No matter when or where, teach your children to care about God.

POINTS TO PONDER

- Who taught you about God?
- How did they teach it?
- How are you teaching it?

KEEP THE FAITH

Let us draw near to God with a sincere heart and with the full assurance that faith brings.
HEBREWS 10:22

We all need to continually draw near to God. Life, and especially parenting, will lead us to occasionally feel lonely. There will be times you won't want to talk to anyone about what you are going through. Other times you may be embarrassed by your children and uncertain of yourself. When you might not feel like drawing near to God, this is probably the time when you should.

When we do this, we have the full assurance from God that only faith brings. We can find hope and confidence in the fact that faith can do so much more than we realize. It builds us up and keeps us focused on the task at hand. Faith will not "look" like the answer, but it is!

Whatever makes you feel guilty in your shortcomings as a parent can be wiped clean by faith. You can move forward with a clear conscience — confident that God will be able to do awesome things through your life and the lives of your children. Find comfort and peace in these verses today. ✤

PARENTING PRINCIPLE

Draw nearer to God especially when your desire is to pull away.

POINTS TO PONDER

- How do you draw near to God?
- What comfort have you gotten from drawing near to him?
- What situations keep you from drawing near to God?

DO NOT DECEIVE

If we claim to be without sin, we deceive ourselves and the truth is not in us.   1 JOHN 1:8

Everyone sins. It is part of human nature. When we talk with our children about the sins they may be struggling with, it will help them to know we sin too.

Actually accepting the fact that we are sinful and in need of God's grace is a freeing thought. As Christian parents, if we act like we are perfect and continually point out to our children their sins and faults, they will become very discouraged and begin to hide their sins. Too often this leads Christian children to think they must be the only ones who battle with sin. This creates a lot of guilt in them. That's why it is important to share our own struggles. It can help our children understand the grace of God better, and how he can meet our sinfulness with his salvation and grace.

Do not deceive yourselves by pretending you don't sin in order to paint a perfect picture of you and your family. Admit to it and then work together to keep each other accountable to rely fully on Christ and live in truth. ✢

PARENTING PRINCIPLE

Sin keeps us in bondage, while confession sets us free.

POINTS TO PONDER

- What have you taught your children about sin?
- How can you relate to their life and help them?
- What can you tell them to help them overcome sin?

LIGHT UP

God is light; in him there is no darkness at all.   1 JOHN 1:5

There is a little darkness in all of us. Parenting has a way of making that darkness come out! The frustrations that you thought you could manage when dealing with your children can quickly get out of control. No matter how much we yield to Christ, we are still human.

In these times, we need to turn to God because he is the light. There is no darkness in or near him. He calls us to draw near not for his sake, but for our sake. The closer we get to God, the more our life is a light for him.

Teach your children this concept by actually holding a light and then have them walk toward you. They become more illuminated. As they walk away, the darkness begins to close in around them. Always be aware of their age and maturity levels and make sure they understand what you are sharing. It's an easy way to communicate this visually and will help them see the need to stay near to God.

Helping them walk in the light will not only be to their favor, it will bless you too! ❧

PARENTING PRINCIPLE

Stay illuminated by staying close to God.

POINTS TO PONDER

- What do you do to stay near the light?
- How else can you help your children understand the light of God?
- How could you grow in this?

THE ULTIMATE SACRIFICE

If anybody does sin, we have an advocate with the Father—Jesus Christ, the Righteous One. He is the atoning sacrifice for our sins, and not only for ours but also for the sins of the whole world.   I JOHN 2:1–2

Our children need to fully comprehend the vastness of God's grace. Not only does he cover our sins, he covers the sins of the whole world. It's simply mindboggling.

One thing we can be confident in teaching our children is that their sins are covered by Christ's death on the cross. They need to know this because they will face a time in their lives when they will think their sin is too big for God. It may not be while they are living under your roof, but it will come. Our goal as parents is to prepare them for whatever life throws their way, and not just for what they will experience while living at home.

It is those simple truths that our parents and grandparents taught us that ultimately sustain us in our difficult trials of life and will uphold our children. It is also in knowing these truths that we find our greatest joy! ❖

PARENTING PRINCIPLE

Jesus Christ paid the price with his sacrifice!

POINTS TO PONDER

- What has Christ's sacrifice meant to you?
- How are you fulfilling the calling of God to reach the world for him?
- Are your children learning this lesson of reaching the world?

SIBLING RIVALRY

Anyone who loves their brother and sister lives in the light, and there is nothing in them to make them stumble.   1 JOHN 2:10

First John 2:10 is referring to our brothers and sisters in the Christian family, but it certainly can apply to our biological family as well.

Every parent has the dream that their children will grow up to love each other. Those dreams get crushed when one sibling or another makes decisions that hurt the family. Children become protective of their parents, siblings lose patience with each other and all sorts of chaos can ensue.

As a parent, you will have to mediate at times among your children, which can be very tiring. The best response a parent can offer is to encourage your children to repent of any sinful behavior and value one another. Your children may not be best friends but they can still show respect.

Make it your mission to live a life pleasing to God. Do all you can to be peaceful, and pray your children also understand their role in bringing peace to the family. ❖

PARENTING PRINCIPLE

You are not responsible to make your children get along—they are!

POINTS TO PONDER

- How well do you get along with your siblings?
- How do you see your children growing in relationships with each other?
- Where do you see your children struggling in their sibling relationships?

# day**352** december 18

THE WORLD

For everything in the world—the lust of the flesh, the lust of the eyes, and the pride of life—comes not from the Father but from the world. 1 JOHN 2:16

Everything mentioned in 1 John 2:16 can cause us tremendous pain and struggles. Get a good understanding of it and teach your children about the harm it can bring.

Our bodies continually crave something, and that is the lust of the flesh. It cannot be satisfied. Just look to the example of Adam and Eve. They wanted something and they disobeyed God to get it. Many of the cravings of the body come from our eyes and what looks good. Adam and Eve saw the apple, thought it looked good and lost control.

The pride of life is less obvious but more cunning. Adam and Eve were told by the serpent that by eating the apple they would be wise like God. That was their motivation, not physical hunger.

We must always be aware of the temptation around us now that are the same as Adam and Eve faced. The only way to overcome these desires is through the strength of the Lord. ✤

PARENTING PRINCIPLE

God will always provide a way out of every temptation.

POINTS TO PONDER

- How do you guard yourself from these three areas of temptation?
- Are your children growing in their ability to deal with temptation?
- How can you help your children better understand these flesh patterns?

GOD'S PROMISES

And this is what he promised us—eternal life.   1 JOHN 2:25

The thought of dying can be scary for everyone but particularly difficult for a child. The idea of living eternally can be equally scary because no one really knows what heaven will be like. We know it will be wonderful but nobody knows exactly how we get there or what we will look like. Certainly scholars and writers, through their scriptural interpretations, have painted a blissfully happy picture, but that doesn't mean there still aren't lingering questions.

What we don't have to question is that God promises us eternal life in heaven with him. We can count on it. God sacrificed his one and only son so we could have this opportunity and by that sacrifice alone we know it will be beyond our wildest imagination! The days of parenting that are filled with strife are a good reminder that we don't live for this world, but for the world to come.

Do your best to explain this to your children and let them ask questions. If you don't know how to answer them, admit it. Then talk about how sometimes when the answers aren't clear we must simply trust in the promises of God. ✤

PARENTING PRINCIPLE

Eternal life is better than eternal strife!

POINTS TO PONDER

- What are your thoughts on eternity?
- How can you help your children understand these concepts?
- What other promises of God do you trust in?

day354

GREAT LOVE

See what great love the Father has lavished on us, that we should be called children of God.
1 JOHN 3:1

There is no better feeling for a child than to know their father loves them. Psychologists have studied this relationship for years and the one consistent word tied to a father's love is "security." Is it any wonder that Satan has attacked the family and sought to destroy that relationship?

The love our heavenly Father has lavished on us is an overwhelming love! As we experience that love and feel the security it brings, it is a natural next step to pass that kind of lavish love along to our children.

Children who grew up without a father may not understand or experience that love as a child. They may well be into their adult years before they begin to realize what's been missing. Thankfully, God can restore that love to a fatherless child.

As parents, you have the opportunity to build the security of love into your children at an early age. You have the opportunity to show them how God's love mirrors the love a father shows to his children. As they grow, they will be able to experience family security along with God's security. ❖

PARENTING PRINCIPLE

We love because he first loved us.

POINTS TO PONDER

- What was love like from your dad?
- Are your children experiencing a good earthly dad love?
- How has God given you security with his love?

TAKE ACTION

Dear children, let us not love with words or speech but with actions and in truth.

1 JOHN 3:18

It's a lot easier to give lip service to parenting than to actually do it. Lots of parents talk about the goals they ought to set for themselves and their children. They discuss with friends how they could do some things better, but then they never actually do anything. Hopefully, because you are reading these devotionals, you are action orientated. You are interested in more than talk and you are making a difference by getting involved.

Notice there is an emphasis on truth in 1 John 3:18. We must seek the truth and wisdom of God to have guidance into what actions to take as a parent. Should you let your child spend the night at their friend's house? Do you let them go with this or that group of friends? Do you get involved or let them fight this battle on their own? It's difficult to always know the right answer.

Along with taking action, you also need to seek wisdom from the Lord. Be a parent whose words and actions honor Christ and you will be a parent who wins at home! ❖

PARENTING PRINCIPLE

Seeking truth in action will bring a parent satisfaction.

POINTS TO PONDER

- Do you use more action or words?
- How could you be more action oriented?
- How do your children react to either your words or action?

day356

IN HIS SPIRIT

This is how we know that we live in him and he in us: He has given us of his Spirit.

1 JOHN 4:13

Aren't you thankful for 1 John 4:13 and other verses that remind us how God has put his spirit within us? They help to keep us focused on his kingdom and how our little earthly family can make a big impact for Christ!

We can literally live in him. This means he guides, sustains and encourages us in all we do. He sees every parenting moment, and nothing is beyond the scope of his care. What hope and peace we can find in him!

Take time today to celebrate all Christ has done to guide you so far in this parenting journey. Give thanks that he has been faithful before and will be faithful again. The greatest news is that it is not just for our era of parenting. He has been faithful throughout history, including the history that is still being written.

Pray for his spirit to be alive in your children. They will be blessed as they experience his presence grow in their life. ❖

PARENTING PRINCIPLE

If his spirit lives in you, then you will live with access to great wisdom.

POINTS TO PONDER

- Why are you thankful for Christ's spirit?
- What difference has it made in your life?
- How can you explain to your children the importance of his spirit living in them?

A SPECIAL RELATIONSHIP

For you know that we dealt with each of you as a father deals with his own children, encouraging, comforting and urging you to live lives worthy of God, who calls you into his kingdom and glory. 1 THESSALONIANS 2:11–12

Paul is writing to the church in Thessalonica. For us reading it today, he provides insight as to what fathers, in particular, are to provide for their children.

Fathers can encourage their children by speaking positively to and about them, which gives them security and confidence because they know they are loved by their father.

The comfort brought by a father's words or touch is unsurpassed. It is reflective of the care provided to us by our heavenly father. Our children, without realizing it, will associate the love of the heavenly father with us as a father. We need to be responsible to understand this calling and honor Christ by fulfilling it.

Fathers can urge their children to live lives worthy of God by helping them discover their unique gifts and abilities. Once those are uncovered, guide them into the areas where they can be used.

Don't underestimate the importance of this responsibility. Satan is continuously trying to ruin the father-child relationship because he recognizes the power of it. ✤

PARENTING PRINCIPLE

Godly fathers are a true reflection of our heavenly Father.

POINTS TO PONDER

• How are you at encouraging and comforting your children?
• What more could you do to encourage and comfort them?
• How can you protect your family against Satan's attacks?

PASS THE SALT

Let your conversation be always full of grace, seasoned with salt, so that you may know how to answer everyone.   COLOSSIANS 4:6

Answering your children's questions will take on a life of its own as you parent. Their first questions will be funny and cute. The degree of difficulty will increase as they age. You will hear questions you don't know how to answer and questions you won't want to answer. That's part of parenting.

Regardless of what the questions are, keep working at having conversations with your children that are full of grace. If you don't know how to hold your tongue and speak with wisdom, your children will probably never learn that trait either. To season your conversation with salt means it will have taste. Your children will desire to talk with you because they sense you understand them.

If you have difficulty with conversing, seek wisdom and discernment from others who do it well and learn from them. You will avoid lots of conflict if you can have conversations that reflect the grace of Christ. He corrects and teaches us in love.

Be like Christ to your children. Confront the issues, but do so with love. ❖

PARENTING PRINCIPLE

A little salt makes everything taste better.

POINTS TO PONDER

- How are your conversations with your children?
- Where do you struggle most in talking with your children?
- How could you improve conversations with your children?

PRAY, PRAY, PRAY!

Devote yourselves to prayer, being watchful and thankful.　　Colossians 4:2

Being a parent devoted to prayer is a big deal. It's easy to say we believe in prayer and have seen the power of prayer, but do we know what it means to be devoted to prayer?

Devotion means an ardent, often selfless affection and dedication to a purpose or principle. To be devoted to prayer would mean we selflessly seek to pray and have an attitude of prayerfulness in our lives. It's a commitment to doing all we can do and not allowing hindrances in our life that would keep us from this spirit of prayer.

The question is, do we use prayer as a quick fix for situations we face or is it a personal connection and commitment that lives and dwells in us continuously? God is calling us to dedicate ourselves to a life of continuous prayer not only when life gets tough, but also when life is good.

Just as we want our children to live with a dedicated heart toward us, Christ desires that same love and commitment to him and to the wonderful gift of prayer he has made available to us. ❖

PARENTING PRINCIPLE

A life dedicated to prayer will be a life filled with peace.

POINTS TO PONDER

- How are you dedicated to prayer?
- Where do you struggle in your prayer life?
- How do you pray for your children and teach them this dedication?

IN HIS NAME

And whatever you do, whether in word or deed, do it all in the name of the Lord Jesus, giving thanks to God the Father through him. COLOSSIANS 3:17

There are verses, like Colossians 3:17, that are awesome to quote but much more difficult to practice. We would all love to say we do everything in the name of Christ, but the truth is we probably don't and neither do our children. With that in mind, our objective as a family should be to work towards this as a benchmark.

In order to accomplish this goal, we must work hard to keep our minds on Christ. Too often, we default to a worldly way of thinking that leads us to fall into anger, bitterness, frustration and the like. When we transform our minds so that our first thoughts in facing any circumstance are how we can honor Christ through this, we take a significant step toward reaching our benchmark.

This kind of change doesn't happen overnight. It takes prompting and reminding each other to think of Jesus Christ first until it becomes our natural response. Then we begin to experience what Colossians 3:17 is teaching. ❖

PARENTING PRINCIPLE

Honor Christ with word and deed and you will gain great wisdom indeed.

POINTS TO PONDER

- How do you seek to grow in knowing Christ in word and deed?
- How are you helping your children to understand what this means?
- What benefits have you seen from doing this?

EVERYONE'S A STUDENT

Let the message of Christ dwell among you richly as you teach and admonish one another.
COLOSSIANS 3:16

As parents, we primarily think it's our job to teach our children, and yet there is so much we can learn from them. As a family we can all learn from each other.

Children see life through innocent eyes. They often say things that speak truth in profound ways. Since that's true, it's a wise parent who will give their children permission to help you see things you can't see about yourself.

For example, ask them if there is anything about your life that they want to make sure they don't do when they are your age. Just as you saw those things in your parents, they will see it in you. No one knows and sees the real you like your family.

If you are willing to listen with grace and grow from your children's wisdom, you will find they will be much more open to the admonishment and instruction that you give to them. This will be a big challenge for many parents, but those who are secure and wise will see the benefits that come from allowing everyone in the family to teach each other. ❖

PARENTING PRINCIPLE

The wisest teachers can sometimes be the youngest teachers.

POINTS TO PONDER

- What have you learned from your children?
- Do you allow them to speak into your life?
- How could we improve in learning from each other?

day362

december 28

CHOOSE WISELY

A wife of noble character is her husband's crown, but a disgraceful wife is like decay in his bones.   PROVERBS 12:4

Our children need to hear early and often that who they marry is a really big deal. They might not understand it at a young age, but it's important to have it in their mind.

Help them recognize how their spouse can either be a delight and helper to their life or they can have a potentially harmful effect on their life. The example your marriage is currently setting for your children will be very influential in their future. They will either want to emulate your example or do things differently because they don't like what they've seen in your marriage.

Make sure you use your marriage, complete with all the winning and losing moments to let them learn so their relationships will be even better. Be open with your children in the areas that you know will help them learn how to get along with their spouse. Tell them you want them to improve on what you've shown them.

Do what you can to help them keep decay from settling into their marriage. ❖

PARENTING PRINCIPLE

Keep the decay out of your bones and you keep the joy in your home.

POINTS TO PONDER

- Do you see any signs of family decay?
- Are you a crown of disgrace to your spouse?
- What are your children's views for a healthy marriage?

LOOK UP

Set your mind on things above, not on earthly things. Colossians 3:2

It will be difficult to get your children to set their minds on things above because there is so much in the world to capture their attention. They have grown up in an age where technology changes every minute and the next great invention is just hours away. Earthly things will be attractive to your children's senses and won't seem harmful at all to them.

But earthly things don't last while Jesus Christ lasts forever. Having all the technology gadgets in the world cannot replace the peace that comes from a relationship with Christ. Your children may believe that the latest laptop will make them happy, but that happiness will only last until the newer model comes out.

That's why you must teach your children to set their mind on things above because that's what lasts. It doesn't mean they can't enjoy earthly pleasures, but those things won't sustain them over time.

Through Christ comes a peace that surpasses understanding and a joy that is present even in the darkest of times. Material things can't produce those results, they can only be found in Jesus Christ. ✢

PARENTING PRINCIPLE

To help you set your mind on things above, remember to keep looking up.

POINTS TO PONDER

- How attached are you to material things?
- How do your children view material things?
- What can you do to help them set their minds on things above?

BE NEIGHBORLY

Each of us should please our neighbors for their good, to build them up.   ROMANS 15:2

Neighborhoods are interesting places. Depending on where you live, you may know your neighbors intimately, may socialize with them and may even call them friends. In other places you may know your neighbors on sight and chat briefly when meeting, but you can tell they mostly want to keep to themselves. And at other times, and hopefully this isn't your situation, neighbors can be outright hostile to each other. You may also become friends with some families simply because your kids hang out together.

Whatever your situation, it's important to model good neighborly behavior for your kids. When you move into a new neighborhood, make a point to meet your closest neighbors. Take a family walk and knock on a few doors. Take some cookies with you. You will quickly discover who is open to a relationship and who is not. After you've taken your first neighborly steps, it's important to respect the boundaries your neighbors are setting for you but also to let them know you are available to them if they need it. There is nothing more valuable than good neighborhood relations in the case of an emergency.

Also, be sure never to belittle your neighbors to your children. Everyone has a different personality and a different life story. And everyone comes to things in their own time. All you can do is lay the foundation for a good relationship and always treat your neighbors with respect. ✤

PARENTING PRINCIPLE

It takes an understanding spirit to build good neighborly relationships.

POINTS TO PONDER

- What kind of neighbor are you?
- How do you model good neighborly behavior for your kids?

day365

CONFIDENCE BUILDER

For the LORD will not reject his people; he will never forsake his inheritance.

PSALM 94:14

It is heartbreaking to see your child get rejected. Little children are innocent and trusting. They believe the best and can't imagine that someone would not want them around.

Life has a way of teaching some hard lessons in this area. That's why it will be critical to help your child know they won't always be welcomed and will face rejection at some point in their life.

It's also important they understand it might be the result of something they did, but more likely it will be another person who is causing that action. This will be a delicate conversation. Some children will handle it easily, but for others it could jumpstart low self-esteem issues. The ultimate goal is for your child to be secure in who they are, and in those moments when they sense rejection, not to take it personally. That is accomplished by reminding them to put their confidence in who they are in Christ. ❖

PARENTING PRINCIPLE

Remember, if you are rejected, it is not by God.

POINTS TO PONDER

- When have you felt a time of begrudging and how did you handle it?
- How can you continue to help your children prepare for these inevitable moments of rejection that are a natural part of life?
- When have you ever made others feel like you were rejecting them?

SUBJECT INDEX

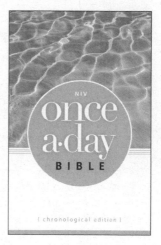

Also Available

NIV Once-A-Day Morning and Evening Prayer Bible

The *NIV Once-A-Day Morning and Evening Prayer Bible* helps you start and end your day in God's Word. This softcover Bible organizes the New International Version — the world's most popular modern-English Bible — into 365 daily readings. Each reading includes daily Scriptures readings from the Old and New Testaments, as well as a selection from the book of Psalms or Proverbs, and a meditative devotion for each morning and evening.

Softcover: 978-0-310-44096-3

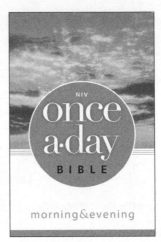

NIV Once-A-Day Bible for Women

This softcover Bible encourages you in your commitment to grow in your relationship with God through daily Bible reading. With Scripture text from the most popular modern-English Bible, the New International Version, this Bible is arranged into 365 daily readings, making it easy to read at your own pace. Each day's reading includes a portion of Scripture from the Old Testament, the New Testament, and a psalm or a proverb, followed by a short devotional thought specifically written for women.

Softcover: 978-0-310-95094-3

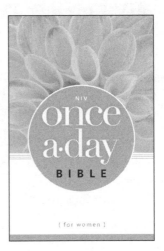